Jesus

The Alpha
and
The Omega

Scriptural references are based on
the New International Version
and the King James Version.

ISBN 0-9668099-1-2

Wake Up America Seminars, Inc.
P.O. Box 273
Bellbrook, Ohio 45305
(937) 848-3322
http://www.wake-up.org

Larry W. Wilson

Jesus

The Alpha and The Omega

Table of Contents

Acknowledgements

This book is dedicated to every person who wants to know more about Jesus.

Deepest appreciation is due to several people who have made this book possible.

First, I would like to acknowledge four women who have dramatically influenced my understanding of Jesus. My mother, Gladys, introduced me to Jesus as I was growing up. Later, my wife, Shirley, demonstrated the compassion and tender love of Jesus to me. For the past thirty-one years my mother-in-law, Opal, has challenged me with excellent questions about the ministry of Jesus, and last but not least, my daughter, Shannon, helped me understand the joy and importance of introducing children to Jesus. I am forever indebted to these four wonderful women for showing Jesus to me.

I am deeply indebted to my staff who have spent many long hours helping me get this book into print. These are people of sterling quality. Shelley has read and reread versions of this book many times. She has made hundreds of corrections and offered many valuable suggestions on making topics and issues clearer. Suzy has also read various versions of this book and her suggestions and comments have been incorporated and deeply appreciated. Marty has proofed and corrected several versions of this book many times and has also managed to put this manuscript into final "page ready" format for the printer. He has overseen the process of getting this book to press. Producing a book of this size is not a casual matter when you consider that these three people carried their full load of daily responsibilities at the time this book was being prepared. I am so grateful these workers for Christ are still speaking to me! May God especially bless these three "musketeers" who have gallantly stood at my side fighting the good fight of faith.

Last, but not least, I am deeply indebted to those who generously support this ministry. Many individuals have sacrificially donated their time and funds for the publication of this book and other materials. Without their generosity, this book could not be a reality. To those who have quietly made this book possible Jesus says, **"But when you give to the needy, do not let your left hand know what your right hand is doing, so that your giving may be in secret. Then your Father, who sees what is done in secret, will reward you."** (Matthew 6:3,4)

There you have it. I am deeply indebted to many wonderful people. I hope every person who reads this book will share in my indebtedness by promoting the gospel of Jesus Christ Everyone who has given something toward creating this book has no other desire than the exaltation of Jesus Christ, the Savior of the world!

Preface

Wake Up America Seminars, Inc. is a non-profit, non-denominational organization dedicated to the purpose of spreading the everlasting gospel of Jesus Christ. Wake Up America Seminars is not endorsed nor affiliated with any religious organization. This ministry was established to herald the salvation and imminent return of Jesus Christ. The words of the apostle Paul are especially timely. He said, **". . . The hour has come for you to wake up from your slumber, because our salvation is nearer now than when we first believed. The night is nearly over; the day is almost here. So let us put aside the deeds of darkness and put on the armor of light."** (Romans 13:11,12)

I wrote this book for four reasons. First, among the gods of this world, Jesus Christ has no equal. There is none like Him. I have found Jesus to be so much more than I ever anticipated. Second, I have found that Jesus is intimately involved in my salvation in ways that I never dreamed possible. Third, I have discovered that life with Jesus is the only way to have a life. Jesus is our only way out from under the curse of sin. It is a deception to believe that life is better with more money. The life that Jesus offers is not based on the currency of the world; instead, it is based on the principles of God's Kingdom as revealed in the currency of Scripture. Last, I believe there are five essential doctrines found in the Bible about Jesus. These are the prerequisites for understanding the imminent fulfillment of the prophecies in Daniel and Revelation.

I hope this book will prove to be interesting enough to read two or three times. The topics discussed are broad and comprehensive, requiring some mental and spiritual processing. Carefully consider the contents of each chapter and notice how each chapter contributes to the biblical tapestry that reveals the love and ministry of Jesus. I readily admit that this book does not begin to surround all that Jesus is, but hopefully it will be a stepping stone for those who want to see more of Him. The study of atomic physics is not simple. The study of molecular biology is not simple. The study of computer science is not simple. Neither is a study about the One who created these sciences simple. How can a study about the Designer of Life, the Creator of the Universe, be a simple subject? Jesus is cloaked in marvelous glory and He sits enthroned at the right hand of the Father. He is the Word of God, He is God Almighty. It is not possible for mortals to fathom all that He is. The best we can do is to try to understand what He has said, what He has done and what He is going to do.   For me, there is nothing more interesting in all of life than Jesus, The Alpha and The Omega!

Larry Wilson
April 2001

Chapter 1
Who is Jesus?

. . . An angel of the Lord appeared to him in a dream and said, "Joseph son of David, do not be afraid to take Mary home as your wife, because what is conceived in her is from the Holy Spirit. She will give birth to a son, and you are to give him the name Jesus, because he will save his people from their sins."

— Matthew 1:20,21

Introduction

Perhaps the most controversial person to ever live on Earth was Jesus Christ. Some people say He was a blasphemer. Others say He was a prophet. Some people say He was a trouble maker and others say He is the Son of God. Not long after He ascended to Heaven, His followers began to disagree about His teachings, prerogatives and identity. So, who is Jesus? Where did He come from? Where did He go? What was He all about? Jesus is a challenge to explain because the Bible says so many things about Him.

Jesus remains a controversial figure because of the claims He made and the things He did while on Earth. If He is not the Son of God as He claimed (Matthew 26:63,64), then He has to be the greatest liar who has ever lived. Conversely, if any person denies that Jesus is the Son of God, the Bible says that person is a liar! (1 John 2:22,23) Jesus leaves no one straddling an ideological fence. He is either all that He says or He is the world's greatest imposter. Interestingly, either people love Him or hate Him. There is no middle ground. The birth, life, death and resurrection of Jesus play a pivotal part in Earth's destiny. One man, Jesus Christ, changed the course of human destiny. Jesus brought the assurance of salvation and eternal life out of the tomb. Of course, the promise of salvation existed before Jesus died on the cross, but after His resurrection, we have "living proof" that the penalty for sin has been paid and the promise of eternal life is a coming reality. Jesus taught that this life is but a prep-school for the life to come. The differences between the life we know right now and the life to come are almost too good to be true. Life will be very different when we finally dwell in God's physical presence because the curse of sin and every blemish on Creation will be removed. Jesus will no longer be veiled from our eyes. We will see His face and rejoice in His instruction. Everlasting life will be filled with everlasting joy and endless vistas of learning. In the Earth made new, we will build houses and inhabit them. We will know each other even as we are known. (1 Corinthians 13:12) The redeemed will live forever without seeing death, sorrow, sickness, injury or suffering! Better yet, the redeemed will live forever seeing the One who made life possible. The experience of everlasting life and all that goes with it is only possible because one man, Jesus Christ, changed the destiny of a planet in rebellion.

The Alpha and Omega

Less than 27% of the world's population claims to be Christian. This indicates Jesus is either unknown to most of the world or He is not considered to be the Son of God by billions of people. Although Christian denominations may not agree on the teachings of Jesus, lively debate has no bearing on who Jesus really is.

The source of disagreement among Christians about Jesus seems to be quite simple. Jesus Christ is so magnificent and so awesome that people cannot understand Him. He is the Alpha and Omega, the beginning and end of everything that exists. Jesus is the artist that paints the sunsets with the properties of light. Jesus is the biological engineer who put the world's ecological systems into operation. Jesus is the designer of life's DNA; the One who put the intricate chemistry of the human body into motion. He is the author of life. He is the executor of God's justice. Jesus Christ is everything. He has no beginning and He has no end. Therefore, it is not possible to fully define Jesus! He is simply too much to comprehend.

Although God has completely demonstrated His love for mankind through the life and death of Jesus, we still have much to learn about God's love. Even more, Jesus Christ is not through revealing the love of God! He has plans. He has authority and power. And most of all, He is not limited by time or space. He lives forever and the people who love Him will someday enjoy His presence forever! I believe that because Jesus Christ is so magnificent, the Bible allows some wiggle room for variations in our understanding of His mission and teachings. Every question that we might have about Jesus is not answered in the Bible, but we will soon be able to ask Him any question that we might have.

Test All Things

When it comes to religious ideas, I have observed that many people use the "sour milk method" for testing. In case you were not raised on a farm, the "sour milk method" of testing works like this: A five-gallon bucket of milk can be tested with one teaspoon of milk – if the milk in the teaspoon is sour, all of the milk in the bucket is sour. It is not necessary to drink five gallons of milk to know whether all the milk is sour. Unfortunately, people often test new ideas with teaspoons or "sound bites." I mention this because you will probably find some new ideas in this book about Jesus, and at first these ideas may appear to be sour, but please do not throw the whole book out just yet. I would prefer you use another farm method for testing. I call it the "rotten apple" exam. This method requires the examination of each apple in the barrel so that bad apples can be separated from good ones. This method of investigation can produce very good results because the good apples are not discarded with the bad! Really, the spiritual difference between these two methods of investigation is attitude. If you find an idea about Jesus that is different from what you have heard before, look up the *Scripture references in your Bible.* Do your best to glean as much from this study as you can.

The God of Both Testaments

For many years, I assumed the God of the Old Testament was the Father and the God of the New Testament was Jesus. In other words, I assumed they were two different Gods. I concluded that the Father was more grumpy than Jesus. Perhaps my assumptions began during childhood because I remember hearing preachers say the God of the Old Testament was more likely to kill people than the God of the New Testament. Today, my view about the Father and Jesus is very different. One is not grumpy and the other gracious. They are both gracious beyond comparison! Jesus said that He and the Father are one. (John 10:30) I know some people interpret this verse to mean that Jesus and the Father are two manifestations of one being, but I disagree. I understand the oneness of the Father and the Son to mean that they are perfectly united in purpose, plan and action. For example, my wife and I are one (Genesis 2:24), yet we are two separate human beings. So, I do not understand Jesus' words to mean that Jesus *is* the Father and Jesus *is also* the Son, as some people believe. My study has led me to conclude that the Godhead has three distinct and separate members in it: God the Father, God the Son, and God the Holy Spirit. Each member of the Godhead shares in the name "God" because each member of the Godhead has the same prerogatives and attributes as the other two, yet they live and function harmoniously in different ways.

What Did Jesus Do before He Was Born?

I did not question my early assumptions about the Father being the God of the Old Testament and Jesus the God of the New Testament until I began to wonder about the life and actions of Jesus before He came to Earth as a baby. As I studied this topic, I made an amazing discovery. The "God" of the Old Testament is not the Father, but actually Jesus! (John 1:1-14; 5:37-40; Colossians 1:17,18) More than 90% of the references found in the Old Testament pertaining to "God" refer to Jesus Christ! This discovery profoundly changed my understanding of the Bible and Jesus. Consequently, I now have a much different perspective about the words and teaching of Jesus. It is wonderful to understand how Jesus discussed themes and issues when He was on Earth (as recorded in the Gospels) that He previously discussed with Moses, Isaiah, Ezekiel, Jeremiah and other Old Testament prophets before He came to Earth. As we proceed through this study on Jesus, I will provide scriptural references that demonstrate why I believe, in most cases, the God of the Old Testament is Jesus.

One Theme

Most Christians do not question why the Bible is divided into the Old and the New Testaments, but after studying both testaments for many years, I have concluded the division is artificial. Actually, the New Testament is a continuation of the Old Testament. Neither Testament should be exalted above the other nor is one book in the Bible inferior to another. The Jesus I find in the Old Testament is a Jesus of love, compassion and long-suffering. This is consistent with what I find about Him in the New Testament. The Old Testament reveals a history of God's people repeatedly rejecting their Benefactor, but the same story is also found in the New Testament (and throughout church history, I might add). I find a God of justice and deadly judgments in the Old Testament, and I also find the same thing in the New Testament. As I wrote before, I believe the New Testament is simply a continuation of the Old Testament. The actions and testimony of Jesus in both Testaments reveal what the Godhead is like. (John 5:37-40)

Jesus, the Creator of Heaven and Earth

The Bible begins, **"In the beginning God created the heavens and the earth."** (Genesis 1:1) The first verse in the Bible explains Earth's origin. This verse also introduces our Creator and we call Him by several titles or names: Jesus, God, Lord, The Word, Son of God, Master, Jehovah and Savior. Did you know that the creative agent of the heavens and Earth is not the Father, but the Son? Notice what Paul wrote, **"In the past God spoke to our forefathers through the prophets at many times and in various ways, but in these last days he has spoken to us by his Son, whom he appointed heir of all things, and through whom he made the universe."** (Hebrews 1:1,2) Jesus is the "hands-on" creative agent of the Godhead. The Father, Son and Holy Spirit were in perfect harmony about the creation of Earth, and yes, all three were present! The Father was observing, Jesus was creating, and the Holy Spirit was hovering over the Earth, ready to dwell within the hearts of a new creation called man. (Genesis 1:2) Notice this statement by Paul affirming that Jesus is the creative agent within the Godhead, **"For by Him** [Christ] **all things were created: things in Heaven and on earth, visible and invisible, whether thrones or powers or rulers or authorities; all things were created by him and for him. He is before all things, and in him all things hold together."** (Colossians 1:16,17, insertion mine.) In the fourth command- ment, the creative works of Jesus are recognized: **"Remember the Sab- bath day by keeping it holy. . . For in six days the Lord made the heavens and the earth, the sea, and all that is in them, but he rested on the seventh day. Therefore the Lord blessed the Sabbath day and made it holy."** (Exodus 20:8-11) John places the creative handiwork of Jesus beyond dispute by writing, **"He was in the world, and though the world was made through him, the world did not recognize him."** (John 1:10)

Three points need to be highlighted in the texts just presented. First, Jesus is the creative agent of the Godhead. Second, Jesus is called by many different names or titles because one title cannot describe all that Jesus is! Last, Jesus is a name that we use to identify a member of the Godhead *after* He was born of Mary. In other words, the name "Jesus," as it applies to the Son of God, is only 2,000 years old. Jesus, of course, is much older.

The Bible and Holy Spirit Agree

The Bible uniquely reveals information about Jesus that cannot be found in any other place. Yet, the Bible is incomplete. John says an infinite and omnipotent Jesus cannot be adequately described on paper. (John 21:25) Knowing *about* Jesus is not the same as personally knowing Jesus. There may be hundreds of millions of people who claim to be Christian, but a loyal follower of Jesus is known by *love* and obedience to God and by love for each neighbor. (Matthew 22:37-40; John 13:35) To help us understand what the Godhead is all about, Jesus promised to send the Holy Spirit to help us. Jesus said, **"But when he, the Spirit of truth, comes, he will** guide you into all truth. He will not speak on his own; he will speak only what he hears, and he will tell you what is yet to come. He will bring glory to me by taking from what is mine and making it known to you." (John 16:13-14)

If it takes time and experience to understand what a friend is really like, you can understand why it might take a very long time and many diverse experiences to grasp what Jesus is like. For this reason, the historical record in the Bible covers a period of about 4,000 years. If we study the whole Bible, we can get a good picture of what Jesus is really like. In the Old Testament Jesus says, **"I the Lord do not change."** (Malachi 3:6) In the New Testament Paul wrote, **"Jesus Christ is the same yesterday and today and forever."** (Hebrews 13:8) The nice thing about studying 4,000 years of Jesus' behavior is that the Bible presents many separate situations and issues. By thoughtfully examining a range of events and experiences, we begin to understand how Jesus deals with human beings. Far too many people make the mistake of defining Jesus with a small sample of His words or actions. Jesus does not live in our dimension or operate on our timescale. If we limit our research about Jesus to the four gospels or the book of Psalms, we will not understand all that Jesus is. We must examine every book in the Bible.

Eternal God Revealed in Old and New Testaments

The Old and New Testaments are inspired by the same Holy Spirit, have the same authority and reveal the same Jesus! Pay close attention to what John says about Jesus. **"{1} In the beginning was the Word, and the Word was with God, and the Word was God. {2} He was with God in the beginning. {3} Through him all things were made; without him nothing was made that has been made. {4} In him was life, and that life was the light of men. . . {10} He was in the world, and though the world was made through him, the world did not recognize him. {11} He came to that which was his own, but his own did not receive him. {12} Yet to all who received him, to those who believed in his name, he gave the right to become children of God – {13} children born not of natural descent, nor of human decision or a husband's will, but born of God. {14} The Word became flesh and made his dwelling among us. We have seen his glory, the glory of the One and Only, who came from the Father, full of grace and truth."** (John 1:1-14)

These verses contain profound information. If you reread the verses in reverse order, you will discover some interesting things about Jesus. For example, many people are confused about the title "God" as it relates to Jesus in verse one. How can "the Word be God" and be "with God?" Think of "God" as a last name: Father God, Son God, and Holy Spirit God. These three entities have the same last name because they are equal in every way, but they each have different roles. (Matthew 28:19; John 15:26; 16:5-11; 17:1-5.) In this light, John 1 reveals that Jesus was God and He was a part of the Godhead from the very beginning.

After reading John 1:14, you may ask, "Why is Jesus called the Word in verse one?" In simple terms this title says volumes about Jesus as the creative agent of the Godhead. The Psalmist says, **"For He [Jesus] spoke, and it came to be; he commanded, and it stood firm."** (Psalms 33:9, insertion mine.) If the person who baked the cake is called "the baker," and the person who performed the surgery is called "the surgeon," then the One, who through the breath of His mouth, spoke the world into existence should be called "the Word." The disciples were amazed at the power of His words. He calmed a terrifying storm on the Sea of Galilee by speaking the word! (Mark 4:39)

Jesus is God just like the Father

The idea that Jesus is equal in every way to God the Father may be hard to grasp at first, but it is true. Jesus has all the power, authority and glory the Father does. Jesus is not a lesser God. Somehow the title "Son of God" seems to make Jesus a lesser God in some people's minds, but this is not the case. I will explain later how the *title* "Son of God" refers to the state of submission that Jesus entered to save man. Jesus has existed forever. He was not created. Just like the Father and Holy Spirit, Jesus is an eternal member of the Godhead. Jesus is as worthy of honor and worship as is the Father! (John 5:23) Paul wrote, **"For in Christ all the fullness of the Deity lives in bodily form . . . who is the head over every power and authority."** (Colossians 2:9,10) In Revelation Jesus said to John, **"I am the Alpha and the Omega, says the Lord God, who is, and who was, and who is to come, the Almighty."** (Revelation 1:8) Remember, this same John wrote, **"In the beginning was the Word, and the Word was with God, and the Word was God. He was with God in the beginning. Through him all things were made; without him nothing was made that has been made."** (John 1:1-3) Peter wrote, **"He [Jesus] was chosen** [as the one who could die for man] **before the creation of the world, but was revealed in these last times for your sake."** (1 Peter 1:20, insertions mine.)

In the Old Testament, Isaiah quotes Jesus saying, **"Listen to me, O Jacob, Israel, whom I have called: I am he; I am the first and I am the last. My own hand laid the foundations of the earth, and my right hand spread out the heavens; when I summon them, they all stand up together . . . This is what the Lord says – your Redeemer, the Holy One of Israel: I am the Lord your God, who teaches you what is best for you, who directs you in the way you should go."** (Isaiah 48:12,13, 16,17) Near the end of Job's suffering and distress, Jesus revealed just how little Job and his friends knew about His purposes. Jesus said, **"Where were you when I laid the earth's foundation? Tell me, if you understand. Who marked off its dimensions? Surely you know! Who stretched a measuring line across it? On what were its footings set, or who laid its cornerstone – while the morning stars sang together and all the angels shouted for joy?"** (Job 38:4-7)

For some readers it may be hard to grasp that it was actually Jesus who said to Abraham, **". . . I am God Almighty; walk before me and be blameless."** (Genesis 17:1) When the Jews argued with Jesus about His claim that He was greater than Abraham, Jesus responded, **"Your father Abraham rejoiced at the thought of seeing my day; he saw it** [in vision] **and was glad."** [The Jews sneered,] **"You are not yet fifty years old . . . and you have seen Abraham! 'I tell you the truth,' Jesus answered, 'before Abraham was born, I am!' "** (John 8:56-58, insertion mine.)

One last point. Old Testament writers were well acquainted with Jesus even though they did not know Him by the name "Jesus." The writer of Hebrews stated that **"He** [Moses] **regarded disgrace for the sake of Christ as of greater value than the treasures of Egypt, because he was looking ahead to his reward."** (Hebrews 11:26, insertion mine.) How did Moses know Christ before Christ was born? John knew that Jesus had revealed His glory to Isaiah 700 years before Jesus was born. John wrote, **"Isaiah said this because he saw Jesus' glory and spoke about him."** (John 12:41) How did Isaiah know about Jesus before He was born? When Jesus was upon Earth, notice what He said about Himself by repeating Isaiah's words: **"He** [Jesus] **replied, 'Isaiah was right when he prophesied about you hypocrites; as it is written: "'These people honor me with their lips, but their hearts are far from me. They worship me in vain; their teachings are but rules taught by men.' You have let go of the commands of God and are holding on to the traditions of men."** (Mark 7:6-8, insertion mine.) When Jesus began to select His disciples, Philip excitedly ran to Nathaniel and said, **". . . We have found the one Moses wrote about in the Law, and about whom the prophets also wrote – Jesus of Nazareth, the son of Joseph."** (John 1:45)

What do these verses confirm? Jesus lived in Heaven before He was born to Mary. Obviously, He did not go by the name Jesus before His birth, but all the Old Testament prophets knew Him as God Almighty or Jehovah God. (Exodus 6:3) Enoch, Job, Noah, Abraham and Moses even talked with Him. Jesus is fully God and the creative agent of the Godhead. Jesus does so much! He is so much!

Mary Told to Call Him Jesus

Here is a point to consider. The angel instructed Mary to call her child by the name "Jesus." (Matthew 1:21) In other words, Mary and Joseph could not choose the name of the Messiah. It is my opinion that the loss of this privilege gently imposed Heaven's higher ownership of this baby boy. In ancient times, the mother usually had the privilege of naming her offspring at birth. (Genesis 29:32-35; 30:6-13; 1 Samuel 4:21) This privilege was suspended for both Elizabeth and Mary (mothers of John the Baptist and Jesus) because these sons were not to be under the dominion of their respective mothers. Like the prophet Jeremiah, the Holy Spirit set them apart from birth. (Luke 1:15,35; Jeremiah 1:5)

The Bible is very clear that Jesus lived in Heaven before He created the world. Jesus was not called by His earthly name though, until He was born to Mary. It makes sense then that we do not find Jesus called by His earthly name in the Old Testament. Remember, more than 90% of the references to God in the Old Testament are references to the person we now call Jesus! For example, in Gethsemane Jesus prayed to the Father saying: **"And now, Father, glorify me in your presence with the glory I had with you before the world began."** (John 17:5) Clearly, Jesus shared glory with the Father before the world was created. On another occasion, Jesus revealed where He had come from: **"For I have come down from heaven not to do my will but to do the will of him who sent me. And this is the will of him who sent me, that I shall lose none of all that he has given me, but raise them up at the last day."** (John 6:38,39) On more than one occasion, Jesus told the Pharisees that the Old Testament specifically focused on Him: **"And the Father who sent me has himself testified concerning me.** [The Father spoke at the baptism of Jesus saying, 'This is my Son . . .'] **You have never heard his voice nor seen his form, nor does his word dwell in you, for you do not believe the one he sent. You diligently study the Scriptures because you think that by** [knowing] **them you possess eternal life.** [But] **These are the**

Scriptures that testify about me, yet you refuse to come to me to have life." (John 5:37-40, insertions mine.) Remember, the "Scriptures" at the time of Jesus were the books we now call the Old Testament. (Luke 24:27) Jesus' remarks confirm that the Old Testament is a testimony about Himself.

Progressive Revelation

The truth about Jesus is continually unfolding. In fact, the last book in the Bible is appropriately called "The Revelation of Jesus Christ" because it describes *how* Jesus will be fully revealed to the world at the end of time. Our knowledge about Jesus is based on progressive revelation. In other words, the revealing of all that Jesus is – has been progressively unfolding over thousands of years. Early prophets did not know as much about Jesus as people who came later. Each succeeding prophet stood on the shoulders of the earlier prophet, providing a more complete picture of Jesus and His work. Notice one instance of this progression in the Bible: **"God** [Jesus] **also said to Moses, 'I am the Lord** [Jehovah]. **I appeared to Abraham, to Isaac and to Jacob as God Almighty** [El-Shaddai]**, but by my name the Lord** [Jehovah] **I did not make myself known to them.' "** (Exodus 6:2-3, insertions mine.) This text presents a bit of a problem because Abraham and Jacob knew about God's Hebrew name *Jehovah*. Notice these two texts: **"And he** [Jehovah] **said unto him** [Abraham]**, I am the Lord** [Jehovah] **that brought thee out of Ur of the Chaldees, to give thee this land to inherit it."** (Genesis 15:7, KJV, insertions mine.) Later, God spoke to Jacob in a vision as he was fleeing from his brother Esau: **"And, behold, the Lord** [Jehovah] **stood above it** [the ladder reaching to Earth]**, and said, I am the Lord** [Jehovah] **God of Abraham thy father, and the God of Isaac: the land whereon thou liest, to thee will I give it, and to thy seed . . ."** (Genesis 28:13, KJV, insertions mine.) These two texts, as well as Genesis 22:14, indicate that Abraham and Jacob knew of the name Jehovah. So, what did Jesus mean when He said to Moses, **"by my name the Lord** [Jehovah] **I did not make myself known to them."** I understand Jesus to mean that Abraham, Isaac and Jacob did not understand the *meaning* of His name Jehovah. In ancient times, Hebrew names were carefully selected to describe character, emotions, or an event at the time of birth. In this sense, although Abraham and Jacob knew the title "Jehovah," they could not understand that the awesome *meaning* of the name would not be revealed until the time of the Exodus.

At the time of the Exodus, Jehovah (Jesus) performed a series of astonishing miracles. These miracles established the Hebrews as a nation under

His sovereign leadership. Jehovah sent Moses and Aaron to speak to Pharaoh. Jehovah sent ten plagues on Egypt. Jehovah "passed over" Egypt at midnight and killed all the firstborn of Egypt, both man and beast. Jehovah destroyed Pharaoh and his army in the Red Sea. At this time, the Deliverer of Israel began to identify Himself with the Hebrew name *Jehovah*. Jesus did this so that all nations would know the King of the Jews was Jehovah God. About 1,400 years later, Jehovah was born to Mary and He died on the cross with this title written above His head: "The King of the Jews." (John 19:19-21)

Sacred Name

Some Christians today *insist* that Jesus must be called by a Hebrew name such as "Yashua," "Yehoshua," "Jehovah," "Yahweh," etc. I find these claims to have no merit. From secular history and Bible history, we know that the name "Jesus" was a common Jewish name used at the time of Christ's birth. (Acts 13:6; Colossians 4:11) If it is inappropriate to call Jesus by His given name, why was Mary required to give her son the name "Jesus?" The basis for insisting on one sacred name for Jesus stems from Jewish superstition. The Jewish people became so superstitious about God that they refused to speak or even write the names "Yahweh" and "Jehovah." Actually, one name is no more sacred than any other title or name which God uses. It is God Himself who makes a name and title holy, not a specific name that makes Him holy. Regardless of the name or title you may find in the Bible to identify Jesus, we should never use any of His names or titles carelessly. (Exodus 20:7). One of the highest and most exalted titles given in the Bible for God is "Father" and Jesus instructs us to address the Ruler of the Universe with the endearing title, "Our Father." (Matthew 6:9) Furthermore, because "Father" is an exalted title for God, Jesus forbids anyone from calling a clergyman, "Father." (Matthew 23:9)

So, Who is Jesus?

Jesus is all of the following:

> Jesus is Jehovah God. (Exodus 6:3)
>
> Jesus is the Lord thy God. (Isaiah 48)
>
> Jesus is King of kings and Lord of lords. (Revelation 19:16)
>
> Jesus is the Angel of the Lord. (Genesis 22:11-18; Exodus 3:2-6; Judges 2:1-5)

Jesus is the Creator of Earth. (Exodus 20:8-11; Colossians 1:16; John 1:10; Hebrews 1:1,2)

Jesus is our Redeemer. (Isaiah 48; Ephesians 1:7)

Jesus is our Friend. (John 15:13-15)

Jesus said to His disciples, **"Do not let your hearts be troubled. Trust in God; trust also in me. In my Father's house are many rooms; if it were not so, I would have told you. I am going there to prepare a place for you. And if I go and prepare a place for you, I will come back and take you to be with me that you also may be where I am. You know the way to the place where I am going."** (John 14:1-4) Do you think our trust in the Father should be any different from our trust in Jesus?

Chapter 2
The Angel of the Lord

After forty years had passed, an angel appeared to Moses in the flames of a burning bush in the desert near Mount Sinai. When he saw this, he was amazed at the sight. As he went over to look more closely, he heard the Lord's voice: " 'I am the God of your fathers, the God of Abraham, Isaac and Jacob.' Moses trembled with fear and did not dare to look. Then the Lord said to him, 'Take off your sandals; the place where you are standing is holy ground.' "

— Acts 7:30-33

A Controversial Point

Some readers may consider the following remarks to be blasphemy, but let me say that nothing could be further from the truth. Unfortunately, many people believe that it is slanderous to say that Jesus lived in the form of an angel before He came to Earth. Surprisingly, these same people have no problem accepting the fact that Jesus lived in the even lower form of a man while He was on Earth. Do not misunderstand my statement that Jesus lived in the *form* of an angel before He came to Earth. Jesus *is not* a created being. He is eternal God, just like the Father is God, and He has existed from time everlasting. (John 1:1-14; Colossians 1:17; 1 Chronicles 16:36) The Bible plainly teaches that Jesus lived in Heaven before He lived on Earth. (John 14:24; 17:5; Hebrews 1:1-3)

Angelic in Form

Consider this possibility: Prior to taking on the form of a man, Jesus lived in Heaven in the form of an angel and the angels called Him "Michael" (which means "One who is like God"). Before we get too involved in this topic, I ask that you prayerfully consider a simple concept about the Godhead. I am not asking you to agree with me, but I would like to present a summary statement first, allowing you to see the big picture before demonstrating from Scripture that Jesus is Michael.

Here is the concept: Three Gods rule over the Universe; the Father, Son and Holy Spirit. Each God is separate and distinct in His own right. They have the same authority, power and ability, but they function in different roles according to a mutual covenant between themselves. The role of the Father is universal *focus*. He is the object of worship and the Supreme Ruler of the Universe. (The "out front" position of the Father also makes Him the focus of litigation should a contest over governance arise.) The role of the Son is to live *among* the created beings as one of them, to faithfully instruct and demonstrate God's love to all beings. The role of the Holy Spirit is to live *within* the soul of each created being, making intimate communion between God and creature simultaneously available to every-one – everywhere – anytime. This concept of the Trinity establishes that God is above us (the Father), beside us (the Son) and within us (the Holy Spirit). If this view of the Godhead is correct, the following information about Michael should be easier to understand.

Michael

Jesus is called by many names in the Bible. Each name is like a prism that reflects something new about His marvelous wisdom and ways. Whether He is called "The Word," "The Lamb of God," or "The Rose of Sharon," each name reveals another aspect of His beautiful character. The name "Michael" also reveals something very important about Jesus. It indicates how closely He identified with the angels before He took on the form of a man. The subject of Christ's preexistence is important because the disclo-sure of Jesus, His authority, power, love and humility is a very encompass-ing subject. To the angels, He is Michael *the* archangel (the prefix *arch* means "over" or "above" all angels). To man, He is Jesus, Savior, King of kings and Lord of lords, the "archman," if you will. A revealing of all that Jesus is also exposes the other members of the Godhead since the mem-bers of the Godhead are one in purpose, plan and action. The Father and the Holy Spirit are keenly interested in the actions and testimony of Jesus because as "The Word," He represents them, too. Since Jesus is the Creator/Heir of Earth, He will take possession of Earth at an appointed time. People who trust in Him for salvation should be willing to understand all they can about Him and His ways since He is Lord and Master to all who call on Him.

There is one Archangel in Heaven. Four books in the Bible offer informa-tion about Him:

1. **"But even the archangel Michael, when he was disputing with the devil about the body of Moses, did not dare to bring a slanderous accusation against him, but said, 'The Lord rebuke you!' "** (Jude 9) In this text, Michael is identified as *the* archangel. Some people are offended by the idea that Michael, the archangel, is another name for Jesus, the Son of God. Sometimes, a portion of this text is used to prove that Michael is not Jesus because Michael says to the devil, **"The Lord rebuke you."** The argument goes like this: "If Michael is Jesus, why would He refer to Himself in the third person?" This objection is not valid. Notice what Zechariah 3:2 says, **"The Lord said to Satan, 'The Lord rebuke you, Satan! The Lord who has chosen Jerusalem, rebuke you!' "**

   The language of Zechariah 3:2 is identical to Jude 9. In both cases, Michael is speaking of Himself in the third person. He speaks with divine authority in the argument over the body of Moses and ends the argument without slandering the devil. This is Jude's point in verse nine. Jude contrasts the words of Jesus with men who are like "unreasoning animals," carelessly slandering celestial beings without realization of their wrong doing. We also know that when the devil tempted Jesus in the wilderness, Jesus did not slander the devil nor rail against him. Speaking to Lucifer, Jesus said, **"Do not put the Lord your God [me] to the test."** (Matthew 4:7, insertion mine.) Jesus knew who He was. So did the devil and he retreated.

2. **"For the Lord himself will come down from heaven, with a loud command, with the voice of the archangel and with the trumpet call of God, and the dead in Christ will rise first."** (1 Thessalonians 4:16) Before we examine the details of this verse, we need to consider two other texts. Notice what Jesus said about Himself, **"I tell you the truth, a time is coming and has now come when the dead will hear the voice of the Son of God and those who hear will live."** (John 5:25) Whose voice did Jesus say the dead will hear at the resurrection? Jesus also said, **"For my Father's will is that everyone who looks to the Son and believes in him shall have eternal life, and I will raise him up at the last day."** (John 6:40)

   These three texts harmonize only if the archangel is Jesus Himself. The Lord Himself *will speak with the authority of the archangel* and call the dead to life. When Jesus comes in glory, all of the angels will be with Him. (Matthew 25:31) The dead will hear His voice at the last day. Some people try to ignore the weight of textual evidence by saying the archangel joins with the Lord in raising the dead. Why does Almighty God need an archangel to help Him raise the dead? Jesus alone has the keys to the grave and He alone has the authority to redeem man! (Revelation 1:18; 5:9)

Read 1 Thessalonians 4:16 again and notice how Paul connects two important themes. First, the Lord Himself is the Redeemer coming down from Heaven to gather up His saints. Second, the Lord Himself is also the archangel, Michael, leading Heaven's angelic host. Paul merges two perspectives about Jesus in this text. From man's point of view, Jesus is the Redeemer. From the angel's point of view, Michael, the archangel, is the Commander-In-Chief who leads the heavenly host. In other words, Jesus has great authority rising from both identities – He is the Redeemer of man and Commander-in-Chief of angels.

3. **"At that time Michael, the great prince who protects your people, will arise. There will be a time of distress such as has not happened from the beginning of nations until then. But at that time your people – everyone whose name is found written in the book – will be delivered. Multitudes who sleep in the dust of the earth will awake: some to everlasting life, others to shame and everlasting contempt."** (Daniel 12:1,2) These verses reveal two impressive facts. First, the Great Tribulation commences when Michael *stands up*. This suggests that at the present time, Michael must be seated and Scripture verifies this point, **". . . We do have such a high priest, who *sat down* at the right hand of the throne of the Majesty in heaven, and who serves in the sanctuary, the true tabernacle set up by the Lord, not by man."** (Hebrews 8:1-2, italics mine.) In other words, when Michael stands up, His work of intercession at the right hand of the Father (Hebrews 7:25) will be finished and a time of distress will then begin on Earth. Do not overlook the fact that Michael is the great *prince* who protects His people. It is well known that a prince becomes a king when the kingdom is actually handed over to him. The same is true for Jesus. At the present time He is "a prince in waiting"– waiting for Earth to become His dominion. (Hebrews 1:13; Revelation 11:17) According to the Bible, the Father will hand over the kingdom to Jesus during the Great Tribulation, at the time of the seventh trumpet. (Revelation 11:15-19) His first action (as King of kings) will be to pour out seven bowls of vengeance upon the wicked people of Earth. (Revelation 15 and 16) Therefore, when Jesus appears in the clouds of glory He will appropriately wear the title, "King of kings and Lord of lords." (Revelation 19:16)

The second impressive fact found in Daniel 12:1-2 is that Michael, the archangel, is associated with a resurrection of the righteous. (Paul confirms this point in 1 Thessalonians 4:16.) Yet what makes the book of Daniel so amazing is that it was written about 600 years *before* Paul even appeared on the scene. From Daniel's perspective, Michael had not become "Jesus" yet! When studying the Old Testament, keep in mind that the name "Jesus" was not associated with the second member of the Godhead. This did not happen until He was born to Mary. These texts from Daniel suggest that Michael is actually Jesus and His position in Heaven is "Archangel."

One text in Daniel is sometimes used to support the idea that Michael is not Jesus. **"But the prince of the Persian kingdom resisted me twenty-one days. Then Michael, one of the chief princes, came to help me, because I was detained there with the king of Persia."** (Daniel 10:13) This text describes an event when Gabriel needed Michael's help to overcome the devil's influence over the king of Persia. At first, it may seem strange that Michael is called "*one* of the chief princes," especially if He is *the* archangel. However, this use of language can be easily harmonized if the reader can accept two concepts. First, Jesus lived among the angels as "one" of them, just like He lived among men as "one" of us. In other words, Michael looked like the other chief princes of Heaven. Second, in Heaven's administrative order, the highest rank is that of a servant leader. Jesus said, **"The greatest among you will be your servant."** (Matthew 23:11) For example, when Jesus lived on Earth, did He awe the multitudes with His glory? Did He lord His divine authority over mortals or rule from an exalted throne? Did He surround Himself with an entourage of 10,000 servants? The answer to each question is "No." Even though Jesus is Almighty God, He chose to subject Himself to the Father, the Plan of Salvation, and even death itself. He lived as a humble servant of man and Michael lived the same way in Heaven among the angels. Servant leadership is the highest order in God's kingdom and Gabriel refers to Michael as one of the chief princes because He functioned as that. Keep this parallel in mind: From man's perspective, Jesus *appeared* to be one of us and from the angel's perspective, Michael *appeared* to be one of them.

4. **"And there was war in heaven. Michael and his angels fought against the dragon, and the dragon and his angels fought back. But he was not strong enough, and they lost their place in**

heaven." (Revelation 12:7,8) I believe this war took place on Resurrection Sunday. This text describes Michael and His angels fighting against Satan and his angels. Michael and Satan are commanders, each having an army of angels. Lucifer is the Prince of Darkness and sin. Michael is the Prince of Righteousness and light.

This battle on Resurrection Sunday had a long history that preceded it. Before Lucifer sinned, Michael was the *arch*angel, the ruler over all angels. When one-third of the angels defected and joined Lucifer in rebellion against Christ, Satan became the self-appointed *arch*angel over his followers. Thus, the great controversy between Christ and Satan is actually a contest between two powerful archangels who were once best of friends. *It is interesting to note that each time the name Michael is used in the Bible, it is used in the context of an angelic conflict between the devil and Jesus.*

After examining the four texts in the Bible that refer to Michael, the evidence indicates that Michael is Jesus. But continue reading because there is better evidence still to come!

Michael, the Angel of the Lord, is Jehovah

Many people are surprised to learn that in the Old Testament, Jesus is often identified as "the angel of the Lord." Three excellent examples follow. Pay careful attention to who is speaking in each text. When Abraham was about to slay Isaac as a sacrifice, the Bible says, **"But the angel of the Lord called out to him from Heaven, 'Abraham! Abraham! . . . Do not lay a hand on the boy,' he said. The angel of the Lord called to Abraham from Heaven a second time and said . . . 'I swear by myself, declares the Lord** [Jehovah]**, that because you have done this and have not withheld your son, your only son, I will surely bless you and make your descendants as numerous as the stars in the sky and as the sand on the seashore. Your descendants will take possession of the cities of their enemies, and through your offspring all nations on Earth will be blessed, because you have obeyed me.' "** (Selections from Genesis 22:11-18, insertion mine.) Did you notice in these verses that "the angel of the Lord" is actually God, the Lord Jehovah?

The second example is even more illuminating. One day when Moses was tending his sheep, he noticed a bush blazing with flames of fire. **"There the angel of the Lord appeared to him in flames of fire from within the** bush. **Moses saw that though the bush was on fire it did not burn up. So Moses thought, 'I will go over and see this strange sight – why the bush does not burn up.' When the Lord saw that he had gone over to look, God called to him from within the bush, 'Moses! Moses!' And Moses said 'Here I am.' 'Do not come any closer,' God said. 'Take off your sandals, for the place where you are standing is holy ground.' Then he said, 'I am the God of your father, the God of Abraham, the God of Isaac and the God of Jacob.' "** (Exodus 3:2-6) Did you notice again that "the angel of the Lord" is actually God?

The third text removes all doubt. **"The angel of the Lord went up from Gilgal to Bokim and said, 'I brought you up out of Egypt and led you into the land that I swore to give to your forefathers. I said, 'I will never break my covenant with you, and you shall not make a covenant with the people of this land, but you shall break down their altars. Yet you have disobeyed me. Why have you done this? Now therefore I tell you that I will not drive them out before you; they will be thorns in your sides and their gods will be a snare to you.' When the angel of the Lord had spoken these things to all the Israelites, the people wept aloud, and they called that place Bokim. There they offered sacrifices to the Lord."** (Joshua 2:1-5) I have to ask again, who is "the angel of the Lord?" There is only one angel who is God, has the authority of God and speaks for God. His name is Michael. He is the archangel. He was with the Israelites day and night and provided for all their needs, including their food and water. Notice what Paul wrote, **"They all ate the same spiritual food and drank the same spiritual drink; for they drank from the spiritual rock that accompanied them, and that rock was Christ."** (1 Corinthians 10:4) After reviewing these verses, the mystery is easy to solve. The angel of the Lord is God. He is the Archangel and His name is Michael, which means "One who is like God."

Michael/Jesus

When Michael was born to Mary, the Father gave Him an earthly name. The birth of Jesus was a profound miracle. Michael became Jesus. This transition says much about the role of servant leader in God's order because Jesus stooped even lower in the order of creation to become a man. Paul was overwhelmed with the submission of Jesus. He quotes a song by David (Psalm 8:4,5) saying, **"What is man that you are mindful of him, [even] the son of man that you care for him? You made him a little lower than the angels; you crowned him with glory and honor and put** everything under his feet . . ." "But we see Jesus, who was made a little lower than the angels, now crowned with glory and honor because he suffered death, so that by the grace of God he might taste death for everyone." (Hebrews 2:6-9, insertion mine.) Jesus may appear to be a man – Michael may appear to be an angel – but He is none other than a member of the Godhead dwelling among His created beings. This may be hard to comprehend, but Jesus left Heaven to live among sinful men for the express purpose of revealing the marvelous ways and unfathomable love of the Godhead.

The Bible is dedicated to revealing the love which the Godhead has for man and understanding Jesus Christ is the only means through which this revelation can occur. In other words, the truth about God begins and ends with the Word, i.e., Jesus. No wonder He is called the Alpha and the Omega. At the end of sin's drama, just before the wicked are destroyed, God will show everyone – including all fallen angels and all mankind – the fullness of all that Jesus really is. After Earth is purified, the King of kings and Lord of lords is going to do a very amazing thing. Paul says, **"Then the end** [of sin's drama] **will come, when he** [Jesus] **hands over the kingdom to God the Father after he has destroyed all dominion, authority and power . . . When he has done this, then the Son himself will be made subject to him who put everything under him, so that God may be all in all."** (1 Corinthians 15:24,28, insertions mine.) Can you believe this? After conquering sin and destroying evil, after receiving the Earth as an inheritance, after redeeming billions of saints, Jesus returns all that He has to the Father so He can live with humanity as one of them. What a servant leader!

Think about this. Michael/Jesus has the same power, authority and glory as the Father, but He humbled Himself to live among the angels as one of them. Then, when sin entered the universe He stooped even lower to live as a man. Even more, He was willing to be cursed and bear the shame of the cross to pay the penalty for our sins. (Hebrew 12:2) He was willing to perish for eternity if it meant that sinners could have the possibility of eternal life. To His glory, He succeeded in His rescue of humankind and was exalted to the highest position in all the universe. Then, in one act of incomprehensible love, a victorious Jesus returns His crown and great possessions to Father God so He may live among His people. The kingdom of God is all about serving others. Jesus said, ". . . **Whoever wants to become great among you must be your servant, and whoever**

wants to be first must be your slave – just as the Son of Man did not come to be served, but to serve, and to give His life a ransom for many." (Matthew 20:26-28) **"If I then, your Lord and Master, have washed your feet; ye also ought to wash one another's feet. For I have given you an example, that ye should do as I have done to you."** (John 13:14,15)

Closing Thoughts

One of the saddest verses in the Bible is found in John 1:11. **"He came to that which was his own, but his own did not receive him."** Reflect for a moment how it must have been when Michael bent down on His knees to affectionately create Adam out of the soil of the Earth. (Genesis 2:7; Hebrews 1:1-3) Later, He personally spoke with Abraham, sharing with him God's plans for a future nation dedicated to His purposes. He personally spoke with Moses and cancelled Pharaoh's authority, delivering the children of Israel from Egyptian bondage. Tenderly, He watched over Israel, feeding them with angels' food – manna from Heaven. True to His word, He gave them the promised land and prosperity which had peaked during the reigns of David and Solomon. He sent Nebuchadnezzar to destroy His temple, but He later sent Cyrus to free His people. After all He had done, His own people totally rejected and crucified Him. John says, **"He came to that which was his own, but his own did not receive him."** The story of His rejection, of course, does not end with the Jews. It continues among the Gentiles, even to the last generation. What have you done about Jesus Christ? Do you believe His words? Do you love Him and do you want to be a part of the kingdom He represents? Have you accepted His authority as the Lord of your life? Are you willing to reflect His character and be one of His representatives on Earth? Are you willing to do what He asks? Are you willing to become what He wants you to be? Are you willing to go where He commands? If your answer is, "Not right now," then when will it be? If you surrender your will to the yoke of Christ, you have the Son, and those who have the Son have life! (1 John 5:12) If you surrender your life to Him, He will clothe you with His righteousness. Surrender is the first step toward Heaven. Think of it! All who surrender to the Son will have the privilege of embracing this most wonderful person who is fully God, who is the archangel, Michael and who is the man, Jesus!

Chapter 3
The Author and Finisher of Salvation

**Looking unto Jesus the author and finisher of our faith;
who for the joy that was set before Him endured the
cross, despising the shame, and is set down at the right
hand of the throne of God.**

— Hebrews 12:2 KJV

Jesus is called the author of the Christian faith because He has demonstrated the true meaning of faith in God. Consider His destiny for a moment. Jesus did not want to go to the cross. (Luke 22:42) He had done nothing to deserve death. (Hebrews 4:15) Yet, it was the Father's will that He go to the cross – so He obediently submitted and went to His death. This is a perfect demonstration of living by faith in God. The knowledge that sustained Jesus during the terrible ordeal of the cross was the joy of knowing that many human beings would receive the gift of eternal life. So, Jesus obediently laid His own life down and allowed cruel men to nail Him to the cross. He accepted the shame and humiliation associated with dying as a criminal. The penalty for sinners was laid on Him. Just before He died, Jesus uttered words that demonstrates the depth of His great faith. He cried out, "**. . . Father, into your hands I commit my spirit.**" (Luke 23:46) In such trying circumstances, His words reveal something very beautiful.

Paul says that Jesus is the finisher (Greek: *teleiotes*) of our faith. The word *teleiotes* means completeness or perfection. In this sense Jesus is a perfect example of what faith in God should be. As Jesus hung on the cross, He became totally separated from the Father. Never before had He felt the depth of despair that comes from God's silence – He had always had the assurance of the Holy Spirit's presence. Now, the Father actually put Jesus in the position of those sinners who will experience the second death. "**God made him who had no sin to be sin for us, so that in him we might become the righteousness of God.**" (2 Corinthians 5:21) In other words, Jesus actually experienced the death required by God to pay for the penalty of sin. During His darkest moment, Jesus did not know if He would be resurrected. Yes, He had predicted His resurrection on the third day (Luke 9:22), but His prediction was a statement of faith, not fact. He knew that His resurrection was contingent on receiving the Father's approval of His entire earthly ministry. Therefore, when Paul says that Jesus is the finisher or perfecter (NIV) of our faith, few of us grasp the importance of these words. Jesus stepped across the portal from life to the second death maintaining perfect faith in God even though He did not know if He would be restored to life. Wow! What incredible love – what incredible faith!

Jesus, the Centerpiece of Bible Prophecy

Jesus is the centerpiece of Bible prophecy. (Colossians 1:18) Bible prophecy predicts a time will come when Jesus Christ is fully revealed to this world. (Matthew 26:64; Revelation 1:1-3) The revelation of all that Jesus is unfolds in a sequence of events – a grand process built into the Plan of Salvation. As the revelation of Jesus unfolds, it illuminates what the Godhead is all about. Jesus is the Word, the Spokesperson for the Godhead. (John 1:1-14) Jesus is the beginning and the end of information about God. He is the Alpha and the Omega. (Revelation 1:8) The Greek alphabet *begins* with a character called an alpha and it *ends* with a character called an omega. The character of the Godhead begins and ends with Jesus. In other words, we cannot correctly understand the ways of the Godhead without knowing and understanding Jesus. The wonderful thing about the Plan of Salvation is that a person can be saved from eternal death without understanding the Godhead or even knowing about Jesus! This is very good news when you consider that billions of people live (and have lived) on this planet who have never heard of Jesus or His offer of salvation. This is a profound topic and worthy of consideration.

Salvation is not Based on Absolute Knowledge

For some people, the following concept is a completely new thought: Salvation is not based on an absolute knowledge of God. Many Christians are taught that in order to receive salvation they *must* know about Jesus and His offer of salvation. Instead, man's salvation is based solely on the merits of something that Jesus Christ did for the whole world AND our willingness to obediently submit to the authority of the Holy Spirit. When Jesus died on the cross, He reconciled the whole world to God. **"For if, when we were God's enemies, we were reconciled to him through the death of his Son, how much more, having been reconciled, shall we be saved through his life! Not only is this so, but we also rejoice in God through our Lord Jesus Christ, through whom we have now received reconciliation."** (Romans 5:10,11) This verse says that mankind was reconciled to God through Jesus when we were still God's enemies! This reconciliation does not mean that everyone on Earth will receive eternal life as some people claim. Rather, it means that Jesus paid the penalty due each sinner so that each sinner can receive the gift of eternal life, but only if he is willing to obediently surrender to the authority of the Holy Spirit. The "born again" experience occurs whenever a person obediently surrenders his heart to the control of the Holy Spirit. Jesus said, **". . . I tell you the truth, no one can see the kingdom of God unless he is born again."** (John 3:3) Paul wrote, **"Those who live according to the sinful nature have their minds set on what that nature desires; but those who live in accordance with the Spirit have their minds set on what the Spirit desires. The mind of sinful man is death, but the mind controlled by the Spirit is life and peace; the sinful mind is hostile to God. It does not submit to God's law, nor can it do so. Those controlled by the sinful nature cannot please God."** (Romans 8:5-8)

God examines our mind, He knows our motives because He knows our heart. The Spirit knows whether we obediently submit to His demands in faith or whether we are living in rebellion. God cannot be fooled. The greatest of all sins and the only one that cannot be forgiven is an attitude of continuing stubbornness that refuses to submit to the authority of the Holy Spirit. Jesus said, **"And so I tell you, every sin and blasphemy will be forgiven men, but the blasphemy** [rebellion] **against the Spirit will not be forgiven. Anyone who speaks a word against the Son of Man will be forgiven, but anyone who speaks against the Holy Spirit will not be forgiven, either in this age or in the age to come."** (Matthew 12:31,32, insertion mine.)

The bottom line is this: If a person allows the Holy Spirit to live within his or her heart and soul, God considers that person a child of the kingdom. Salvation is not based on an absolute knowledge of God. Instead, it is based on submission to the Holy Spirit. This is ground zero. This is where *every human being starts* his or her walk with God. The Spirit approaches every person to see if He can find residence there. If He can, life begins to change. A new character begins to develop as desires begin to change. This is how knowledge fits in. Paul wrote, **". . . Faith comes from hearing the message, and the message is heard through the word of Christ."** (Romans 10:17) Paul does not say that salvation comes by simply agreeing with truth. Paul says that our faith in God increases as we learn more from the teachings of Christ. A person wants to know more about Christ because the Spirit creates the interest! Again, notice the order of events. First the Spirit dwells within, followed by an obedient submission to His dominion, and then a thirst for more knowledge begins. There is an enormous difference between living in obedient faith to God and merely agreeing with certain statements about God. The demons know that God is omnipotent and they tremble! (James 2:19) This knowledge does not save them from their destined destruction. Knowledge does not save, but knowledge will increase our faith in God if the Holy Spirit has gained entrance into our heart.

God Created Diversity

Because God ordained it, billions of people currently live (and have lived) on the Earth. Paul said, **"From one man he** [God] **made every nation of men, that they should inhabit the whole earth; and he determined the times set for them and the exact places where they should live. God did this so that men would seek him and perhaps reach out for him and find him, though he is not far from each one of us. 'For in him we live and move and have our being.' As some of your own poets have said, 'We are his offspring.' "** (Acts 17:26-28, insertion mine.) God knows there are billions of people who truly love a divine entity they call God. These sincere people serve their God to the best of their knowledge and ability. Honesty and sincerity in serving God are evidence of the indwelling Spirit. This is true for the Muslim, for the Jew, for the Catholic, or the Protestant. According to Jesus, the Godhead accepts all people as "children of the kingdom" if they obediently submit to the authority of the Holy Spirit, even though they may not know about Jesus. (John 4:23; 10:16; Romans 2:14,15) This truth reveals how great God's love is. Because mankind has been reconciled to God through Jesus, God accepts everyone who allows the Holy Spirit to have dominion in their lives.

Many Will Be Surprised

At the last day, Jesus will resurrect many people who have never heard of His name and give them eternal life! This is possible because God offers salvation on this generous basis: Anyone who submits to the indwelling authority of the Holy Spirit will mature into the kind of person that God wants to live within His eternal home. People who obediently submit to the Holy Spirit live by faith. (Romans 1:17; 8:5) The ministry of the Holy Spirit is a gift from God to all people. (See Joel 2:28,29; Romans 3:28-30 and Romans 12:3) The Holy Spirit attempts to reside in every heart. His mission is to draw people near to God, even if some of them have no knowledge about God. (John 3; Romans 2:14,15; Acts 10:34,35) The Holy Spirit creates a hunger for knowledge about God and a desire for a relationship with Him. Just because the presence of the Holy Spirit dwells within us does not mean we have an automatic infusion of knowledge about God. Instead, the first work of the Spirit is to develop a new attitude within a person's character. He wants to produce a joyful, obedient, submissive heart, that will hunger to know God and His truth! Just like steel is attracted to a magnet, any person who allows the Holy Spirit to direct his or her life will be irresistibly drawn to greater truth about God and His will. (John 3:21; 16:13) In fact, the presence of childlike humility and a thirst for the living water of truth about God is one of the most obvious signs of a "born again" person. (Matthew 5:6)

Attitude – First and Foremost

Every teacher knows that conduct is a reflection of inner attitude, and if a good attitude is established first, problems can be solved within the class-room faster and more permanently. Jesus certainly understands this process. This is why He offers salvation to man without the necessity of works. If God's goodness and generosity do not soften our rebellious attitude toward His authority, eternal life with a bad attitude would be hell for a sinner and for everyone around him or her! Our attitude toward God's authority is inherently rebellious because we are born under the influence of sin. The law of sin goes to work within our brain the day we are born. (Romans 7:17,23) Therefore, God sends the Holy Spirit to create a sweet spirit within each of us to prepare us for His presence. Eternal life would be pointless if our attitude toward God is not amicably and warmly reconciled to the fact that He has sovereign authority over us. **"I the Lord search the heart and examine the mind, to reward a man according to his conduct, according to what his deeds deserve."** (Jeremiah 17:10) God's interest and love for humankind are incomprehensible. For example, whenever a person follows the Holy Spirit's prompting – even if that person does not understand everything there is to know about the Father, Jesus, or even the Holy Spirit – the Godhead accepts that person as a member of the kingdom. The Godhead accepts a person when his or her heart becomes willing by faith to obey the Holy Spirit and do whatever the Spirit requires. God knows that if this person knew more, he or she would do more. From God's point of view, the essential problem with fallen man is the stubborn refusal to submit to the Holy Spirit! (Matthew 12:31) When the Holy Spirit is allowed to stay within a person's heart, that person exhibits the childlike *attitude* God is looking for. (Matthew 18:3) Although my understanding of God has changed dramatically during the past 30 years of study, my thirst for truth about God remains the same. It is very assuring to know that God's love for us is not proportionate to our knowledge of Him. Jesus loved me long before I ever knew Him. Even more, Jesus loves me even though I do not know even 1 percent about Him!

Knowledge is Constantly Eclipsed

Some well meaning people believe they know "the whole truth" about God and His will for all mankind, but this is not possible. No created being on Earth or in Heaven knows "the whole truth" about the Godhead. No, not one. Even if a person knew everything about God that could be known today, his or her knowledge would have to be updated tomorrow because the truth about God is ever unfolding. Today's advancing knowledge constantly eclipses the limits of what was known yesterday. Since we cannot comprehend "the whole truth" about an Infinite God at any given time, it is even more important to live by faith. Many people in every religion live up to all they know to be right and they thirst for greater truth. These are God's children. Remember that we are not saved by knowledge, but by our faith in God. (Romans 3:21-26) So, whether a person is a Moslem, Jew, Hindu, Catholic, Protestant or even an atheist, religious persuasion is secondary in matters of salvation. A person is given Christ's righteousness as long as he or she submits to the authority of the Holy Spirit. If a Hindu is seeking greater truth about God and is honestly living up to all that the Holy Spirit has put in his or her heart, God accepts that person as His child. If you are still a bit skeptical about this matter, consider the story of the Jewish zealot, Saul. Jesus called Saul into His service while he was on his way to Damascus to destroy Christians. The conclusions Saul had in his head were totally wrong, but God could see that his heart was right. (Acts 9) It may be hard to comprehend, but consider God's magnificent grace of accepting all people from all walks of life on the basis of obedient faith alone!

Knowledge Has a Place

You may ask, what is the point of having knowledge about Jesus if you are saved through faith *alone*? Furthermore, what is the point of promoting the gospel of Jesus to the world if the Holy Spirit already lives within people of all religious systems? These are good questions and I believe the answers center on this point: To *correctly* understand the will, ways and plans of the Godhead, man has to know Jesus Christ. There is no other way. **"Jesus answered, 'I am the way and the truth and the life. No one comes to the Father except through me. If you really knew me, you would know my Father as well. From now on, you do know him and have seen him.' "** (John 14:6,7) Jesus is the Alpha and the Omega enlightening man's understanding of an infinite God. He speaks for God. He is the Word of God. Humanity must correctly understand the will, ways and plans of the Godhead for two important reasons: First, the truth about God sets man free of superstitious burdens (nonsense) and false guilt. (John 8:32) Religion at its best is a mixture of partial truth, degenerate culture, foolish speculation and superstition. The older religion gets, the more corrupt it becomes. In general, religious leaders become more concerned with authority and control over people than with the advancement of truth and spiritual growth within their congregations. Jesus was crucified because His teachings weakened the control of the religious authorities over the people. (John 11:50) Historically, religion has caused more wars, separated more people and produced more grief than any other institution on Earth. On the other hand, greater truth about God sets people free from the heavy burden that religion can impose. (Matthew 11:28) The second reason man needs a correct understanding of God is this: Fullness of life is discovered only through knowing the Lord Jesus. Jesus is the Alpha – Architect of life and the Omega – Overcomer of every problem. The more we know about the Designer and His designs for life, the higher and more fulfilling the human experience will be. If a person adopts God's principles of life, then his or her life will be noble and honorable. Each person will enjoy the benefits of respect, and integrity will produce many rewards. So, the knowledge of Jesus Christ and His teaching is important. With this knowledge comes freedom and a higher and more fulfilling human experience.

Eternal Jesus

The Bible teaches that Jesus has existed forever. (Colossians 1:17; Isaiah 48:12,13) It is hard for finite minds to comprehend that Jesus has no beginning and no end. He is an eternal being just like the Father and the Holy Spirit. He was not created and He is not a lesser God or inferior to the Father. (Colossians 1:15-19; John 5:23; 10:30) Jesus is Almighty God just like the Father and the Holy Spirit are Almighty Gods. (Genesis 17:1; Isaiah 44:6; 47:4; Matthew 28:19; Acts 5:3; Revelation 1:8) If you are willing to see it, the Bible teaches that there are three distinct and separate eternal Gods in Heaven. The plurality of the Godhead is introduced in the first chapters of Genesis, supported throughout the Bible and summarized in the final chapters of Revelation.

The progressive revelation of Jesus is the focal point of the Bible because the Godhead predetermined that the process of revealing all that Jesus is was the best way to illuminate their purposes, plans and actions.

Be assured, Jesus is not self-seeking or self-promoting. On the contrary, no being has sacrificed more or shown more genuine humility than the Author and Finisher of our faith. When He was here on Earth, He did not travel in a gold-plated chariot with hundreds of heralds announcing His appearance. He did not dress in kingly robes of purple or wear costly jewels. He did not seek the approval or endorsement of religious and political leaders with weasel words or compromise. Even during the donkey-back parade into Jerusalem, King Jesus was not beguiled by the pseudo-praise of a spontaneous crowd. Instead, He immediately angered religious authorities by going straight to *His* temple to remove the horde of greedy thieves who were conducting "business" in *His* house of prayer. (Matthew 21:7-14) For almost 30 years Jesus traveled the dusty roads of Galilee as a poor carpenter. He did not seek position and fame, and even when the devil offered to give Him the kingdoms of the world, Jesus would not bow down and worship him. (Luke 4:5-8) Jesus was not on a mission to capture the wealth and glory of this world. He did not come to entertain the carnal heart and win its affection, but to transform it. The miracles He performed were not done to impress the people with His prowess, but to reveal the Father. He came on a mission to seek and save a lost world. Every miracle He performed was calculated to confirm His testimony about the ways and love of the Godhead. If you really want to get a good snapshot of what Jesus was like on Earth, read the entire gospel of John in one sitting. You will be amazed at the conflict He faced and the courage and tenderness He expressed! You will also be amazed at the stubbornness and meanness of carnal hearts.

The Greatest Sacrifice

Consider this point: When Adam and Eve sinned, Jesus immediately offered Himself to the Father as man's substitute. Jesus offered to become a man and die in man's place. Carefully evaluate what this means. First, Jesus was willing to become a man. This is an act of humility that boggles my mind. Think of it! The Creator of the universe became a mere mortal and subjected Himself to death, just like man is subject to death! The human race was created lower than angels. Jesus is God, as well as the Archangel Michael, and His offer to become the second Adam was an immeasurable condescension. (1 Corinthians 15:45; Hebrews 2:7-9) Second, we know the wages of sin is eternal death. (Genesis 2:17, Romans 6:23; Revelation 20:15) When Jesus offered to die for humanity, He was not only willing to die as people do, but also willing to cease to exist *forever* so that we could have the opportunity of eternal life. This selfless offer from Jesus truly reflects the heart of our Father. This condescension reveals so much about the character of the Godhead. They were willing to disrupt their eternal union to redeem fallen humanity! (John 3:16) Yes, the Father did promise to resurrect Jesus, but His promise was conditional.

Jesus had to succeed – live a perfect sinless life – in order to regain eternal life. (John 10:18; Acts 2:32,33; Hebrews 5:7-10) If Jesus had failed, He would have come under the penalty of the same law which condemns all sinners. The risk and sacrifice were great. Jesus, eternal God and Creator of Heaven and Earth, was willing to take the risk. If necessary, Jesus was willing to perish forever – just so man could have an opportunity to be restored to the Garden of Eden. It was the ultimate gift . . . the ultimate sacrifice! Because Jesus offered so much, the Father has decreed that Jesus will be exalted above everyone in the universe. (Psalms 2; 1 Corinthians 15:24-28; Revelation 5:1-12) This exaltation is an ongoing process. As time passes, the revelation of Jesus Christ becomes greater and greater. The Plan of Salvation requires that Jesus be fully disclosed, verifying that He has all the prerogatives of God. The revelation of Jesus will be accomplished by the end of the 1,000 years and every being in the universe will know that "Michael the Archangel," "Jesus the man," is Almighty God.

Jesus Reveals It before It Happens

Jesus told Isaiah, ". . . **I am God, and there is no other; I am God, and there is none like me** [on Earth]. **I make known the end from the beginning, from ancient times, what is still to come . . . What I have said, that will I bring about; what I have planned, that will I do.**" (Isaiah 46:9-11, insertion mine.) Jesus also told His disciples, **"I am telling you now before it happens, so that when it does happen you will believe that I am He** [the One sent from God]." (John 13:19, insertion mine.) Contrary to what many people say, Bible prophecy cannot be separated from the Plan of Salvation. Prophecy plays an integral role in salvation. Even the birth, death, ascension and return of Jesus to Earth are expressed in the Bible as prophecies. The Bible teaches that salvation comes by faith in Jesus (Ephesians 2:6-10), but it is difficult to have faith in Someone we have not actually seen or heard. It is also difficult to love Someone we have never met. Therefore, God sent the gift of the Holy Spirit so we could come to know and love Jesus. (John 16:7) The Spirit makes Jesus real in our minds. Furthermore, Jesus provides us with enough reasonable evidence to demonstrate that He is God. The fulfillment of Bible prophecy provides this evidence. Bible prophecy is history stated in advance. Jesus declares what He will do and history confirms what He did. Prophecy is a progressive record and by studying it, we can observe the marvelous work of Jesus through many centuries. History confirms God's constant vigil to verify that His promises are kept. When understood correctly, Bible prophecy demonstrates and explains the character of Jesus in many wnderful ways. Peter said, **"And we have the word of the prophets made more certain, and you will do well to pay attention to it, as to a light shining in a dark place, until the day dawns and the morning star rises in your hearts. Above all, you must understand that no prophecy of Scripture came about by the prophet's own interpretation. For prophecy never had its origin in the will of man, but men spoke from God as they were carried along by the Holy Spirit."** (2 Peter 1:19-21)

Present Truth

On or about the time of fulfillment, Bible prophecy "suddenly becomes understandable and applicable." This is an interesting phenomenon. For example, when Jesus was born, the prophecies surrounding His birth suddenly became clear to the honest in heart, such as the wise men. The sudden understanding and fulfillment of prophecy is sometimes called "present truth." A good example of "present truth" is demonstrated by Paul's preaching. (Romans 16:25-27) The arrival of present truth always centers on some new truth or event concerning Jesus. Therefore, when students of the Word understand what Jesus is about to do, they know how and when to prepare for His actions! For example, Jesus told Noah to build an ark because He was going to destroy the world with a flood. The message Jesus gave Noah was present truth at that time because Jesus was about to do something He had not done before! Because Noah lived by faith, he obeyed Jesus. With great expense and tremendous effort, Noah built an ark, thereby saving himself and his family. (Hebrews 11:7)

Having Ears That Hear

One of the biggest problems students face with Bible study is that some elements of the Bible have to be believed before they can be understood, and other elements have to be understood before they can be believed. It is important to approach Bible study with both perspectives in mind. We may have to stretch our minds to do some possibility thinking because some answers are a long time in coming. In the end, it is reassuring to know that faith and truth are inseparable – they are brother and sister. For this reason, we should not feel threatened when the big picture does not snap into focus right away. In our search for truth, we must have a humble attitude and teachable spirit. My prayer for 30 years continues to be: "Lord, I do not care what the truth is or where it may lead, just let me see it!"

Jesus said to the Pharisees, **"He who belongs to God hears what God says. The reason you do not hear is that you do not belong to God."**

(John 8:47) In Revelation 2 and 3, Jesus emphasized seven times, **"He that has an ear to hear, let him hear what the Spirit says to the churches."** This phrase indicates that those people who honestly listen for God's voice will eventually hear and understand what the Holy Spirit says! Jesus said, **"But when he, the Spirit of truth, comes, he will guide you into all truth. He will not speak on his own; he will speak only what he hears, and he will tell you what is yet to come."** (John 16:13)

Afraid of Two Things

The carnal heart is afraid of two things: the truth and the future. The born again heart has nothing to fear because Jesus is the truth and He stands today where we will be tomorrow. This is the beauty of living by faith. If we are willing to confess our sins and move forward, truth is not a fearful thing. Likewise, there is nothing to fear about the future because our Savior sees the future and has made every provision for it. Jesus said, **"Everyone who does evil hates the light, and will not come into the light for fear that his deeds will be exposed. But whosoever lives by the truth comes into the light, so that it may be seen plainly that what he has done has been done through God."** (John 3:20,21) The Apostle Paul wrote, **"The man without the Spirit does not accept the things that come from the Spirit of God, for they are foolishness to him, and he cannot understand them, because they are spiritually discerned."** (1 Corinthians 2:14) Even more, Daniel says of the wicked: **"Many will be purified, made spotless and refined, but the wicked will continue to be wicked. None of the wicked will understand, but those who are wise will understand."** (Daniel 12:10)

These verses confirm the complete harmony between the operation of the Holy Spirit and the Word of God. One is not antagonistic toward the other. The members of the Godhead are in one accord. The Holy Spirit will never lead a person into rebellion against a plain "thus saith the Lord" stated in Scripture. Never! The Holy Spirit always nudges a person to obediently submit to God's higher authority. (Acts 5:29) Whenever we face a difficult situation where sin appears to be the best solution, we are on treacherous ground. Remember Abraham. He and Sarah concluded that having a child by Hagar was the only answer to Sarah's infertility, but look at the price of their sin. Daniel 12:10 also confirms that if we are not obedient to the leading of the Holy Spirit, we will not be able to grow spiritually and understand even greater truths about God.

Even though we may be honest seekers of truth, there will always be portions of the Bible that will be unclear and challenging to understand. Do not feel intimidated. We stand on the shoulders of many honorable men and women who have experienced this same dilemma. No person can understand everything written in the Bible. However, everyone who seeks truth will find it and will be able to understand the basics. (Matthew 7:7) Even more, everyone who seeks truth will see God (Matthew 5:8) and He will reward everyone who diligently seeks Him. (Hebrews 11:6; Revelation 1:3) Just as God's infinite love is greater than we can ever hope to understand, many Bible concepts are simply too broad, deep and large to be completely understood in one lifetime. Jesus reads the mind and heart of each person and all that He requires is a surrendered heart, an honest inquiry, a diligent effort and an open mind. If we cooperate with the leading of the Spirit each day, Jesus will produce a spiritual maturity that is otherwise impossible to attain. (Ephesians 4:13)

Forever Immature?

Too many Christians stay on the merry-go-round of basic elements and never mature into the deeper and intricate concepts about Jesus. The Author of our Faith did not produce a third grade primer on salvation. He produced a library of 66 books that offers something at every level of spiritual development. Paul observed the fact that some people would not grow up spiritually and he chastised the Hebrews saying, **"We have much to say about** [the ministry of Christ]**, but it is hard to explain because you are slow to learn. In fact, though by this time you ought to be teachers, you need someone to teach you the elementary truths of God's word all over again. You need milk, not solid food! Anyone who lives on milk, being still an infant, is not acquainted with the teaching about righteousness. But solid food is for the mature, who by constant use have trained themselves to distinguish good from evil. Therefore let us leave the elementary teachings about Christ and go on to maturity, not laying again the foundation of repentance from acts that lead to death, and of faith in God."** (Hebrews 5:11-6:1, insertion mine.) Did you notice the subjects that Paul called "elementary truths?"

Of course, Paul believed that we should understand the basics of salvation first and then move on to practice them in our lives. But he did not stop there! He encouraged all of us to grow up and continue learning more about the ways and plans of Jesus. If we are satisfied with "just enough religion" to be saved (the basic truths about salvation), could it be that we are more interested in saving ourselves than knowing Jesus? How foolish!

The Plan of Salvation is not an insurance policy, nor is it a scheme to obtain eternal life. Instead, the Plan of Salvation is a comprehensive way of life. When a person enrolls in the Plan of Salvation, he or she wants to grow up spiritually and reflect Jesus' character. A hunger for spiritual food drives a born again person to the Bible.

"Prophecy is not Essential to Salvation"

When people insist that Bible prophecy is not essential to salvation, they tacitly admit they are spiritually immature and still fascinated with the milk of elementary things. (Remember Hebrews 5:11-6:1.) Keep in mind that Jesus is neither mindless nor shallow about the things He does or says. He is the Creator of molecular physics, as well as the Revealer of the mysteries of God. He would not have included electrons in atoms nor apocalyptic prophecy in the Bible if these elements were not important. Jesus would not have instructed John to write the Book of Revelation if it was meaningless and useless. On the contrary, the Book of Revelation is the only book in the Bible that offers a blessing to everyone who reads it. **"Blessed is the one who reads the words of this prophecy, and blessed are those who hear it and take to heart what is written in it, because the time is near."** (Revelation 1:3) The Book of Revelation will become, at the right time, a marvelous "road map" of present truth for the people of Earth. Prior to the Great Tribulation, the Book of Revelation will not enjoy preeminence because it will not be the time for its fulfillment. But this will suddenly change and overnight, the most complicated book in the Bible will become an important roadmap explaining the actions of Jesus. Do not lessen the importance of Bible prophecy simply because you do not understand what it says. Paul wrote, **"Do not treat prophecies with contempt."** (1 Thessalonians 5:20) Jesus condemned the Pharisees for not recognizing the fulfillment of prophecy right before their eyes! He said, **"Hypocrites! You know how to interpret the appearance of the earth and the sky. How is it that you don't know how to interpret this present time?"** (Luke 12:56)

False Prophets

John warns us to be aware of false prophets. **"Dear friends, do not believe every spirit, but test the spirits to see whether they are from God, because many false prophets have gone out into the world."** (1 John 4:1) Jesus warned His disciples, **"For false Christs and false prophets will appear and perform great signs and miracles to deceive**

even the elect – if that were possible." (Matthew 24:24) Think about it. According to these texts, if a person performs great signs and miracles, does it necessarily make them a true prophet? No! (See Deuteronomy 13:1-5.) If a great sign or miracle is not proof of truth or a true prophet, then the proof of a true prophet must be found in the validity of his message. A prophet's message will conform to Bible truth and be a plain "thus saith the Lord." A prophet is not a god. True, prophets sometimes perform miracles to confirm their testimony, but a miracle is not enough. There has to be something external (that is, a witness) to validate the testimony of the prophet. (John 8:13-20)

If a person is not acquainted with the Bible, it becomes very difficult to use the "gold standards" set forth in the Bible to test a prophet. If we are left with nothing but our senses – he or she looked good, spoke authoritatively and appeared to know a lot about the Bible – we become very vulnerable to deception. The devil knows the Bible very well and this makes it imperative that we know God's Word, too. In days to come, a great contest will occur between the prophets of God and the prophets of the devil. Many people who currently claim to be "led of the Spirit" will painfully discover they were led by their foolish imaginations. (Ezekiel 13) The Spirit ever leads us toward truth – to carefully examine God's Word. Then, as we discover more truth, the Spirit confirms it in our minds by connecting more dots to form a growing picture of truth.

Wrong Conclusions and Terrible Consequences

If we interpret prophecy with faulty presuppositions, we will produce faulty conclusions. Notice how faulty presuppositions led Jewish leaders to a faulty conclusion in Jesus' day. Malachi predicted, **"See, I will send you the prophet Elijah before that great and dreadful day of the Lord comes. He will turn the hearts of the fathers to their children, and the hearts of the children to their fathers; or else I will come and strike the land with a curse."** (Malachi 4:5,6) This prophecy was given to Malachi about 400 years before Jesus was born and the Jews commonly interpreted this prophecy to mean that Elijah would *physically* come down from Heaven and introduce the Messiah when the time came for Him to appear. (Remember, Elijah was taken to Heaven in a whirlwind approximately 450 years before Malachi wrote these words. See 2 Kings 2:11.)

John the Baptist

This prophecy has an interesting setting. According to Luke 3:1,15, many Jews anticipated Messiah would arrive during the 15th year of Tiberius Caesar. This anticipation was based on the fact that A.D. 27 marked the commencement of the 70th week since the decree to restore Jerusalem was issued by Artaxerxes on Nisan 1, 457 B.C.[1] (Ezra 7,8) The Jews were not alone in their expectations, even the Samaritans anticipated the appearing of Messiah! (See John 4:25.)

Interest in the appearing of Messiah had been fueled by the appearance of a strange and powerful man whom many people regarded as a prophet. His name was John. It was the custom of John the Baptist (John the baptizer) to hold services out in the desert, near the Jordan River. He preferred the sobriety of the wilderness to the din of the city and many of the curious ventured into the wilderness to hear him. John's preaching created a sensation for he spoke with power and penetrating insight. He claimed the kingdom of God was at hand and many people believed him. His prophetic message debunked the teaching of the religious leaders and the superstitions imbedded in Judaism. People and priests were "pricked in the heart" because of their sins. As they listened to this man of God, they realized the Messiah would appear and establish His kingdom very soon! John made it very clear that sinners with a rebellious attitude could not be a part of God's kingdom. "Therefore," he cried, "repent of your sins and be baptized." Holy Spirit power rested on John the Baptist. His words carried much weight. They deeply stirred the hearts of his listeners and as his popularity grew, the clergy in Jerusalem became increasingly troubled with him.

---

[1] A.D. 27 is the 15th year of the reign of Tiberius according to the Jewish method of inclusive reckoning. Inclusive reckoning means that any part of a unit counts as a unit. In this example, any part of a year counts as a year. The following list demonstrates how Luke counted the 15th year of Tiberius using the Jewish civil calendar which starts a new year on Tishri 1 (October/November):

Year 1 = A.D. 14/14 (Tiberius was granted sole authority on September 17. From September 17 to November 11 [Tishri 1] is counted as one year.)
Year 2 = A.D. 14/15 (Tishri 1 to Tishri 1)
Year 3 = A.D. 15/16 (Tishri 1 to Tishri 1)
Year 4 = A.D. 16/17 (etc.)
Year 5 = A.D. 17/18
Year 6 = A.D. 18/19
Year 7 = A.D. 19/20
Year 8 = A.D. 20/21   *(Footnote continued on following page)*

"Who Are You?"

One day, the *Religious Affairs Department* in Jerusalem sent a group of priests to the Jordan River to question the uneducated "wild-man" who was causing such a stir among the people. (See John 1:19-23.) Notice the sequence of the priests' questions, because the questions were based on their understanding of prophecy. Their first question to John was, "Are you Messiah?" John answered, "No." Then, they asked if he was Elijah. Again, John answered, "No." They asked if he was the prophet that Moses had predicted. (See Deuteronomy 18:15.) John again responded, "No." In desperation, they finally asked, "Who are you?" John answered by quoting from Isaiah 40:3, "**I am the voice of one calling in the desert, 'Make straight the way for the Lord.'** " (John 1:23)

Satisfied that John the Baptist was not the Messiah, Elijah, or the prophet predicted by Moses, the priests returned to Jerusalem with their report. As you might guess, the problem was their misunderstanding of whom John represented. They *assumed,* based on their interpretation of Malachi, that the physical appearing of Elijah was a mandatory fulfillment before Messiah could appear. This interpretation helped the Pharisees to reject Jesus as Messiah because John the Baptist plainly declared that he was not Elijah. They concluded that if there was no Elijah, there could be no Messiah. Look again at the prophecy of Malachi 4 on page 48. How do you interpret it? If you had been a Pharisee at that time, would you have doubted that Jesus was the Messiah since Elijah had not physically appeared?

"Where is Elijah?"

The only way to reach an accurate prophetic conclusion is to combine the harmony of the Scriptures with the help of the Holy Spirit. In other words, spiritual things are spiritually understood. (1 Corinthians 2:14) About two years after the priests had questioned John the Baptist, Peter, James and

---

(Footnote Continued)

Year 9 = A.D. 21/22
Year 10 = A.D. 22/23
Year 11 = A.D. 23/24
Year 12 = A.D. 24/25
Year 13 = A.D. 25/26
Year 14 = A.D. 26/27
Year 15 = A.D. 27/28 (Jesus baptized sometime after Tishri 1.)

John went with Jesus to a mountain top now called the Mount of Transfiguration. There they saw Jesus visit with Elijah and Moses. (Matthew 17:1-9) The disciples thought this was the Elijah that Malachi had predicted! But Elijah did not stay on Earth, in fact, only those men on the mountain saw him. They must have wondered why Elijah and Moses made the trip from Heaven to see Jesus. The Father sent Elijah and Moses as representatives of the human race to encourage Jesus as He was about to meet His rendezvous with death. The salvation of the human race depended on Jesus obediently going to the cross. Elijah was a representative of people who will be saved without seeing death and Moses represented those who will be resurrected from death and the grave. Of course, at the time, the disciples did not comprehend that Jesus was about to die. In fact, they were waiting for Him to establish a glorious kingdom. A short time after the mountain top experience they asked Jesus about Elijah and the prophetic argument the Pharisees used to negate the possibility that Jesus was the Messiah. They asked, **"Why then do the teachers of the law say that Elijah must come first?"** (Matthew 17:10) Jesus responded, **"'To be sure, Elijah comes and will restore all things. But I tell you, Elijah has already come, and they did not recognize him, but have done to him everything they wished. In the same way the Son of Man is going to suffer at their hands.' Then the disciples understood that he was talking to them about John the Baptist."** (Matthew 17:11-13)

Was John the Baptist the promised Elijah? The answer is both no and yes. No, John the Baptist was not the *physical* person of Elijah. Everyone knew that John was the son of Zechariah and Elizabeth. But yes, John the Baptist was a *spiritual type* of Elijah. Notice what the angel Gabriel said to John's father, Zechariah, before his son was born, **"And he will go before the Lord, in the spirit and power of Elijah, to turn the hearts of the fathers to their children and the disobedient to the wisdom of the righteous – to make ready a people prepared for the Lord."** (Luke 1:17)

Jesus Applies the Prophecy

Jesus clearly understood the importance of John's work. He said, **"Among those born of women there has not risen anyone greater than John the Baptist; yet he who is least in the kingdom of Heaven is greater than he . . . And if you are willing to accept it, he is the Elijah who was to come. He who has ears, let him hear."** (Matthew 11:11,14) There is that phrase again, **"He who has ears, let him hear."** Notice that Jesus said, **". . . if you are willing to accept it, he** [John the Baptist] **is the Elijah who was to come."** (insertion mine.) In other words, the prophecy of Malachi was fulfilled by John the Baptist. The fulfillment of the prophecy was not based on the appearing of Elijah in the flesh, but the ministry of John in *the spirit and power* of Elijah. (Luke 1:17) There is a very important reason for using this particular example of Bible prophecy. If faulty presuppositions are used to interpret Malachi's prophecy, the prophecy contributes to the rejection of Jesus as Messiah. If Elijah does not appear, Messiah cannot appear. But according to Jesus, John the Baptist fulfilled Malachi's prophecy because he appeared in the spirit and power of Elijah. This is an important lesson. We must be very careful to use the correct methods of prophetic interpretation. A wrong turn in interpretation can have very serious consequences!

Summary

Jesus is the Word, the Alpha and Omega in all things pertaining to the Godhead. He is the Revealer of love and truth about the Godhead. There is no other flawless source. Jesus is a perfect demonstration of what faith in God is all about. The role of the Holy Spirit is also central in the Plan of Salvation. His mission and work are to draw each person into a faith relationship with God. A faith relationship is defined as an obedient surrender to God's will – to go where the Spirit directs, to do as the Spirit convicts and to become all that the Spirit urges. When the Holy Spirit is allowed to live within our heart, He creates a thirst for knowledge about God. As we learn more about the life, teaching and doctrines of Jesus Christ, we also begin to understand more about the will, ways and truth of God. (John 16:14,15) Finally, Bible prophecy is a form of present truth that becomes understandable and applicable on or about the time of fulfillment. When rightly understood and combined with progressive historical fulfillment, Bible prophecy proves that God keeps vigil over Earth. It also proves that God has a plan to save man. The good news is that very soon, the plan will be completed.

Chapter 4
Salvation through Justification

Therefore, since we have been justified through faith, we have peace with God through our Lord Jesus Christ, through whom we have gained access by faith into this grace in which we now stand. And we rejoice in the hope of the glory of God.

— Romans 5:1,2

The Way to Eternal Life Is Through Jesus

Consider these five statements:

1. The only way a sinner can receive eternal life is through justification.

2. Justification is a legal standing in the court of Heaven in which a sinner is viewed as though he has not broken the law (is without sin).

3. Justification occurs when a person becomes willing to obey the authority of the Holy Spirit and live a life of faith.

4. Justification can be illustrated in the following way: Angels record the words, actions and motives of every person. Within the book of records is a faithful record of each sinner's life. When a sinner becomes willing to obediently submit to the authority of the Holy Spirit and live by faith, Jesus justifies that sinner by placing His perfect life over the record of the sinner. As long as the covering life of Jesus remains intact, that sinner is not under the penalty of sin. He is free of the condemnation which God's law demands.

5. An absolute knowledge of God is not required for justification. However, a sinner's ongoing obedient submission to the Holy Spirit is required for the continuation of justification.

Blessed Assurance

Any sinner can receive the assurance of eternal life *right now, this very minute,* if he or she agrees to obediently submit to the demands of the Holy Spirit. If you are willing at this very moment to go, to be, and to do all that the Holy Spirit asks of you, rejoice! The assurance of eternal life is yours through a heavenly process called justification. Whenever this transforming moment occurs, a new life of faith begins. Of course, a sinner can return to his sinful ways at any time because the power of choice still remains. (Ezekiel 18) Just because we are willing to submit to the demands of the Holy Spirit today does not mean that we have to submit to His sanctifying demands tomorrow. To a large extent, the internal authority of the Holy Spirit is limited by our desire and cooperation. If a person so desires, He can be permanently turned away. (Matthew 12:31,32)

How can we tell if the Holy Spirit is pressing us for submission? How can we distinguish between the guilt produced by the Holy Spirit or some kind of false guilt? The urging of the Holy Spirit always conforms to Heaven's constitution of love. We are to love the Lord with all our heart, mind and soul, and we are to love our neighbor as we love ourselves. The difference between false guilt and guilt imposed by the Holy Spirit becomes easier to differentiate as we learn more about Jesus. Jesus is the Author and Finisher of our faith. His example helps us understand many things about the properties of life. A growing knowledge of Jesus Christ sets us free of unnecessary guilt and burdens which God has not imposed.

The process of entering into the assurance of eternal life happens in a rather predictable way, although it is not limited to this process. Here's my experience: The Holy Spirit produced a strong feeling and relentless conviction that I was guilty of sin before God. My guilt and condemnation weighed often on my mind, because unbeknown to me at the time, the Holy Spirit was trying to motivate me to "get right" with God. Eventually, I recognized my condemnation as a sinner and I wanted pardon for my sins. I desired to know God. I had heard enough to know that people who do wicked things have no hope of a future life and I did not want to miss out on Heaven. I did not know much about God in those days, but I believed God would be pleased with me if I stopped doing things which I knew were wrong. I also knew that it was impossible for me to stop sinning and I wondered how God dealt with human beings like me. The problem was simple: He wanted me to stop sinning, but I could not stop sinning. How could I be saved and go on sinning? In those days, I did not understand the wonderful offer of justification.

Over time as my spiritual maturity developed, I became *willing* to go, to be and to do as God directed in my life – no holds barred. I did not become a Christian by invitation. That is, I did not decide to become a Christian by walking down the aisle to the front of a church. One day I made a commitment to God and became a Christian. I was at work when I resolved that from now on, I would be a follower of Jesus Christ, no matter what it cost. If I remember correctly, one of my first decisions involved restitution. I understood that God's grace and forgiveness were not a whitewash for wrong doing. From my personal Bible study, I concluded that God required me to make restitution to those whom I had defrauded in the past. So, I began to make restitution for past wrongs as best I knew how. This was expensive, and it required several hundred dollars. After reviewing my past and making every wrong right as far as possible, I confessed my sins to God and have had perfect peace about them ever since. I was happy and truly free of guilt, which made me feel much closer to God. I resolved, by God's grace, not to do those things again. Do not be fooled! Sin is always expensive! Sin will take you farther than you want to go and cost you more than you want to pay. During this transforming process in my life, some of my friends fled. They thought I had become a religious fanatic.

By faith, I accepted God's assurance that He was pleased with my actions. I was happier and felt closer to God, although my understanding of God and His will was very limited. Thirty years later, my peace and joy remain. As long as I continue to obey the demands of the indwelling Holy Spirit, I know Jesus *justifies* me before the Father as though I am without sin, even though I am a sinner. Because of this, I am at peace with God and have the joyful assurance of salvation. Yes, I still sin, but now I understand a few things about dealing with sin. First, accidental or unintentional sin does not bring eternal death. John says, **"All wrongdoing is sin, and there is sin that does not lead to death."** (1 John 5:17) Second, I am prone to sin and rebellion because I am under the curse of sin. Paul noticed the same thing after being a Christian for almost 25 years. He wrote, **"But I see another law at work in the members of my body, waging war against the law of my mind and making me a prisoner of the law of sin at work within my members."** (Romans 7:23) Last, when I do sin there is a process that I must obediently follow. First, I have to acknowledge to the Holy Spirit that I understand the guilt He is imposing in my heart because I have sinned. Next, I have to confess to my neighbor that I have sinned against him and I must provide restitution as far as possible. Last, I turn to Jesus. John says, **"If we confess our sins, he is faithful and just and will forgive us our sins and purify us from all unrighteousness."** (1 John 1:9) This order of events is well stated in Scripture. (Matthew 5:23-26) If I am faithful in dealing with the sin problem, my willingness to go, to be and to do God's will is affirmed. Jesus sees the evidence of my faith and He, my Savior and Lord, grants me the covering of His righteousness.

Justification is possible for three reasons. First, God's offer of justification is based on nothing but God's love for man. **"For God so loved the world that he gave his one and only Son, that whoever believes in him shall not perish but have eternal life. For God did not send his Son into the**

world to condemn the world, but to save the world through him.”
(John 3:16,17) Second, Jesus came to Earth and He lived a perfect life so
that He might cover us with His righteous life! **“For if, when we were
God's enemies, we were reconciled to him through the death of his
Son, how much more, having been reconciled, shall we be saved
through his life!”** (Romans 5:10) Last, Jesus is qualified to justify repentant
sinners because He paid our penalty for sin. In other words, sinners cannot be
justified as sinless people if the penalty upon sinners has not been removed.
Jesus provided the necessary restitution for every sinner. The merits of this
restitution are transferred to sinners when they submit to the demands of the
Holy Spirit. When I became *willing* to submit to God's will, Jesus covered my
sinful life with His perfect life. (Romans 5:17) Notice, I emphasized the
word willing. We are not justified by works. Works are a reflection of the
motives and desires of our heart. We can do right for the wrong reason
(legalism) and we can attempt to justify wrong doing (rebellion). Making
restitution in order to be saved is a corrupt motive. An honest motivation
that prompts appropriate restitution comes from a deeper understanding of
what loving our neighbor is all about.

A parallel between all sinners and Adam and Eve's Garden of Eden experience provides an excellent illustration. When Adam and Eve sinned, they
lost the covering of light that covered their bodies. Realizing their shame,
they ran and hid from God. They tried to cover their nakedness with some
large itchy fig leaves, but Jesus used this opportunity to present a wonderful object lesson. Jesus killed a flawless sacrificial lamb and I presume He
covered the naked pair with its skin. (Genesis 3:7-21) The parallel for every
sinner is that we too, stand naked before God. He knows who we are,
where we are, and He knows all of our sins. Any attempt to cover up (or
justify) sin is foolish. Jesus offers “His perfect skin” as the Lamb of God, the
spotless wedding garment of His righteousness, to all of us. If we surrender
our will to God and daily submit to the demands of the Holy Spirit, Jesus
covers our nakedness with His perfect righteous life. Therefore, when the
Father sees us wearing the robe of Jesus' righteousness, we stand before
God fully clothed, as though we never sinned! This is the profound beauty
of “justification through faith!” (Ephesians 2:8,9) Justification is available to
every person who has lived, regardless of religious background.

Just As Though I Have Never Sinned

My joy and peace is full because I know that when the Father looks at me,
He sees me as though I am without sin. Christ's perfect life of righteousness can cover the worst sinner. Justification does not require works,

deeds or proof that I am a changed man. The thief on the cross did not prove that he was a changed man, but he was granted the righteousness of Jesus that very day. (Ephesians 2:8,9; Luke 23:43) I am sure the thief would have become a different man if he could have lived longer. The profound beauty of justification is that it begins in Heaven the moment we become willing to submit to the authority of the indwelling Spirit. As long as we continue in a submissive attitude (to be, to go, to do) toward God's authority over our lives, we have the assurance of eternal life.

This, in a nutshell, is how my justification and yours begin before God through Christ. Even though the process is simple, it is a miracle! How the Holy Spirit transforms a rebellious heart into a submissive heart is a mystery that God alone knows, but it does happen! (John 3; Romans 8) So, if you are missing the joy and peace that comes from "letting go and letting God," if you have not experienced the full assurance of God's salvation through the justification that Jesus offers, if you have not grasped something about God's great love for you, review the process and implement those portions that remain unfinished in your life. If the Holy Spirit is not beating you up with that strong and relentless conviction that you need salvation, perhaps you need to slow down and ask God to speak to your heart! The Spirit will reveal your true condition before God if you open your heart. I have been there, and my testimony is not unusual. Submit to the Holy Spirit's prompting, confess your sins, provide restitution where possible and joy and peace will surely follow.

That's Not All!

Now comes the scary part! When a person receives the assurance of salvation through justification, he or she begins a faith-journey. The journey may seem frightening at times, because you do not know where the journey will lead, but you know Who is leading. You may not know which road you will take, but you know where you will end up. You do not know how you will get there, but you know a way will be made. In short, walking with Jesus is a scary experience at times, because The Good Shepherd leads His sheep over dangerous mountain trails and through the deepest ravines to take them home. The scary part should not be the travail of travel, but the possibility of losing sight of The Good Shepherd. When two people stand at the marriage altar and unite their lives by agreeing to vows of fidelity, they begin a journey of a lifetime that will take them through uncharted waters. So it is when we join ourselves to Jesus. People who join themselves to Jesus begin a journey that is uncharted to the human eye. Marriage requires fidelity, loyalty, faith and love and so does the journey with Jesus.

Basic Law

By definition, "basic law" is an instinct or inherent ability to rationally determine right from wrong. This phenomenon is exhibited by most young people at an early age. When a child has achieved enough maturity to determine right and wrong on his or her own, that age is often called the age of accountability. Thomas Jefferson eloquently noted the presence of "basic law" in the "Introduction" of the *Bill of Rights* for the *U.S. Constitution*. He wrote, "We hold certain truths to be self evident . . ." In other words, intelligent people can determine right from wrong because "basic law" is operating and this feature is self evident within all of humanity. Yet, the opposite is just as true. If someone does not want to understand or agree with the truth, no one can show them the truth! In fact, people who want to justify evil are the first to deny what is right. (John 3:20)

God created human beings with reasoning powers. Even before Eve tasted the forbidden fruit, God wanted man to distinguish between good and evil. If people strive to live right and be honorable – no matter what religion they belong to – they are doing all that God asks of them.

God does not hold a person guilty who does not know His will, but God will condemn a person who refuses to accept the truth! This is a critical point in understanding how salvation operates. Man is not saved by knowing or agreeing with absolute truth, instead man is saved by faithfully living up to all he believes to be righteous and true. Closely study Paul's comments: **"Indeed, when Gentiles, who do not have the law** [e.g. the knowledge of God penned by Moses, but they], **do by nature things required by the law, they are a law for themselves, even though they do not have the law, since they show that the requirements of the law are written on their hearts, their consciences also bearing witness** [when they do wrong], **and their thoughts now accusing** [them of their wrong deeds], [this confirms they know right from wrong and their conscience is] **now even defending them. This** [is how the judgement] **will take place on the day when God will judge men's secrets through Jesus Christ, as my gospel declares."** (Romans 2:14-16, insertions mine.)

The word *law* as used by Paul in this context is a reference to Moses' writings. The point Paul is making is that God judges the heart and takes into consideration the knowledge base that is in the heart. Therefore, Gentiles who know nothing about the true God and His ways will be judged by the *same process* as Jews and Christians who have had every opportunity to know God and His ways. God righteously judges each person on the basis of his or her knowledge base and the resulting actions. (Ecclesiastes 12:13,14) People who live up to the high ideals of what they honestly believe God wants of them demonstrate the kind of *faith* that pleases God! James also supports the concept of basic law. He says, **"Anyone, then, who knows the good he ought to do and doesn't do it, sins."** (James 4:17)

I do not want to leave you with the impression that God is not concerned with absolute right and wrong. He is very concerned about absolute right and wrong. The Ten Commandments are ten absolutes. Period. They are not "Ten Suggestions" or a place to begin negotiation. Jesus Himself wrote the Ten Commandments on tablets of stone and His eternal law is more enduring than stone. Still, God understands that everyone on Earth does not know about His absolutes or the terms and conditions within the Plan of Salvation. Therefore, He righteously judges each person on their knowledge base, actions *and* willingness to search for and submit to higher truths as the Holy Spirit leads. God does not require that we know or understand all His marvelous truths in order to receive salvation, for no one on Earth understands everything there is to know about God! However, God does require that we submit, by faith, to a growing spiritual process so we might know His will. (1 Thessalonians 4:1-8) If we honestly submit to the leading of the Holy Spirit as we understand it, to go, to be and to do His will, God is pleased. If we endeavor to grow in knowledge and understanding, Jesus will bless us with a deeper understanding of truth!

Nothing on Earth compares to walking with God. He is anxious to reveal the issues and ways of life! God knows our knowledge base and the motives that prompt our actions and still loves us in spite of our great ignorance. But, and this is an emphatic "but," God is not pleased when we compromise our beliefs or shrink back from the demands of faith. Jesus said, **"If anyone is ashamed of me and my words, the Son of Man will be ashamed of him when he comes in his glory and in the glory of the Father and of the holy angels."** (Luke 9:26)

While we are on the topic of ignorance and law, consider the practical side of ignorance of the law. Since one man cannot read the heart or determine the motives of another man, man has to take an opposite approach to the issue of ignorance and law. Man's laws take the perspective: "Ignorance is no excuse for breaking the law." So when a person gives the excuse, "But officer, I did not know the speed limit was 35. . .," we should not be surprised when the officer writes a traffic citation.

Salvation Includes Full Restoration

The Plan of Salvation begins with "basic law." Realization that we need a Savior comes after we sense guilt and become aware of sin's penalty. Without the presence and operation of basic law, there would be no guilt and salvation would not be deemed necessary or desirable! In other words, an infant does not find salvation necessary or desirable, because an infant cannot reason. The Bible does not support infant baptism. The notion of infant baptism originally began from a distortion of Christ's teaching. **"Jesus answered** [Nicodemus], **'I tell you the truth, no one can enter the kingdom of God unless he is born of water and the Spirit.' "** (John 3:5, insertion mine.) A superficial reading of this text can result in this twisted meaning: "Unless a person is baptized by water, he or she cannot receive eternal life." In ancient times, the Christian Church abused this text and unfortunately, the tradition continues today. History reveals that the early Church used baptism and other rituals to control access to salvation. If people were cut off (or excommunicated) from the rituals offered by the Church, they were not considered eligible for eternal life. Since adherents believed the rituals were mandatory for salvation, this gave a great deal of control to the Church. The Church implemented infant baptism because infant mortality rates were very high. To insure that every infant would enter Heaven, the Church taught that children had to be baptized as soon as possible. Of course, an appropriate "gift" to the Church was also expected. Obviously, an infant does not know one thing about basic law, guilt or salvation, and the Bible clearly teaches that salvation does not come through rituals or works of the flesh. (Ephesians 2:8,9)

Let us examine the meaning of John 3:5. No one can enter the kingdom of God unless (a) his or her heart is made alive to spiritual matters by the Holy Spirit, and (b) he or she is washed clean of rebellion. During the time of Nicodemus, it was customary to immerse Gentile converts who wished to become citizens of Israel in the Jordan River. The Jews regarded baptism by immersion as a symbolic act indicating death (burial) to the past and resurrection to a new life. In other words, a Gentile went down into the water and a Jew came out! Jesus used the symbol of baptism to make His point to Nicodemus that if a person wants to become a member of God's kingdom, he or she too, must to be "born of water" to become a member of a new kingdom. (Romans 6:1-7)

The Bible reveals that children are born with the assurance of salvation *until* they chose otherwise. In other words, God does not hold children accountable for sin until they know better (accountability begins when basic law starts working within a young person - James 4:17). Since Jesus paid the price for each sinner and children are not held accountable for sin, what prevents them from having the assurance of salvation? Some Christians believe just the opposite, believing that a child is born condemned to eternal death. This was the reasoning used in ancient times when infant baptism began. But consider this: If God considers an adult sinner a saint because of his or her faith in Jesus Christ's atonement, why not a mere child, who is simply too young to know right from wrong? God is much more geerous than man and God loves every child – for of such is the kingdom of Heaven! (Matthew 19:14)

How Man Became Unsaved

Why is justification necessary in the Plan of Salvation? What makes salvation necessary in the first place? Why did Jesus have to die on the cross? What issues are involved between God and man? These are very important questions and we will examine them.

According to the book of Genesis, God created man in His image, forming him out of dirt. God placed man in the Garden of Eden, where he had unrestricted access to the Tree of Life. As long as man had access to the fruit on the Tree of Life, man's life was sustained indefinitely. The point must be made that Jesus created man (and even the angels) as mortal beings. The word "mortal" means to be subject to death, having a beginning and the possibility of an end. The word "immortal" means to have no beginning or end and is a term that applies only to God. (1 Timothy 6:15,16; Hebrews 7:3; Revelation 1:18) Many people are surprised to learn the Bible teaches that human beings are mortal because they have a beginning and the possibility of an end. Genesis 2:7 says, **"The Lord God formed the man from the dust of the ground and breathed into his nostrils the breath of life, and the man *became* a living being."** (Italics mine.) Adam did not exist as some intelligent entity prior to his creation. The soul of Adam came into existence on the sixth day of Creation when God put the breath of life into a body made of dirt. In a similar manner, the soul of Adam ceased to exist when the breath of life was taken from his body of dirt. After his death, Adam does not exist as some intelligent entity. The soul of man is mortal. **"The soul who sins is the one who will die. The son will not share the guilt of the father, nor will the father share the guilt of the son. The righteousness of the righteous man will be credited to him, and the wickedness of the wicked will be charged against him."** (Ezekiel 18:20)

Jesus told Adam, "**. . . You are free to eat from any tree in the garden; but you must not eat from the tree of the knowledge of good and evil, for when you eat of it you will surely die.**" (Genesis 2:16,17) It may surprise you to learn that Adam and Eve were to perish *the very day* they ate the forbidden fruit. The Hebrew text expresses the immediacy of death saying, **"in the day of your eating from it surely you will die,"** the King James Version says: "**. . . for in the day that thou eatest thereof thou shalt surely die.**" (Genesis 2:17) For me, the Bible is clear. Adam and Eve were to be executed the very day they sinned. The penalty for sin is death *by execution.* Most Christians overlook this important point. There are two types of death. Death caused by disease, accident or "natural causes" is the *consequence* of sin, but the *penalty* for sin is death by execution. This is why it was necessary for Jesus to be executed at Calvary and this also explains why the wicked will be executed by fire at the end of the 1,000 years. Many Bible students have difficulty interpreting Genesis 2:16,17 because Adam and Eve did not die the day they sinned. The reason they were not slain *that very day* is this: Jesus immediately went before the Father and offered to die in man's place. The Father accepted the offer of Jesus and their execution was stayed. Ever since that fateful day, Jesus has fulfilled two roles in Heaven. He is our Intercessor and He is the Lamb of God. Later in this book, we will consider how these two roles reflect two unique processes that are necessary for man to be fully reconciled with God.

Sin Begins

Genesis 3:6 says, **"When the woman saw that the fruit of the tree was good for food and pleasing to the eye, and also desirable for gaining wisdom, she took some and ate it. She also gave some to her husband, who was with her, and he ate it."** I believe the devil schemed and planned his approach at the tree for some time and he was unbelievably successful. He gained Eve's full attention and ultimately her confidence. The fruit was beautiful and desirable, and after he had beguiled Eve with his comments, she tasted it. The serpent quickly left the tree and Eve, no doubt, felt strange and uncomfortable inside. For the first time she felt the guilt of sin. Quickly she gathered up some of the fruit and ran to Adam. Adam recognized the forbidden fruit Eve was holding and knew she was in deep trouble. She excitedly explained the course of events and then, in an innocent way, sought his companionship by offering him some fruit. Adam must have thought: "God will strike Eve dead today because she ate the fruit and if she is taken from me, life will be miserable and lonely." Eve was created to perfection, she was beautiful and she had been his "soul mate" since the day of their creation. She was part of him, they were of one flesh and spirit, and he was deeply distressed. Therefore, out of love and devotion for Eve, he chose to eat the fruit and share God's punishment with her. Unfortunately, Adam loved Eve more than he trusted God to resolve the problem.

A very important distinction can be made between the sins of Adam and Eve. Eve believed a lie and she sinned in ignorance. Adam, chose to disobey God and eat the forbidden fruit because of his love for Eve. Even though Adam's sin was not an act of defiance, it was intentional and willful. Remember the text? **"And the Lord God commanded the man, 'You are free to eat from any tree in the garden; but you must not eat from the tree of the knowledge of good and evil, for when you eat of it you will surely die.' "** (Genesis 2:16,17) Adam knew better, his sin was deliberate, whereas Eve's sin was not. Therefore, Paul concludes that Adam is responsible for the entrance of sin on Earth and not Eve! **"Therefore, just as sin entered the world through one man, and death through sin, and in this way death came to all men, because all sinned. . . ."** (Romans 5:12) This verse explains why Jesus could not overlook the sin of Adam and Eve. It would have been great if God could have said, "O.K. Adam and Eve, we will overlook your sin this one time, but you had better not sin again!" God could not say these words for two reasons: First, Adam and Eve were now subject to the penalty of sin. They had violated God's law. God's law cannot be cancelled or altered because His universal government is based on the rule of unchanging law. Second, after Adam and Eve sinned, they were not the same. They were immediately transformed by sin and their minds and hearts suddenly became hostile to the authority of the Godhead.

Passing the Blame

Adam and Eve were confronted with their sin that evening. When they heard Jesus approaching, they ran and hid. They were ashamed, naked and defensive. When confronted with their deeds, they were strangely unrepentant! Eve blamed her actions on the serpent. She said, **"The serpent deceived me, and I ate."** (Genesis 3:13) Even worse, Adam blamed his rebellion on his Creator and then on Eve! Adam said, **"The woman *you* put here with me - *she* gave me some fruit from the tree and I ate it."** (Genesis 3:12, italics mine.) The moment Adam and Eve became sinners, their natures changed. Instead of having a predisposition toward righteousness, they became rebellious and carnal. The Creator listened and then He spoke. He addressed the serpent first, then He placed a curse upon the woman, and last, He turned to Adam and said,

". . . because you listened to your wife and ate from the tree about which I commanded you, 'You must not eat of it,' Cursed is the ground because of you; through painful toil you will eat of it all the days of your life . . . By the sweat of your brow you will eat your food until you return to the ground, since from it you were taken; for dust you are and to dust you will return." (Genesis 3:17-19)

Access Denied

God drove Adam and Eve from the Garden of Eden for one simple reason. They could not have access to the Tree of Life! Read the following text carefully, as it contains a conversation between the members of the Godhead: **"The Lord God said, 'The man has now become like one of us, knowing good and evil. He must not be allowed to reach out his hand and take also from the tree of life and eat, and live forever** [without end].**' So the Lord God banished him from the Garden of Eden to work the ground from which he had been taken. After he drove the man out, he placed on the east side of the Garden of Eden cherubim and a flaming sword flashing back and forth to guard the way to the Tree of Life."** (Genesis 3:22-24, insertion mine.)

Two Types of Death Created

At this point in the story, it is very important to consider a development that occurred that fateful day. Remember, God had warned that Adam and Eve would be executed the very day they ate the fruit of the forbidden tree. If the execution had been carried out, that would have been the end of the story. However, when Jesus stepped "in the way" of their execution, offering to die in man's place, an important development occurred: Two types of death were created. It became possible for man to die twice. We know the *penalty* for sin is death by execution, but the *consequence* of being shut away from the Tree of Life is also death. The "first death" occurs as a consequence of sin. People die of cancer, accidents or old age. This type of death is called "sleep" 53 times in the New Testament because in God's eyes it is a temporary death. (See John 6 and 11.) The second death, that is, death by execution, is a future event. The second death is reserved for people who remain defiant against God's authority during their life. The annihilation of the wicked occurs at the end of the 1,000 years. (Revelation 20:14) Currently, no one has experienced the "second death" (except Jesus) because God has not executed the wicked. The second death occurs by fire and the results are eternal and final.

The reason Adam and Eve had to be banished from the garden and denied access to the Tree of Life was because God did not want sin to live forever. Notice how this works: Man was created a mortal being (man has a beginning and the possibility of an end). If man cannot obtain the fruit from the Tree of Life, he dies. Have you ever considered how the rebellious predisposition of Adam and Eve, like a biological trait, has been passed down to all the offspring of the guilty pair for nearly 6,000 years? The heritage and power of sin were quickly revealed in their firstborn son, Cain, who became a murderer!

Think of Adam and Eve's suffering outside the garden. The Bible says that Adam lived 930 years. (Genesis 5:5) Imagine living that long and observing the terrible consequences of your own sinful choice! Adam had to watch the consequences of his own deed for an extended period of time. He had lived *within* that glorious garden before sin began, now he survived by the sweat of his brow *outside* the garden. He saw the effects of the infectious blight of sin within his family and on all of nature. Think of Adam's mental and emotional agony – living nine centuries to witness the degenerate effects of his wrong doing – all this to be with Eve. And, of course, Eve painfully experienced the degenerate effects of sin within her own body during childbirth, not to mention the disappointing behavior of her children. I am sure that as she held in her arms the lifeless body of her second son, Abel, she was overwhelmed with grief as she began to choke on the bitter taste of sin.

Jesus Not Caught by Surprise

The sins of Adam and Eve did not catch Heaven by surprise. In fact, the very day Adam and Eve sinned, Jesus became man's intercessor by stepping "in the way" of the executing angel. (Isaiah 53:12; Job 16:20,21; Hebrews 7:25) Jesus stepped between the wrath of God's law (death by execution) and the guilty pair when He offered to die in man's place. In my mind's eye, I can visualize the scene. The executioner was preparing to leave Heaven to slay Adam and Eve, but Jesus ran to the Father. Jesus petitioned the Father to allow Him to die in man's place. The Father agreed to the petition of Jesus and the work of execution was delayed. Jesus came to Earth and shared with Adam and Eve that a way had been provided for them to one day be restored to their Eden home. Ever since that day, the way back to the Garden of Eden has been called the "Plan of Salvation." The plan includes many features that reveal a Godhead of love. One marvelous feature about the plan is the Father's willingness to justify sinners with the righteousness of Christ.

What Must I Do?

" 'Sirs, what must I do to be saved?' They replied, 'Believe in the Lord Jesus, and you will be saved – you and your household.' " (Acts 16:30,31) A frightened jailer cried out for his life in the middle of the night and an assuring response came from two prisoners. The words that Paul and Silas spoke that night have echoed from that prison cell for almost 2,000 years. However, Paul and Silas' response includes much more than many Christians understand! To understand this passage of Scripture the student has to take off his Nike's and put on the sandals of Paul and Silas. In other words, we have to consider the circumstances during which these words were spoken.

The setting in Acts 16 begins a few years before the Romans destroyed Jerusalem in A.D. 70. The mutual hatred between the Romans and Jews was fierce. To make matters worse, the Romans regarded Christians as just another Jewish sect because most Christians were former Jews who continued to observe a number of Jewish customs even after they became Christians. While in the Macedonian city of Philippi, Paul cast a demon out of a young slave girl, who was "a fortune teller." She had earned large sums of money for her owners and when the owners realized their financial loss, they initiated a riot saying, **" '. . .These men are** [those rebellious] **Jews, and are throwing our city into an uproar by advocating customs unlawful for us Romans to accept or practice.' The crowd joined in the attack against Paul and Silas, and the magistrates ordered them to be stripped and beaten. After they had been severely flogged, they were thrown into prison, and the jailer was commanded to guard them carefully."** (Acts 16:20-23, insertion mine.)

Notice in the previous text that Paul and Silas were identified as Jews – their nationality was the inflammatory word that justified the riot. The instigators of the riot did not need to say more. However, in the mob's angry rush to assault two more Jews who were not welcomed, city leaders failed to consider whether Paul and Silas were Roman citizens – a significant oversight since Roman law mandated that Romans could not be punished or imprisoned without a fair trial. Non-Romans could be punished on the spot.

After Paul and Silas were flogged severely, they were placed under the care of a Roman jailer. The jailer understood the rules of Roman guardianship and he was paid good wages to guard well. If prisoners escaped from his jail, he was automatically guilty of negligence – end of discussion and end of life. Such were the no-nonsense, ironclad rules of Roman government. The jailer had heard Paul and Silas preach. No doubt, the jailer was also a good judge of character. He was fascinated with their teachings about Jesus Christ and their miracle working power, but he was foremost a public servant and prisoners were his highest priority.

"About midnight Paul and Silas were praying and singing hymns to God, and the other prisoners were listening to them. Suddenly there was such a violent earthquake that the foundations of the prison were shaken. At once all the prison doors flew open, and everybody's chains came loose. The jailer woke up, and when he saw the prison doors open, he drew his sword and was about to kill himself because he thought the prisoners had escaped. But Paul shouted, 'Don't harm yourself! We are all here!' The jailer called for lights, rushed in and fell trembling before Paul and Silas. . . ." (Acts 16:25-29) When the jailer reached the open cell of Paul and Silas, he uttered the most important question on Earth, **"Sirs, what must I do to be saved?"** When I consider his question in the light of his immediate circumstances, I have wondered if the jailer's concern was focused on the receipt of eternal life. In fact, could the jailer really be asking, "What must I do to save my present life and that of my family, because I will be promptly executed if any prisoners escape?" If this was the case, then Paul and Silas' response was instruction leading to justification in God's sight – "Put your trust in Jesus *right now* and you will not lose your life, nor will your household perish." Look at the verse again: **" 'Sirs, what must I do to be saved?' They replied, 'Believe in the Lord Jesus, and you will be saved – you and your household.' "**

I have yet to meet one Christian who says this verse actually means, "Mr. Jailer, if you will believe in the Lord Jesus this very minute, you and your entire household will be granted eternal life." In other words, most Christians do not believe that one person's acceptance of Jesus saves other family members. So, what did Paul and Silas mean when they said, "Believe in the Lord Jesus"? Here are two choices: First, they could have meant, "Believe that Jesus Christ is a real person. Believe this simple historical truth and He will give you eternal life." I mention this option because some Christians actually believe this to be the intent of Paul and Silas. I find this view makes a mockery of the biblical definition of faith. Second, they could have meant, "Believe that Jesus Christ is your Savior and *submit* your life to His authority. All who do will receive life eternal *at the last day.*" (John 6:39-44) My study leads me to believe that the last choice is the correct answer. Paul and Silas invited a desperate man to immediately submit to the authority of Jesus Christ (as they had done in their own lives) and allow Him to work out the details. This story is paradoxical. Paul and Silas are telling the jailer to submit his life to the Lord Jesus as they had done. However, consider their misfortune – sitting in prison stocks covered with cuts and bruises – inviting the jailer to submit his life also. The point Paul and Silas were making was that when you submit your life to the authority of the Lord Jesus, your life and future are in God's hands. But truthfully, after considering the issues of life and all the options, it really is the only way to go. This story reaffirms that justification begins with total and complete submission. If it takes a life-threatening experience or even an earthquake to produce submission, then so be it. (Remember, Paul himself had a life-threatening encounter with the Lord Jesus on the road to Damascus. This experience led Paul to surrender his life to Jesus immediately. See Acts 9.)

Will Words do the Trick?

Some Christians claim that salvation comes only after a person *publically confesses* faith in Christ as Savior. In other words, to become saved a person has to publicly state that "Jesus is Lord." While this may sound good among church members, the flip side of this concept is a doctrine teaching that most of the world is eternally doomed because more than 70% of the world's population has not confessed, "Jesus is Lord." Carefully notice these texts: "**. . . If you confess with your mouth, 'Jesus is Lord,' and believe in your heart that God raised him from the dead, you will be saved. For it is with your heart that you believe and are justified, and it is with your mouth that you confess and are saved.**" (Romans 10:9,10) "**Salvation is found in no one else, for there is no other name under heaven given to men by which we must be saved.**" (Acts 4:12)

While "proof texts" sound good in a Christian environment, what about the remaining 4.4 billion people who are not Christian? Are people doomed to destruction simply because they were born in a place where there are no Christians or any knowledge of Jesus? Be careful how you answer this question, because God's offer of salvation to the world is not as narrow and simplistic as some Christians claim. There is more to the concept of salvation than first meets the eye. For example, what does a loving God do with:

(a) billions of people down through the centuries who have lived and died without having an opportunity to hear about Christ's generous offer of salvation?

(b) billions of people who rejected Christianity because the "Christians" they knew were disgusting examples of immoral and uncivil behavior?

(c) billions of people who have never honestly considered the teachings of Christianity because they were born into another religious system or culture that taught their religion was superior to Christianity?

(d) billions of good people living right now, as well as in ages past, who never showed serious interest in religion because their parents were not religious?

Are All Four Groups of People Doomed for Destruction?

Through the years I have asked people about these four groups of people and a disappointing number of Christians have callously said that all four groups are doomed for destruction because they never gave their heart to Christ. When I respond, "But billions of people have never had the opportunity to know about Jesus! What does God do with them?" Sometimes I just get an irritated look because it seems unreasonable to say that God would destroy people who have not had a chance to know about salvation. If the frown is not too bad, I have dared to asked further, "Who will receive greater condemnation: The Christian who did little or nothing to propel the gospel of Jesus throughout the world, or the pagan who did not hear the gospel because a Christian did not share the good news with him." These questions are important to consider, because the Bible says that God's love for each person on Earth is the same! (John 3:16; Acts 10:34,35; Romans 2:14,15)

Far too many Christians have a view regarding salvation that is too narrow. Many church members believe that salvation requires sameness. Consider the logic: "If others are going to be saved, they must become like me for I am convinced that I am saved." This concept is the mainspring of many evangelical efforts. However, the larger idea behind justification is that God can justify anyone, anywhere, and at any time a person becomes willing to obediently submit to the authority of the Holy Spirit. Consider the magnanimity of God! When a man (or woman) experiences the "born again" miracle in his heart and receives the assurance of eternal life, he becomes motivated to help others experience the joy and peace that he has received. For example, if he finds the "born again" experience within a particular denomination, it is only natural that he would want others to find the same joy he has found when attending his church. This is not inherently bad. The misunderstanding occurs, however, when one denomination concludes that God will not save people who understand His will in a different way. Unfortunately, this is the basis for Christian exclusivity. In reality, the Christian experience should be one of inclusiveness because the Christian life is a mixture of doctrine and experience. If the balance is right, there will be joy and happiness from wholeheartedly serving God and man. Remember this: Good doctrines stimulate good faith. Bad doctrines produce toxic faith.

Which Church is the Right Church?

A large number of Christians believe that salvation is church specific; that is, you must believe the right things and belong to the right church to be saved. As a result, some Christians will brazenly say that members of other churches are doomed for destruction because they do not follow God correctly! Interestingly, every Christian denomination on Earth claims to be the true church of God. For example, the Roman Catholic Church believes it is the *only* true church of God on Earth. Notice this recent comment: "The fullness of religious truth, unmixed with error, is found only in the Catholic Church, the very Church which Jesus Christ Himself established." (Joel Peters, "*Scripture Alone?, 21 Reasons to reject Sola Scriptura*," p. 64, 1999, Tan Books and Publishers, Inc.) Mr. Peters also concludes that neither the pope nor the Catholic Church can lapse into error. "The Holy Spirit was given to the Church by Jesus Christ, and it is exactly the same Spirit who protects the Church's visible head, the Pope, and the teaching authority of the Church by never permitting him or it to lapse into error." (*Ibid*, p. 26) I use these quotes by a recent Catholic author to demonstrate that Catholics are not reluctant to declare everyone else wrong and themselves the only inerrant depositories of God's truth. However, I must quickly add that every Christian church does the same thing (more or less), even though they may not be as "up front" or boastful about their claims as this Catholic writer.

Religions Differ, but They are Similar

Even though the religions of the world differ, they share certain characteristics. Although we may be a world of many languages, religions, governments and cultures, the ways of humanity are surprisingly similar. Whether we realize it or not, certain laws govern the exercise of religion on Earth and this similarity among diverse religions proves the presence and operation of "basic law." Consider these five laws and the effects they produce:

Law #1: Religion usually limits a person to one view or perspective of God. For this reason, 95% of the world's population stay within the religious system they were born. Moslems tend to stay Moslems, Jews tend to stay Jews, Catholics tend to stay Catholics, Protestants tend to stay Protestants, etc. Why does this phenomenon exist? Ideas about God become a part of a person's conscience at an early age and many people cannot have their views about God challenged without feeling threatened or becoming hostile. Unfortunately, for 95% of the world's inhabitants the only exit from an inherited religion is death.

Law #2: Religion does not change very fast. People who decided to follow Christ were expelled from Judaism because Jewish leaders could not update their thinking. Protestants were expelled from the Roman Catholic Church because papal leaders refused to change their thinking. For a more modern example, the Worldwide Church of God (Armstrong) literally disintegrated during the 1990's when leaders suddenly changed key doctrines. This also reveals that laymen, too, cannot adopt new ideas or change their views very fast either.

Law #3: Religion usually encompasses a body of knowledge that is far larger than laymen care to understand. For this reason, few laymen thoroughly investigate the origin and teachings of their religion. People usually submit (more or less) to the views of their religious authorities unless or until there is a divisive controversy. The confidence, allegiance and trust laymen place in their religious authorities is so great that they usually will not consider a contradicting point of view no matter how logical or well-presented it may be. Often, religious controversies are more about social issues than theology. Because religion is a complex influence that integrates with culture, churches often establish their own publishing houses because laity prefer to read material produced by their own denomination. Of course, this self-indoctrinating process tends to keep the views of the reading laity in line with church tradition.

Law #4: Every religion is inherently self-exalting. Each denomination concludes it has *the* truth about God and all other religions have less truth or no truth. No religious system on Earth will concede that another church has greater truth about God than itself. Christ's experience with the religious leaders of His day should be a warning to religious leaders today. Be careful not to become so devoted to your religion that God Himself cannot open your mind to greater truth.

Law #5: Everyone born on Earth inherits three basic elements of religion, whether institutional religion is practiced or not. Just as we inherit a carnal nature from our parents, we also inherit a basic need to know God. Because Jesus created human beings this way, we should not be surprised that adversarial religions flourish all over the Earth. The basic elements of religion are:

> a. adoration of someone or something greater than self
> b. submission to someone or something greater than self
> c. association with others who share similar adoration

These five laws help to explain *why* religious forces are so strong, why they exist, and why they plague the *entire* human race. These laws explain, in part, why human beings are diverse, yet similar. These laws also explain why a religious gridlock exists throughout our world. Every religion is self exalting; therefore diverse people from all over the world cannot discuss *truth* because there is no common authority from which to start. Every definition of God is different. The Jew has no common ground with the Moslem. The Moslem has no common ground with the Christian, etc. Do not despair; there is good news! God has a plan that will soon break up the religious gridlock of the world. Jesus has a plan that will show the world how each religious system is not the answer to salvation. Jesus is the answer for man's need of salvation. He will extend the offer of salvation to every human being alive during the Great Tribulation. He will save hundreds of millions of people from every nation, kindred, tongue and people who love truth. God will use the world's religious diversity to make a profound point about the way He loves humanity! Here's how: Jesus will send a *powerful* testimony throughout the world during the Great Tribulation. Individuals who love truth and are currently living up to all they know to be right will quickly see the beauty of this simple, but powerful testimony. Millions of people will accept God's truth, even at great peril to life itself. Jesus has carefully designed this final exam. At the end of the Great Tribulation, the people of Earth will be separated into two groups: the sheep and the goats. The sheep will be following The Good Shepherd. The goats will be corralled by the Antichrist.

Confessing that Jesus is Lord

I would like to go back to the text, "**. . . If you confess with your mouth, 'Jesus is Lord,' and believe in your heart that God raised him from the dead, you will be saved. For it is with your heart that you believe and are justified, and it is with your mouth that you confess and are saved.**" (Romans 10:9,10) Some people read this text with the same disregard for its setting, as they do the earlier text in which Paul and Silas told the jailer to trust in Jesus and his household would be saved. To say that eternal life comes by merely stating, "Jesus is Lord" is to miss the essential point of what Paul was saying. When Paul wrote these words, the believers in Rome were in serious trouble. As far as the Romans were concerned, the only difference between the hated Jews and the Christians was words. Consequently, many Christians in Rome lost their possessions, homes and freedom because they would not bow down to Caesar and worship him as Roman law dictated. The Caesars believed they were gods among men. To face Caesar (or one of his governors) and testify with your mouth that "Jesus is Lord" was a surefire recipe for the severest punishment, even death. The Apostle Paul himself died at the hands of the

Romans for his confession that "Jesus Christ is Lord." So, Paul's point in Romans 10 is about faith and loyalty to Christ in the face of life-threatening circumstances. Paul is encouraging the believers to stand firm in their faith, and like the jailer, God will honor your faith and reward your commitment to Him when He returns or maybe sooner! (John 6:39-54) God *eventually* rewards everyone who puts their faith in Him. (Romans 8:28, Hebrews 11) Standing up in a Christian church and confessing that Jesus is Lord is not exactly what Paul had in mind when he penned these words, although there is certainly nothing wrong with doing this. However, Paul is encouraging all believers like you and me to stand firm when your life and the lives of your family members are being subjected to severe punishment. Continue to confess that Jesus is Lord, and through faith alone, you will be justified and ultimately saved.

Summary

The Bible is full of good news. God uses a legal and fair process in Heaven called justification to justify sinners on Earth. Justification is not a white-wash for rebellion against God. Justification is an enormous gift which the Father is willing to bestow upon any sinner if that sinner is willing to live in obedient submission to the Holy Spirit. Justification was made possible through the perfect life and death of Jesus. Every person who has lived on Earth, except Jesus, is a descendant of Adam and Eve. (Acts 17:24-27) Therefore, sin and rebellion are part of every generation because of our grandparents. Of course, our Creator foreknew that sin would rise, just as He knew that when He created the world it would someday be populated with billions of people speaking different languages, following different customs and having many religious beliefs. Therefore, from the beginning of time, the Plan of Salvation has been inclusive of *all* people, even though most of Earth's population at any given time does not know the truth about God. The Plan of Salvation includes Chinese, Indians, Russians, Americans and all humankind in every nation – even if they are not Christian. The receipt of God's offer for justification does not require that we first know the whole truth or absolute truth about the Father or Jesus. Remember, "Christians" did not exist prior to Christ's ministry on Earth, yet everyone before Christ who placed their faith in God was justified by faith! (See Romans 2 - 4 and Hebrews 11.) It might be said that they were justified on the promise that Jesus would be forthcoming. Nevertheless, justification is the only way to life eternal and if you are willing to submit to the authority of the Holy Spirit, the assurance of eternal life will be yours absolutely free!

Chapter 5
Salvation and Predestination

"Before I formed you in the womb I knew you, before you were born I set you apart; I appointed you as a prophet to the nations." "Ah, Sovereign Lord," I said, "I do not know how to speak; I am only a child."

– Jeremiah 1:5,6

Omnipotence and Our Power of Choice

Members of the Godhead are omnipotent. This means that if it were not for the rule of law, they could do anything they please with anything or anybody and no one could prevent their abuse. As Omnipotent Rulers of the universe, they are not subject to anyone. However, they are willing to be closely studied and observed because they are willing to abide by the laws they have put in place. Without law there is chaos and arbitrary rule. The presence of law imposes order and accountability for everyone. Even though the Godhead has the prerogatives of omnipotence and other incredible powers, these prerogatives are not exercised according to whim. When the Godhead does exercise their prerogatives, their actions are lawful! The Godhead submits their actions and decisions to their created beings for careful study and analysis. The Godhead wants all of us to see that they are singularly motivated by love and righteousness. Additionally, they want their freewill creatures to choose to follow their example!

As our Creator, Jesus is the source of life. He could have created slaves or robots, but instead He created intelligent beings that are free to exercise the power of choice. Think about this privilege for a moment. Human beings can choose to obey God or rebel against Him. Jesus speaks and worlds appear. He is capable of doubling the size of our infinite universe in a split second by simply commanding it. He could also speak Earth's entire solar system out of existence and we would cease to exist the very moment the words left His lips. Through Him everything exists. Without Him, there is nothing. He creates matter. He destroys matter. He sets limits and no one can change them. (Colossians 1) Although Jesus has omnipotence, He will not violate the power of choice granted to any person. Jesus said to Isaiah, **"This is what the Lord says – your Redeemer, who formed you in the womb: I am the Lord, who has made all things, who alone** stretched out the heavens, who spread out the Earth by myself, who foils the signs of false prophets and makes fools of diviners, who overthrows the learning of the wise and turns it into nonsense. Remember the former things, those of long ago; I am God, and there is no other; I am God, and there is none like me. I make known the end from the beginning, from ancient times, what is still to come. I say: My purpose will stand, and I will do all that I please. From the east I summon a bird of prey; from a far-off land, a man to fulfill my purpose. What I have said, that will I bring about; what I have planned, that will I do." (Isaiah 44:24-25, 46:9-11)

Omniscience

Members of the Godhead are also omniscient. This means they know everything about the past, present and future. And yes, the Godhead knew before the world was created the names of the individuals who would choose eternal life and those who would not. This fact bothers a lot of people because they cannot reconcile God's omnipotence with His omniscience. Some people believe that God has already decided who is going to live forever and who is going to die forever, so no matter what we do, the outcome has already been predetermined. This concept is called "fatalism." Fatalism interprets everything that happens as the predetermined will of God and it is a false doctrine. The devil would like people to believe that they have no choice about their eternal destiny. He also wants us to believe that Jesus created some people simply for destruction. Both ideas are false.

Some Things are Predestined

According to Webster, predestination means, "to decree beforehand." Because the members of the Godhead are omnipotent, they can predestine anything they want to. (Notice, I did not say *anyone* they want to.) For example, when Jesus agreed to die in man's place, His death was predestined long before the actual event took place. Because of God's foreknowledge, the Plan of Salvation was prepared and waiting before He created the world. The Godhead foreknew the rise of sin on Earth and when the rescue was needed, they instituted the Plan. To put divine foreknowledge into perspective, let us say it is something like carrying a diaper bag when you have a newborn baby in your arms. You know the baby will soon need a fresh diaper and you are prepared for that eventuality. This is foreknowledge. However, notice in this simple illustration that your foreknowledge does not predetermine the need for a fresh diaper.

Predestination simply means that God can decree beforehand anything to happen, and it will happen because He has the power and authority to make it happen. Again, Jesus said, **"I say: My purpose will stand, and I will do all that I please. From the east I summon a bird of prey; from a far-off land, a man to fulfill my purpose. What I have said, that will I bring about; what I have planned, that will I do."** (Isaiah 46:10,11) Predestination is a function of God's omnipotence and foreknowledge is a function of God's omniscience. Foreknowledge simply means God knows everything. He knows what our choices will be – not because He makes them happen, but because He knows what we will choose to do. Everything that happens is not, I repeat, *is not* predestined by God. God did not predestine the rise of sin. Therefore, we should not interpret every event in life as a predestined event. God did not predestine Adam and Eve to sin, but He knew they would sin. In the same way the Father knows who will choose or forfeit eternal life.

Jesus Lays Divine Prerogatives Aside

When Jesus stepped "in the way" of the executing angel who was preparing to execute Adam and Eve, Jesus became the "Son of God" that very day. According to the provisions of the plan to save humanity, the day Adam sinned Jesus agreed to lay aside His prerogatives at an appointed time. Even though He was an equal member of the Godhead, He agreed to become subject to the will of the Father at the time of His birth. (John 6:38) Therefore, Jesus is often called the Son of God. (See Psalm 2 and Hebrews 1:5,5:5.) During Old Testament times, Jesus sometimes exercised omniscience and omnipotence, but at the time of His birth, He laid these powers aside to become a man.

How could Jesus lay these powers of divinity aside? This is a mystery, but He put aside a number of divine prerogatives for our salvation. For example, He put aside His immortal life so He could die for sinners. Jesus became subject to death (mortal) and completely experienced sin's penalty when He was put to death by execution! (Hebrews 2:17; 10:12-14; 1 Corinthians 15:3; 2 Corinthians 5:21) After He put these prerogatives aside, He returned to Heaven and was found worthy to receive them back on the basis of His perfect compliance with the Plan of Salvation and the will of the Father. (Revelation 4 and 5) Remember, when Jesus was born of Mary, certain limitations were placed on Jesus' power for a period of time. For example, He said, **"No one knows about that day or hour, not even the angels in heaven, nor the Son, but only the Father."** (Matthew 24:36) In other words, in His human form, Jesus did not know the date He would return to Earth, because the Father had not revealed this information to Him. However, Daniel 7 and Revelation 4 and 5 reveal that a time came when Jesus' omnipotence and omniscience were returned to Him. (Daniel 7:13,14) It is obvious that Jesus increases in power and authority throughout the process of saving man, just like the infant Jesus grew in wisdom and favor with God and man! (Hebrews 2:8; Luke 2:52) At the end of all things, when Jesus has acquired all that Heaven can offer, He gives it all back to the Father so He can live among His subjects as one of them. (1 Corinthians 15:24-28)

Careful! Easy to Distort!

God has not predestined some people to be lost and others to be saved. The Bible says, **"He** [the Father] **predestined us** [fallen human beings] **to be adopted as his sons through Jesus Christ, in accordance with his pleasure and will . . ."** "He [God] **is patient with you, not wanting anyone to perish, but everyone to come to repentance."** (Ephesians 1:5, 2 Peter 3:9, insertions mine.) Be careful! These texts are easy to distort. Ephesians 1:5 does not say that God predestined a certain number of people to be adopted as sons through Jesus Christ – implying that all others are predestined for eternal death. This text says that God has predestined fallen man *to be adopted* as His sons through Jesus. In other words, God predestined the adoption process. It is called justification! **"Now when a man works, his wages are not credited to him as a gift, but as an obligation. However, to the man who does not work but trusts God who justifies the wicked, his faith is credited as righteousness."** (Romans 4:4,5) Did you notice whom God justifies in verse five? To say that God predestines our eternal reward makes a mockery of the Plan of Salvation. If God predestined the eternal reward of a man without recognizing man's actions or power of choice, the Plan of Salvation would be a deceptive trick. If God predestined people to be saved and others to be lost, a Plan of Salvation would not be necessary. Think about it – what is the point of choosing to follow the Holy Spirit if you are predestined to be lost? In simplest terms, the difference between predestination and foreknowledge is the following: Predestination (decreeing beforehand) is setting the alarm clock to ring at 5:00 a.m. the next morning. Foreknowledge (knowing beforehand) is looking at a clock and observing that the alarm setting indicates it will ring at 5:00 in the morning. God does not predestine eternal destiny, but He does predestine events, such as making the process of adoption as His sons available to all mankind.

God Predestines People for Service

God sometimes predestines people to do certain things. Notice these three texts:

"The word of the Lord came to me [Jeremiah]**, saying, 'Before I formed you in the womb I knew you, before you were born I set you apart; I appointed you as a prophet to the nations.' "** (Jeremiah 1:4,5, insertion mine.)

"This is what the Lord says to his anointed, to Cyrus, whose right hand I take hold of to subdue nations before him and to strip kings of their armor, to open doors before him so that gates will not be shut: I will go before you and will level the mountains; I will break down gates of bronze and cut through bars of iron . . . I am the Lord, and there is no other; apart from me there is no God. I will strengthen you, though you have not acknowledged me. . . ." (Isaiah 45:1,2,5)

"He [the man of God] **cried out against the altar by the word of the Lord: 'O altar, This is what the Lord says: A son named Josiah will be born to the house of David. On you he will sacrifice the priests of the high places who now make offerings here, and human bones will be burned on you.' "** (1 Kings 13:2, insertion mine.)

I chose these particular verses because they represent certain extremes. In the first text, Jeremiah, the Jew, was appointed to be a prophet for God before he was born. In the second text, Cyrus, the pagan, was appointed to be a great king that would conquer the Babylonians. In the third text, the birth and reformation of King Josiah was foretold. We know that God is no respecter of persons. (Acts 10:34) He loved Jeremiah, Cyrus and Josiah and they were born with a destiny of service for God. However, God's appointment to service has nothing to do with their eternal reward. That choice remains their exclusive privilege to decide.

These texts demonstrate that God has a plan for our life even before we are born! (See also Psalm 139:16.) However, God's appointment does not mean that we are forced to fulfill His calling. He respects our power of choice and if we so choose, we can turn our backs on God as King Saul did. Although God appointed Saul to be Israel's first king (1 Samuel 15:1), Saul became evil in God's eyes because of his rebellion. Eventually, the Lord refused to have anything further to do with him. (1 Samuel 28:6) Remember, God may predestine a person for certain tasks, but He does not predestine anyone for eternal life or death.

Critical Difference

There is a critical difference between God's foreknowledge and God's power to predetermine an event. Predestination *pre-decrees* the outcome, whereas foreknowledge *knows* the outcome of all things in advance. The future is to the Godhead what the past is to us. It is unchangeable. We may have a perfect view of our past, but we are powerless to change one word, thought or deed in the past. Likewise, the Father is powerless, under the rule of love, to alter or change the future in any way. Can He be trusted to leave the future unchanged? *This is the critical question.* Any manipulation of the future would be a malicious act by God because He claims that His universe is governed by the rule of love. The presence of Lucifer and sin proves, among other things, that intelligent creatures have the power of choice. Is God love? Yes, the death of Jesus proves His love for mankind. The rebellion of one-third of His angels, the fall of Lucifer and the dire consequences of Adam and Eve's sin prove that God will not interfere with the inalienable right of all intelligent beings to exercise their power of choice. This is why the future, as far as God is concerned, is unchangeable. He allows it to unfold according to the choices of His subjects and He responds accordingly.

Perhaps one more illustration will demonstrate the critical difference between foreknowledge and predestination. Suppose an airplane pilot can look down from 10,000 feet and see the twists and turns of a long river. In one glance, he can see the end *and* the beginning. Also imagine that people are traveling down the river in a boat – not knowing where the river leads. The pilot of the airplane can see where the boat will be when it reaches the end of the journey, but the pilot of the airplane has nothing to do with the travelers reaching that destination. Instead, he can only see where the boaters will be when they reach the end of the river. Knowing the end from the beginning without interference is foreknowledge. On the other hand, predestination is pre-decreeing that an event will occur, such as setting an alarm clock to go off at a certain time.

In short, God predestines *events* to happen. He also predestines people for service, but He does not predestine the eternal destiny of people. Because He has foreknowledge, God knows what people are going to do. He not only grants us the power of choice, He insists that we use it! (John 3:16)

Jesus Foreknew Israel's Apostasy

The Old Testament story of Israel illustrates how Jesus does not use His foreknowledge to change the outcome of events, even when they run contrary to His will! Notice this prophecy, **"And the Lord said to Moses: 'You are going to rest with your fathers, and these people will soon prostitute themselves to the foreign gods of the land they are entering. They will forsake me and break the covenant I made with them. On that day I will become angry with them and forsake them; I will hide my face from them, and they will be destroyed. Many disasters and difficulties will come upon them, and on that day they will ask, 'Have not these disasters come upon us because our God is not with us?' And I will certainly hide my face on that day because of all their wickedness in turning to other gods.' "** (Deuteronomy 31:16-18)

Jesus knew what the nation of Israel would do in the future and He shared this information with Moses. The Old Testament record confirms what Jesus knew. However, it also confirms that Jesus did not use His foreknowledge to make Israel a stubborn and stiff-necked people. (Ezekiel 3:7; Jeremiah 7:26) In fact, just the opposite is true! The Old Testament verifies that God did everything possible to redirect Israel from its terrible ways – time after time He sent His servants the prophets – but Israel *chose* to rebel against God! (See Jeremiah 3.) Jesus knew that Israel would rebel before they rebelled! The essential point is that Jesus does not deal with His creatures on the basis of His foreknowledge. Instead, He deals with man on the basis of love and our current needs. Aren't you glad! Although He can see the end from the beginning, He does not use that knowledge to manipulate us. God can be trusted. He will not change the future to protect Himself or His universe. He carefully respects our power of choice. Jesus is the only parent who would send His child through four years of college at the enormous cost of $80,000, knowing in advance that the child is going to fail. Taking this simple point to its logical conclusion we can only conclude that God's love was profoundly amazing! Who else but God would create the cherub Lucifer and give him everything that Heaven could offer – knowing in advance that Lucifer would eventually choose to become His worst enemy?

From the Creation of the World

Consider the contents of this text: **"The beast, which you saw, once was, now is not, and will come up out of the Abyss and go to his destruction. The inhabitants of the earth whose names have not been written in the book of life from the creation of the world will be astonished when they see the beast, because he once was, now is not, and yet will come."** (Revelation 17:8) This text indicates the wicked, whose names were not written in the Book of Life from the creation of the world, will be amazed when they see the beast (the Antichrist) that will rise up out of nowhere (the abyss). My point is that the Bible student can interpret this text to say, "God knew in advance who was going to be lost from creation to the final moment of Earth's history and He left their names out of the Book of Life." This statement is true, but understand that the wicked are not lost because God left their names out of the Book of Life. The wicked are lost because they chose to rebel against God's authority! A profound point found within this text is that during the Great Tribulation, Jesus will do everything possible to save men and women. He will save to the utmost. Jesus will present the terms and conditions of salvation so clearly and so powerfully that no one will be able to justify rebellion against God or claim ignorance of His will. Jesus said, **"And this gospel of the kingdom will be preached in the whole world as a testimony to all nations, and then the end will come."** (Matthew 24:14) John's comment in Revelation 17:8 is set in the context of the final days of the Great Tribulation, after God has done everything possible to save mankind. John is amazed at what length God has gone to save man from the penalty of sin, even though God foreknew who would rebel!

The bottom line is this. The Godhead has omniscience; they know everything, but they do not use their omniscience to manipulate their creatures or alter the oncoming future. If they did, they would be guilty of a terrible breach of confidence. They claim to operate on the principle of love, but any power play to manipulate their subjects would suggest otherwise. From their comprehensive perspective of the universe, the future is clearly laid out, even though their creatures create the future as each day arrives. The good news is that the Godhead can be trusted with this incredible power. As events unfold during the Great Tribulation it will be demonstrated and proven that they are righteous, pure, above reproach and trustworthy. God's omnipotence, omniscience and omnipresence mean that wherever we are in the grand march of time, God is already there. Throughout the endless corridors of eternity, nothing surprises God. He knows everything and He is prepared for every eventuality that His creatures will choose. This fact should be most reassuring to finite beings who put their trust in Him. **". . . From everlasting to everlasting the Lord's love is with those who fear him."** (Psalm 103:17)

Chapter 6
The Sealing

Then I saw another angel coming up from the east, having the seal of the living God. He called out in a loud voice to the four angels who had been given power to harm the land and the sea: "Do not harm the land or the sea or the trees until we put a seal on the foreheads of the servants of our God." Then I heard the number of those who were sealed: 144,000 from all the tribes of Israel.

– Revelation 7:2-4

Introduction

God showed the prophet John an interesting sight which he describes in Revelation 7. He saw an angel rising in the east who had the seal of God delaying the destruction of Earth. The angel from the east calls out to four angels who are about to harm Earth, **"Do not harm the land or the sea or the trees until we put a seal on the foreheads of the servants of our God."** What does this vision mean? What is the seal of God? How does the sealing relate to the 144,000 and the salvation of man?

The Carnal Nature

Jesus said, **"Blessed are the pure in heart, for they will see God."** (Matthew 5:8) These words are a promise. Yet, when I look around and also look within myself, I find an overwhelming amount of sin. Why is there so much degeneracy? When it comes to having a pure heart, all human beings have two problems. First, we come from the womb with a sinful nature. Because of this, we are predisposed to rebel against authority from the moment of birth. Second, the devil understands our human predisposition toward sinning and the inherited traits that push us in that direction. Knowing this, he does everything he can to *entice* us into complete rebellion against God's will and authority. All these factors make rebellion against God and His laws easy and submission to the will of God very difficult. In fact, *in our present state it is impossible to consistently submit to the will of God.*

When a person experiences the miracle of spiritual rebirth, God installs a second nature – a spiritual nature – that is antagonistic toward the sinful nature. As a result, every born again person lives in a continual "state of war" because these two natures are diametrically opposed. When asked about his born again experience, Martin Luther summarized the contest between these two natures by saying that even though the carnal nature remains, it does not reign. No doubt his words were borrowed from his favorite Bible writer, the Apostle Paul. Paul reminded the Romans that the carnal nature does not have control over us *if* we allow the Holy Spirit to live in us. He wrote, **"You, however, are controlled not by the sinful nature but by the Spirit, if the Spirit of God lives in you. And if anyone does not have the Spirit of Christ, he does not belong to Christ."** (Romans 8:9)

No writer in the Bible explains these two warring natures as well as the Apostle Paul. After Paul had been a born again Christian for about 25 years, he wrote, **"I do not understand what I do. For what I want to do I do not do, but what I hate I do. I know that nothing good lives in me, that is, in my sinful nature. For I have the desire to do what is good, but I cannot carry it out."** (Romans 7:16,18) Paul's statement confirms the fact that after a person is born again he or she remains in a constant state of war between these two natures. Paul's discovery about his carnal nature is something like the discovery of gravity by Sir Isaac Newton. For thousands of years no one thought it strange that objects fell in a downward direction because they had weight. Over the course of time, however, a new explanation was needed about the direction objects fall because man discovered that Earth was a large sphere spinning on its axis. Then the question begged to be asked, why do objects fall in the direction of *down* on a rapidly spinning sphere when logic suggests they should fall in the opposite direction! Finally, the presence of gravity was discovered and Sir Isaac Newton was among the first to quantify the law of gravity. In a similar way, the Apostle Paul understood the presence of the carnal heart and he quantified the law of sin that operates upon it. Both the law of gravity and the law of sin are predictable and unchangeable. The law of gravity and the law of sin also have one other similarity – both can be thwarted under the right circumstances. The law of gravity can be thwarted *if* a spaceship exceeds 17,000 miles per hour. At this speed, man can overcome the force of Earth's gravity and escape this planet. Likewise, the law of sin can be overcome *if* a person chooses to obediently surrender his or her will to the Holy Spirit. In this situation, the indwelling power of the Holy Spirit will enable a person to escape the control of sin.

What is the law of sin? It is a code of conduct, an inbred or inborn rebellion against authority. The law of sin has dominion over every fallen being. Paul understood that there is no escape from the law of sin except through faith in Christ. He wrote, **"So I find this law at work: When I want to do good, evil is right there with me . . . What a wretched man I am! Who will rescue me from this body of death? Thanks be to God – through Jesus Christ our Lord! So then, I myself in my mind am a slave to God's law, but in the sinful nature a slave to the law of sin."** (Romans 7:21,24,25) Carefully consider the words of this reformed legalist: **"Now if I do what I do not want to do, it is no longer I who do it, but it is sin living in me that does it."** (Romans 7:20) So, this is the explanation. As hard as it may be for some of us to admit, we are sinful from within the core of our being and sooner or later our conduct will prove it!

Somebody Help Me!

Paul lamented the inescapable effects of the law of sin in his own life. He wrote, **"So I find this law at work: When I want to do good, evil is right there with me."** (Romans 7:21) Paul's remarks in Romans 7 are very revealing because he once belonged to a religious body that believed sinlessness, purity and zeal for God were absolute mandates and Paul was as devoted to God as anyone could be. (Philippians 3:4-7) The Pharisees had meticulously defined impurity as a violation of any one of some 600 laws and Paul was zealous to observe every law. He summed up his life as a boastful Pharisee saying, **". . . as for legalistic righteousness, fault-less."** (Philippians 3:6)

Then, Paul met Jesus. Eventually he began to understand that the "righteousness" achieved by rigorous obedience and religious devotion cannot produce a pure heart. Religion had deceived Paul. As a Pharisee he was completely convinced that righteousness came through legalistic obedience – the avoidance of sin. But after he met Jesus on the road to Damascus, he saw how wretched and offensive he really was in God's sight. (Romans 7:24) This remarkable change in his perspective occurred because he caught a glimpse of the righteousness that God requires and it changed everything. God requires a pure heart, but *a heart is not pure until it has absolutely no attraction for sin.* We may avoid sin, we may escape falling into certain temptations, but the avoidance of sin is not to be confused with a pure heart. When Paul met Jesus, the perfectionist discovered his imperfection. The arrogance of Saul the Pharisee was shattered. God transformed him, renamed him and called him into the service of His saints.

When a person experiences a complete "meltdown" over long held religious beliefs, psychologists call this a paradigm shift. A paradigm shift occurs when concepts believed to be true are proven to be totally false. A paradigm shift shakes us to the core of our being and is very emotionally disturbing. When Jesus spoke to Paul, Paul was devastated to learn that his "perfect" religious life was offensive and unacceptable to God. After Paul realized that he could not make himself pure or acceptable before God by good works, Paul had nothing more to boast about. (God sure knows how to silence legalists.) When Paul saw that he had no righteousness in God's sight, he became a meek man. In this new state of mind, he became a mighty champion of the righteousness of Christ. He wrote, **"For in the gospel a righteousness from God is revealed, a righteousness that is by faith from first to last, just as it is written: 'The righteous will live by faith.' "** (Romans 1:17) When Paul finally grasped the idea that salvation requires a righteousness that man cannot produce, only then did he realize his desperate need for Jesus.

The Nature of Sin

Since the law of sin declares that human nature remains rebellious toward God, how can any person ever become pure in heart? It is impossible through human effort. Consequently, *the carnal nature is man's greatest problem.* Our carnal nature makes us rebellious and prevents us from having faith in God or obediently submitting to His commands. We are born with a "spring loaded" carnal nature, ready to do wrong at an early age. Children do not have to be taught to do wrong, and adults cannot achieve the purity of heart that God requires. Since Adam and Eve's sin, the human race has been in trouble. Yet, a miracle happens every time a person experiences a rebirth. A miraculous change occurs within the heart. Whereas the carnal heart was full of rebellion, the born again heart becomes divided. Part of the heart wants to obey God and part of it wants to remain in rebellion against God. This tremendous struggle never ends. This is why Paul, as a mature Christian lamented, **". . . For I have the desire to do what is good, but I cannot carry it out."** (Romans 7:18) Do not despair – there is good news on two fronts!

Peter demonstrated that we can walk on water through the power of Christ. Paul wrote, **"For if you live according to the sinful nature, you will die; but if by the Spirit you put to death the misdeeds of the body, you will live, because those who are led by the Spirit of God are sons of God."** (Romans 8:13,14) This is the key. The presence and work of the Spirit within the heart is crucial. He brings victory to all who live by faith. The victory which the Spirit brings is not man-made and is not merely the avoidance of sin. When the Spirit brings victory, rebellion is removed.

When we become no longer attracted to a specific sin, then the heart has been set free from the law of sin in this area of life. Therefore, the heart is no longer under the dominion of sin! Sometimes, the Spirit will not give us victory where we want victory the most. Instead, the Spirit may focus on other issues that need His attention first, but you can be sure that the purifying process for each person is always controlled by the Holy Spirit. If a person is not gaining victory over sin as he or she wants, it could be the Spirit is wanting control over another aspect of this person's life first. This requires patience and perseverance. James says, **"Consider it pure joy, my brothers, whenever you face trials of many kinds, because you know that the testing of your faith develops perseverance. Perseverance must finish its work so that you may be mature and complete, not lacking anything."** (James 1:2-4)

On the second front, good news comes in the assurance of forgiveness as we admit and confess our sin. John wrote, **"My dear children, I write this to you so that you will not sin. But if anybody does sin, we have one who speaks to the Father in our defense – Jesus Christ, the Righteous One. He is the atoning sacrifice for our sins, and not only for ours but also for the sins of the whole world."** (1 John 2:1)

Can We Become Pure?

Is it possible to have a pure heart if we want one? The answer is a re-sounding "Yes!" But the means and timing of this event may not be what you think. A number of views exist within the Christian community about the topic of purity. At one extreme, people believe that a pure heart comes through an exhaustive struggle with self and take the responsibility for purity upon themselves. They do everything they can to shut out all worldly influences, hoping to avoid corruption. These people often succumb to the temptation of being legalistic about God's definition of righteousness. The concept of isolation from sin contributed to the early formation of monasteries and stems from the idea that man is inclined to be evil. Therefore, in order to be pure, a person must be physically separated from worldly influences. (The truth is, humanity is inclined to do evil because we have a carnal nature. Wherever a person goes, sin is there, for sin is within each person's heart!)

On the other hand, some people believe that a pure heart is not possible or necessary since Jesus paid the price on Calvary for man's salvation. Such Christians shudder at the thought of self-denial or dealing with a cross to bear. Unfortunately, these Christians often succumb to spiritual complacency. They think they are insulated from the penalty and properties of sin by religious rituals, rites and services. But none of this is true. Like the law of gravity, there is only *one way* to escape the relentless control of the law of sin. His name is Jesus – He is the Way!

No doubt our personalities, religious heritage, culture, and family traditions color our understanding on this fundamental subject. There is no purity in isolation because the carnal nature is within and there is no righteousness in religious rituals, rites or services because the carnal nature is ever present. So, what is a person to do? Before answering this question, let us level the playing field for everyone.

A Christian Handicap

There is a serious handicap that can occur among those people who grow up in a Christian home. Let us suppose "Johnny" was born into a Christian home and taught to avoid certain bad habits such as gambling, drugs, smoking, drinking and pornography. Somehow, Johnny becomes an adult without getting hooked on sex, drugs, cigarettes and alcohol. Since Johnny knows nothing about drug addiction or alcohol dependency in his own body, he may conclude that he is purer than "those poor souls captured by these sinful habits." *This is not true.* Johnny still has a carnal nature just like every prostitute and addict. Johnny was fortunate to avoid the prison of addiction and the subsequent consequences because of his good fortune (a Christian home). Johnny cannot understand the power of addiction because he has not been a slave to lust, drugs or alcohol. But, and this is an emphatic *but*, Johnny's nature is no different from that of the worst sinner. His lifestyle may be different, but his carnal nature is the same. Johnny, just like everyone else, could have become an addict *if* his home life and parental guidance had not been as positive. As you may have heard, "But for the grace of God, there go I." Truer words have not been spoken. This illustration is given because "lifestyle" Christians sometimes get vain and self-righteous. Just because Johnny does not have a craving addiction for something grossly evil, this does not mean he has a pure heart! It must be stated again, "Man's greatest problem is his carnal nature." Yes, avoiding sin is good. Yes, religious services can be beneficial. But, neither avoiding sin nor attending church is a substitute for a pure heart.

What to do about the Power of Sin?

Suppose I want to do something that I know is sin. I have at least four options:

1. I can yield to temptation because I cannot help myself.

2. I can resist the temptation and avoid sinning as far as possible.

3. I can pray ahead for help since I know temptation is coming.

4. I can recognize the inner attraction for sin, confess it to Jesus and ask for deliverance.

Of course, all of these options are acceptable except number one. Resisting sin is an important process in character development. However, no person can resist every sin – the carnal nature will not permit it. As Paul said so well, **"What I want to do, I don't do."** In my estimation, option four should be our greatest focus, followed by option number three and then number two. Ask Jesus for deliverance. Ask Him to do something for you that you cannot do for yourself. Even more, ask Him to remove the desire. This is the key. Remove the desire and the attraction is gone! Victory over sin often depends on being prepared for temptation at any given moment. When you fall into sin, quickly admit it, confess your sorrow and do not forget how it happened. The Bible says we have an Advocate who is willing to forgive us. (1 John 2:1,2) But the Bible also cautions that if we continue in willful rebellion against God, He will not forgive us. (Hebrews 10:26,27; Matthew 12:31) The process of sanctification, or the struggle between the carnal nature and the spiritual nature, does not occur without a constant connection and communion with God. Peter quickly sank into the depths of the Sea of Galilee when he took his eyes off Jesus and we will most assuredly sink into the depths of sin for the same reason.

Why the Torture of Sanctification?

The following statements about sanctification are very important:

1. When a person is born again, a sanctifying struggle *begins*.

2. No one is granted eternal life on the basis of human perfection. Everyone who receives the assurance of eternal life must continually submit to the humiliating process of sanctification.

3. The process of sanctification ends at death or when the carnal nature
    is eliminated.

God watches over each one of us. Nothing is hidden from His sight.
(Ecclesiastes 12:13,14; Luke 8:17; 2 Corinthians 5:10) God measures our
love and faith for Him by what we do (or do not do). James wrote,
". . . faith by itself, if it is not accompanied by action, is dead." (James
2:17) Sanctification is a lifelong experience under the tutelage of the Holy
Spirit. When the Bible says that Enoch, Noah and Abraham walked with
God, the Bible does not mean that these men merely walked with God
down a country road. No, it means that these men endured the humiliation
of sanctification and as a result, God was pleased to visit and speak with
them as friends. The carnal heart hates humiliation because it hates
authority. But, Jesus said, **"Blessed are the meek, for they shall inherit
the earth."** (Matthew 5:5) Our response to the sanctification process is our
way of expressing praise, honor and faith in God. God would much rather
see the process of sanctification occurring in the lives of His children than
to hear the praise of 10,000 choirs. (Isaiah 1:13-18) Obedience and submission to authority is the most basic form of praise or glory that a child can
produce! (Ask any parent if you do not believe me.) So remember, that (a)
sanctification does not merit or bring salvation, and (b) our struggle with
sanctification does not end until death or the carnal nature is eliminated.

When is the Carnal Nature Eliminated?

By now, I am sure that you are aware that the greatest problem for an
individual is the carnal nature. This pesky problem is about to come to an
end! God will eliminate the carnal nature from every person who passes
the test of faith that He administers during the Great Tribulation. By the
time the seventh trumpet sounds (Revelation 11:15-19), God will have
placed His seal upon everyone who lives by faith. (Revelation 10:7) The
144,000 will be the first people to experience the elimination of the carnal
nature. Millions of other people will then pass through the fiery test of faith
and also experience this miraculous transformation. Before we consider
God's seal and the importance of the sealing, a few words about the Great
Tribulation are necessary.

One of God's objectives for the Great Tribulation is to set up a global
situation where His authority is diametrically opposed to man's authority. As
these two authorities stand in opposition to each other, God will determine
who loves Him. (See Daniel 3.) This contest is similar to the struggle that

goes on within the heart of every born again person – which nature will reign? Our actions will reveal which nature we favor most.

During the Great Tribulation, the Ten Commandments will stand in clear opposition to the laws of man. In other words, the Great Tribulation involves a great controversy. The contest between God's sovereign will and the will of humanity will be an intense drama. People will be forced by dire circumstances to take sides and this is how the sheep and goats will become separated. Using His servants, the 144,000, God will send a powerful proclamation of the terms and conditions of salvation (the gospel) throughout the Earth. If a person obeys God, he or she will have to disobey the laws of men. Conversely, if a person obeys the laws of men he will have to rebel against God. Every person will make an informed choice. There will be no straddling the fence or middle ground. Into this intense chaos, the Antichrist (the lamb-like beast who is the devil) will eventually appear and the controversy will finally end. The people of Earth will receive either the seal of God or the mark of the beast. Each person will make an intelligent and informed decision regarding his or her allegiance. Each person's choice will reflect the dominate influence within that person's heart. If the nature is carnal, that person will rebel against the authority of God and have no option but to accept the mark of the beast. If the nature is spiritual, that person will be empowered by the Holy Spirit to obediently submit to the commandments of God and be sealed in His righteousness.

Of course, no sane person plans to receive the mark of the beast. The same might be said about the people in Noah's day. No person planned on drowning! Isn't it interesting that almost every Christian *today* sees himself smart enough to "get in Noah's boat?" But do not forget, only eight people went into the boat. Why so few? There is only one answer: The carnal nature. Rebellion is man's greatest problem. Aware of this, God has designed a four-step process that will separate the sheep from the goats during the Great Tribulation. This process is easy to understand once the drama surrounding the sealing is understood.

The Setting

A few days before the Great Tribulation begins, Jesus will personally select, seal and empower 144,000 ordinary people of all religious backgrounds. God will use these servants to proclaim the gospel to the world. (Revelation 7:1-4) When the 144,000 are ready to do their work, Jesus will methodically begin to destroy the Earth with enormous manifestations of

His wrath. The Book of Revelation predicts global earthquakes, meteoric showers of burning hail, asteroid impacts, darkness, sickness, death and destruction beyond our imagination. These horrific events will affect the whole world and will suddenly cause billions of people to consider the enormity of God and His wrath for the first time. In a setting of death, confusion, conflagration and calamity, billions of people will want some answers. God's 144,000 servants will explain what God is doing and why. Currently, because of religious gridlock and religious paradigms, most people will not consider anything about God that disagrees with what they already believe. Therefore, God will empower 144,000 people to speak for Him and after He delivers a series of fatal blows to the ecosystems of Earth, people will become more willing to consider what the 144,000 have to say. The 144,000 will proclaim three messages which are stated in Revelation 14:6-12. The three messages are condensed as follows:

1. Fear God, worship God and obey His Ten Commandments.

2. Have no part in the crisis government that will form to appease God. Reject its laws and false doctrines.

3. Do not submit to the Antichrist or receive his mark. If you do, God will severely punish you.

The 144,000 will present these three messages within the context of fierce opposition. The call to worship God and obey His Ten Commandments will collide "head on" with the religions of the world. The demands of God's Law will be contrary to the laws and demands of the crisis government that will form. This predicament will produce some very tough choices. (See Daniel 3 for an Old Testament parallel to this story.) These three messages contain the "saving" elements of the everlasting gospel, and as surprising as it may seem, will completely separate the people of Earth. People who allow their carnal nature to reign will reject God's authority, just as people who allow the Holy Spirit to reign will submit to God's authority. It is this simple. Notice the four step process that God has predetermined for the gospel during the Tribulation:

1. Everyone must hear the gospel.

2. Everyone must decide for or against the gospel.

3. Everyone must be tested in their decision (faith tested).

4. Depending on the outcome choice, everyone will either receive the seal of God or the mark of the beast.

The first step in the testing process is the **proclamation** of the terms and conditions of the gospel. The second step is the **decision** phase. The honest in heart will make the right choices as the Holy Spirit and the Bible directs them, even though they will be threatened with persecution and death. The point is that everyone will make an informed decision about the will of God because the 144,000 will complete their preaching assignments. Everyone will either submit to the gospel or rebel against it. The third step will be the **testing** phase. This phase will confirm whether our faith in God is firm and loyal. Last, God will remove the carnal nature and **seal** those who pass the test of faith with a spiritual nature that has no propensity toward sin! God will give the sinless nature He originally gave to Adam to the people who pass this test of faith.

What is the Seal of God?

How can we conclude from Scripture that the sealing process described in Revelation 7 is the change that takes place within the heart when God removes our propensity to sin? There are four steps:

1. The doctrine of justification and its supporting texts (discussed in Chapter 4), describes a process whereby the righteousness of Christ is *imputed* to everyone who becomes willing to submit to the dominion of the Holy Spirit. (John 3:16) Because of imputed righteousness, a sinner *appears* righteous in God's sight even though he is not righteous in reality. (Ephesians 2:8,9) In other words, when the righteous life of Jesus covers the life of a sinner, God sees the sinner as though he or she never sinned. The imputing of Christ's righteousness (justification) is God's gift of grace to every born again person. This is our all important "ticket" to Heaven which Jesus paid. (Romans 8:1-9)

2. The doctrine of sanctification and its supporting texts (discussed earlier in this chapter), describe a process that every born again person must submit to. (1 Thessalonians 4:3; Hebrews 12:14) Sanctification is the process of submitting our will to God's will every day of our lives. Sanctification requires patience and perseverance because the law of sin is relentless. Justification is our "title" to Heaven and sanctification is our "preparation" for Heaven. God has made a way to get man to Heaven through justification and He has made a way to put Heaven's government within the heart of man through sanctification.

3. The sealing of the 144,000 occurs shortly before the Great Tribulation begins. (Revelation 7:1-4) The 144,000 are the firstfruits of the great

harvest of souls that will come out of the Great Tribulation! (Revelation 14:4; 7:9-14) This means the 144,000 are examples of what the harvest will produce. Because they are the firstfruits, the 144,000 are sealed first. Believers who receive their testimony and pass the test of faith will be sealed as the 144,000 were sealed during the time-period of the seven trumpets. (The time-period of the seven trumpets is 1,260 days in length.)

4. The mystery of God is finished by the time of the seventh trumpet. **"But in the days when the seventh angel is about to sound his trumpet, the mystery of God will be accomplished, just as he announced to his servants the prophets."** (Revelation 10:7) What is the mystery of God? The mystery of God that is completed during the Great Tribulation is His plan to transform the carnal nature of every willing sinner into a pure heart! God has not seen a sinner that He did not love. God has not seen a sinner that He could not forgive and God has not seen a problem He cannot solve. The mystery of God that will be announced by His 144,000 servants is God's generous offer to remove each man's greatest problem: man's sinful nature.

Notice how various mysteries of God unfold over time: Paul wrote to the church at Ephesus, **"Surely you have heard about the administration of God's grace that was given to me for you, that is, the mystery made known to me by revelation, as I have already written briefly. In reading this, then, you will be able to understand my insight into the mystery of Christ, which was not made known to men in other generations as it has now been revealed by the Spirit to God's holy apostles and prophets. This mystery is that through the gospel the Gentiles are heirs together with Israel, members together of one body, and sharers together in the promise in Christ Jesus. I became a servant of this gospel by the gift of God's grace given me through the working of his power. Although I am less than the least of all God's people, this grace was given me: to preach to the Gentiles the unsearchable riches of Christ, and to make plain to everyone the administration of this mystery, which for ages past was kept hidden in God, who created all things. His intent was that now, through the church, the manifold wisdom of God should be made known to the rulers and authorities in the heavenly realms, according to his eternal purpose which he accomplished in Christ Jesus our Lord. In him and through faith in him we may approach God with freedom and confidence."** (Ephesians 3:2-12)

Now, examine these words by Paul to the church at Colosse: **"Now I rejoice in what was suffered for you, and I fill up in my flesh what is still lacking in regard to Christ's afflictions, for the sake of his body, which is the church. I have become its servant by the commission God gave me to present to you the word of God in its fullness – the mystery that has been kept hidden for ages and generations, but is now disclosed to the saints. To them God has chosen to make known among the Gentiles the glorious riches of this mystery, which is Christ in you, the hope of glory. We proclaim him, admonishing and teaching everyone with all wisdom, so that we may present everyone perfect in Christ. To this end I labor, struggling with all his energy, which so powerfully works in me."** (Colossians 1:24-29)

Paul told the Ephesians that the union of Gentiles and Jews into one body of people had been part of God's plan from the beginning. But, this part of salvation for the human race (the mystery that had been kept secret from ages past) had not been revealed until now. Now that the appointed time had come for this to take place, this mystery was exposed and Paul was empowered to announce this bold new revelation to the world. If you would like to enjoy the fullness of this revelation, read all of Ephesians 2 and 3 from your Bible and reflect on Paul's commission to reveal this "previously unheard" doctrine.

Likewise, Paul told the Colossians that he had become a servant of the gospel, by the commission of God, to present a mystery which had been kept hidden for ages and generations, but was now revealed to the saints. This mystery is that Jesus lives within the hearts of His followers, "Christ *in* you, the hope of glory."

The mystery which the 144,000 will proclaim has been hidden from previous generations. This mystery is that Jesus will remove the carnal heart with its propensity for sin and He will replace it with a pure heart that has no attraction for sin. *If* sinners will put their faith in Christ and obediently submit to the gospel call which the Holy Spirit is pressing upon their hearts, Jesus will generously grant this miracle.

A Pure Heart

The sealing described in Revelation 7 is the gift of a pure heart. God has promised this gift to the human race for almost 3,000 years! God promised His people while in Babylonian exile, **"I will give you a new heart and put a new spirit in you; I will remove from you your heart of stone and**

give you a heart of flesh. And I will put my Spirit in you and move you to follow my decrees and be careful to keep my laws." (Ezekiel 36:26,27) Unfortunately, the people of Israel failed to follow the Holy Spirit. Israel went astray again and again. Israel rejected Jesus as Messiah and the fulfillment of Ezekiel 36 was delayed. But, it is still coming! Six hundred years after Ezekiel's day, Paul declared this promise again, **"This is the covenant I will make with the house of Israel after that time, declares the Lord. I will put my laws in their minds and write them on their hearts. I will be their God, and they will be my people. No longer will a man teach his neighbor, or a man his brother, saying, 'Know the Lord,' because they will all know me, from the least of them to the greatest. For I will forgive their wickedness and will remember their sins no more. By calling this covenant 'new,' he has made the first one obsolete; and what is obsolete and aging will soon disappear."** (Hebrews 8:10-13)

These two texts, one by Ezekiel and the other by Paul, speak about the powerful transformation God has planned. No doubt, both prophets antici-pated the fulfillment of this promise in their day, but the mystery is not fulfilled until we reach the Great Tribulation. For thousands of years God has looked forward to the day when He can remove our carnal heart and give us a pure heart. He longs for the day when rebellion will no longer be within His children! His children also long for this to happen because they are sick and tired of having to deal with the law of sin. (Romans 7:23-25) Yes, both Ezekiel and Paul knew that this transformation was coming, but they did not know its appointed time. The saints who live during the Great Tribulation will understand the timing and they will see and experience this transformation with their own eyes!

God removes the sinful nature during the Great Tribulation because the intercession of Jesus on behalf of sinners comes to a close at the time of the seventh trumpet. For thousands of years, the righteousness of Christ has been *imputed*. During the 1,260 days of sealing, the righteousness of Christ will be *imparted* to every sinner who passes the test of faith. No longer will the saints be reckoned as sinful, for they will be pure! As indi-viduals pass their personal test of faith, God will do something He has not done since sin began. He will replace the carnal nature of every "faith-filled" saint with a pure heart and *seal* it within him or her. Therefore, the struggle with sin and the rebellion it causes *from within* will be finished for all saints by the time the seventh trumpet sounds!

Summary

It is very important that we learn now to recognize the leading of the Holy Spirit in our lives. He often puts us in difficult situations so that we can see the mighty hand of God move within our lives. We need to experience lessons of faith in the school of sanctification right now in order to prepare for the coming test of faith. Jesus is anxious to prepare us for what lies ahead. Our lack of faith, our failure to do right, our rebellion against God's will, our selfishness and stubbornness are all due to our carnal nature, but this will not be the case forever. Think of it! A time is coming when God's children will no longer have a carnal nature. This is what John means when he wrote, **"Dear friends, now** [in our present condition] **we are children of God, and what we will be has not yet been made known. But we know that when he appears, *we shall be like him*, for we shall see him as he is. Everyone who has this hope in him purifies himself, just as he is pure."** (1 John 3:2,3, insertion and italics mine.) Did you notice that John said, **"We shall be like Him?"** Talk about a promise! Remember the words of Jesus: **"Blessed are the pure in heart for they shall see God."** The saints are going to be pure in heart.

The Great Tribulation will be a great testing time. It will also be a time of revelation and reward for those who pass the test of faith! The saints will be rewarded with pure hearts and then they will see the grandest revelation to ever take place, Jesus appearing in all His glory! So, do not give up! If you are struggling with sanctification, persevere – pray without ceasing and ask for God's grace and strength to overcome. People who learn to depend on God's strength today will not fail during the persecution that lies ahead. Why not learn to walk by faith now? Everyone who walks with God lives in a constant purification process – this can be compared to washing our dirty clothes each day. Every day, God is working on the stain of sin that is within us. One day soon, at the appointed time, the mystery of God will be revealed. Jesus will eliminate the carnal nature within every saint. This is what the Bible means when it says of the redeemed, **"These are they who have come out of the great tribulation; they have washed their robes and made them white in the blood of the Lamb."** (Revelation 7:14)

Chapter 7
What was Nailed to the Cross?

When you were dead in your sins and in the uncircumcision of your sinful nature, God made you alive with Christ. He forgave us all our sins, having canceled the written code, with its regulations, that was against us and that stood opposed to us; he took it away, nailing it to the cross. . . .

– Colossians 2:13,14

Since His death and resurrection, believers in Jesus have discussed the question, "What was nailed to the cross?" The simplicity of the question belies the enormity of this subject. This question ultimately concerns each follower of Jesus because the answer reflects our understanding of God's actions and ultimately, His will. Even though there is a relatively simple answer to the question, the process of getting to the answer requires a working knowledge of the Bible and a great deal of commitment to the leading of the Holy Spirit.

For years the disciples of Jesus struggled with the question of what changed at the cross. Their interest was not merely academic for the answer can have profound social and behavioral consequences. (See Acts 15, Galatians 2 and 2 Corinthians 11.) Although there are hints in the Old Testament that help us understand what was nailed to the cross, Jesus spoke through the Apostle Paul (2 Corinthians 12) to make sure His followers had information sufficient to reach the right answer.

Social Ramifications

At times in Earth's history, following Jesus has taken a lot of courage. For the sake of illustration, the following is a fictitious scenario that generally conforms to the beliefs of most Christians today. Even though this scenario does not represent my views, it has merit because it demonstrates certain things that could have happened if *all* of the laws and statutes given in the Old Testament were made void on the Friday afternoon that Jesus died. Such a dramatic change would have put Jewish converts to Christianity in a very difficult situation because fourteen hundred years of culture and religious practice would have suddenly become worthless. A paradigm shift of this magnitude would be extremely hard, if not impossible for converts to accept. With these thoughts in mind, consider the following scenario: Benjamin was a devout Jew from the tribe of Judah. He was a curious middle-aged man (like Nicodemus) who frequently listened to Jesus. As time passed, Benjamin became favorable to the idea that Jesus could be the predicted Messiah, but he was not sure. Benjamin was an eye witness to the death and ascension of Jesus. Benjamin saw the fiery manifestations of the Holy Spirit at Pentecost! Finally, after Benjamin witnessed the stoning of Stephen, he decided that Jesus had to be the promised Messiah. He told his family and friends that he was converting to Christianity on the basis of what the prophets had foretold, as well as the things that he had seen with his own eyes. Assuming that Benjamin immediately began to interpret the will of God as Christians do today, consider some of the religious and social ramifications that Benjamin faced.

As a "born again" Christian, Benjamin was *suddenly* free of the old covenant, so Benjamin stopped taking animal sacrifices to the temple. He stopped supporting the priests and the temple with his tithes and offerings. Benjamin refused to have his newborn son circumcised because his son could be an heir of Abraham without circumcision. Benjamin told his relatives and friends that the office of high priest in Jerusalem was worthless because man's High Priest had ascended to Heaven. Benjamin told his family that pork and shrimp, among other things, were no longer unclean. Benjamin started working on the seventh day Sabbath. He began attending worship services with Gentiles on Sunday. Benjamin refused to observe the feast days or attend Jewish assemblies. In short, when Benjamin became a Christian, he was set free of the culture and religion he had known all his life and most everyone who knew him refused to even speak to him. There is a feature within all religions that says, "If you are not one of us, you are against us." (Mark 9:40) Given the polemical nature of religion, is it little wonder that Jewish relatives persecuted early Christians? It is likely that Benjamin's business was either boycotted or burned because he became a traitor, a "Gentile lover." Eventually, there was no safe place in Jerusalem for Benjamin. He fled to Damascus because the Pharisee, Saul, had heard of his defection from Judaism.

How does a man endure the hatred of everyone he has ever known? How does a Jew suddenly lose his denigrating bias toward Gentiles and consider them to be equals in the Lord? These matters are not exaggerated. If anything, they are understated. There is no greater conflict than that of religious differences. We live in an age when it takes an average of 18 years to put a man to death for first degree murder, but in Benjamin's day, a person could be stoned *the same day* he spoke out against the high priest. All of the issues presented in this scenario are discussed in the New

Testament because becoming a Christian during the first century A.D. was not an easy decision, especially if the individual was born a Jew.

Not Representative

This scenario about Benjamin **does not** represent how Christians began to act the week after Jesus rose from the dead. A person cannot change his or her religion or religious practices in a week. On the other hand, Benjamin's scenario demonstrates what many Christians think was nailed to the cross. However, the New Testament reveals an interesting fact. It took many years and many intense discussions before the disciples of Jesus figured out what was nailed to the cross. Why did (and why does) God permit so much ambiguity on this question? First, if Jesus had declared the facts from the cross as He did from Mt. Sinai few, if any, Jews would have been able to accept the truth. Jesus often spoke in parables so that the people would consider and think about His words rather than be offended by His words. (Matthew 13:11-13) Second, the answer to, "What was nailed to the cross" requires more than a theological answer. At Mt. Sinai, God's will was plainly stated. (Deuteronomy 30:12-15) The history of the Jews confirms that no man can measure up to the will of God. A close look at Jewish history from the Bible reveals an interesting fact. The Jews were either in total rebellion to the "plainly stated will of God" or they made the "plainly stated will of God" a legalistic burden which no one could fulfill. The failure of the Jews explains why God has left the answer of what was nailed to the cross up to the individual. You can answer the question in whatever way you wish. Of course, your answer may have nothing to do with the truth. God knows that if you do not want to know the truth, there is no point in revealing the truth to you. However, if the Holy Spirit is leading you, and you are an honest seeker for truth; if you are a born-again follower of Jesus Christ, you have a hunger and thirst for the whole truth. On this basis, according to God's grace, you are going to discover the truth that God has hidden and joyfully apply it in your life. Jesus has promised this! Jesus told His disciples, **"But when he, the Spirit of truth, comes, he will guide you into all truth . . . ."** (Matthew 13:11) **". . . The knowledge of the secrets of the kingdom of heaven has been given to you, but not to them."** (John 16:13)

The Womb of Judaism

Jesus was a Jew and so were His disciples, so there is no denying that Christianity began in the womb of Judaism. Peer pressure and social conformity have enormous staying power over people. This is why less than 5% of Earth's population converts from their original religious system to another. Therefore, a sudden revelation of all that was nailed to the cross would have been too much at one time for any Jew to thoughtfully consider. Early Jewish converts to Christianity struggled with the question of what was nailed to the cross for years *because* the social consequences were enormous in the family and in the community. (Acts 15) Even after making the transition to Christianity, converts could not make a clean break from their past, culture, traditions or beliefs. Jewish converts carried a lot of Jewish baggage with them into the early Christian faith. Often, the Apostle Paul modified his social conduct to conform to each situation in which he found himself. For example, when he was in Corinth, he lived like a Corinthian. He behaved like a Jew when he was in Jerusalem. (1 Corinthians 9:20-23) Because of its Jewish origin it seemed that Christianity might remain a sect within Judaism, but God had other plans. The Romans surrounded Jerusalem and Titus destroyed it in A.D. 70. This event forced Christians to scatter toward the four corners of the Earth and pushed Christianity out of the womb of Judaism.

The Empire Was Prepared

Thirty-five years before Jerusalem was destroyed, Jesus chose a man whose heart was right and his head was wrong, to become His spokesperson to the Gentiles. After Saul was converted on the road to Damascus, he became an unstoppable ambassador for Jesus. The Apostle Paul prepared the Roman empire for the dispersion of Christians. Paul traveled extensively throughout the Roman empire carrying the gospel of Jesus Christ. Paul established many early churches and on the basis of several revelations from Jesus, Paul laid a theological foundation that explains how God viewed believers in Christ as the heirs of Abraham. As Gentile men and women joined the Christian faith they naturally brought Gentile baggage into the Christian faith with them just as their Jewish counterparts had done in Jerusalem. (This baggage is often the primary reason for Paul's epistles.) In all cases and in each locale, the end result was a hybrid religion – not entirely Christian, Jewish, Grecian, Egyptian or Roman. This religious baggage explains why early Christianity fractured on a many theological issues. Jewish converts were concerned with many of Jewish issues that converts to Christianity in Rome or Alexandria did not have. History confirms that early Christians did not have an absolute answer to the question, "What was nailed to the cross?" Instead, their answers were the result of processing selected epistles of the apostles, Old Testament study, and social ramifications. Church history demonstrates that specific answers were *constructed* to suit the needs of Christians in their respective parts of the world. Remember, the New Testament was not compiled until the middle of the fourth century so early Christians had to use the Old Testament to verify Paul's claims. (Acts 17:11) Strange as it may sound, variances on the question of what changed at the cross ultimately caused Christians in one region of the world to become opposed, even hostile toward believers in other parts of the world. Church history confirms that the Christian community has not been in one accord since the Pentecost that followed the ascension of Christ. (Acts 1:14; 2:1)

A Need for Sameness

By the end of the second century A.D., the Christian Church was growing strong in the North, South and East. The northern version of Christianity was centered in Rome, the southern version was centered in Alexandria, Egypt and the eastern version was centered in the churches of Asia Minor. Each respective area had its own version (or perversion, if you will) of Christianity. If we mix the ancient modes of transportation, the vast distances and the lack of communication between Christians along with the religious baggage carried into regional churches, it is easy to see why major theological differences developed within the Christian movement. About A.D. 312, Constantine became the sole emperor of Rome. The unity of the empire was waning because ethnic populations had changed the political demographics of the world, but Christianity seemed impervious to ethnicity. Although independent of each other, Christian groups were gaining in presence and popularity throughout the empire. Constantine was a brilliant strategist and he saw an opportunity to strengthen and reunify the Roman empire through a political arrangement with Christians. He saw that Christianity needed a centralized authority or it would fracture and suffer the consequences of the empire. Therefore, he converted to Christianity and adopted religion as a formal vehicle through which his empire could be unified and his authority consolidated. Of course, Christians in Rome were very pleased with Constantine's interest. They had been persecuted and treated badly for a long time. Now, Christians began to enjoy the sunshine of the emperor's favor. Well educated and skillful Christian leaders in Rome became intimate advisors to Constantine and they "adjusted" Christian doctrine on an *ad hoc* basis to meet the needs of the Romans and most of all, the ambitious goals of Constantine.

Unequals in the Lord

About a hundred and fifty years before Constantine became emperor, Christians in the South and East began to complain that the bishop at Rome should stop trying to impose his views on other Christians. The bishop at Rome gained higher authority than other bishops for three reasons: First, the church at Rome developed into the largest church system. Therefore, the bishop at Rome directed the largest body of Christians. Second, the city of Rome was the world's center for advanced education at that time. Many of the converts in Rome were well educated and they had wealth and influence. Third, as the office of bishop rose to administrative importance in Rome's version of Christianity, Christians in Rome accepted the necessity of a hierarchy that was similar to the hierarchy of Roman government. These factors helped propel the bishop of Rome into the position of "chief spokesman" for Christians before Constantine came to power. Because the Romans did not bestow power and authority on religious leaders, the bishop at Rome could not enforce his declarations nor control the universal Christian church. But, the Romans did bestow divine power and divine authority upon Caesar. The church at Rome obviously understood the importance that Caesar could play in their cause and they carefully sought to win the favor of the emperors through flattery. Their motto was, "Convert the king, and the kingdom will follow." When Constantine arrived on the scene in A.D. 312, the extensive presence of Christianity throughout the empire and its hierarchal structure were political grapes, "ripe for the picking." The union between Constantine and the church at Rome looked like "a marriage made in Heaven." The church at Rome needed his unimpeachable authority and Constantine needed the unifying force of religion. This marriage produced one offspring, known as the Holy Roman Empire.

First Sunday after the First Full Moon after the Spring Equinox

The observance of Easter is first noted in church history about the middle of the second century A.D. Prior to this time, it is probable that Jewish converts observed the anniversary of Christ's death and resurrection at the time of Passover (Nisan 14/15). As Christianity diversified and more religious baggage was introduced into Christianity, the observance of Christ's death and resurrection became associated with pagan fertility rites (Easter eggs and bunny rabbits). Because Jewish converts insisted on observing the death and resurrection of Jesus at the time of Passover, a serious dispute arose. Christians, principally those in Rome (Pope Pius I, A.D. 142-154), insisted on a perpetual Sunday observance for Easter, the day that Jesus rose from the tomb. The pope insisted that it was more appropriate to celebrate the day of Christ's resurrection instead of the day of His death. But, a Sunday celebration did not solve the whole problem. Which Sunday should be celebrated for Easter? Depending upon the phases of the moon, Passover can vary about 29 days. Should Christians observe the Sunday following the Jewish Passover each year in order to stay close to the date of Christ's resurrection or should they fix an absolute date for Easter?

The bishop at Rome decided that Easter would be celebrated on the first Sunday that followed the first full moon following the Spring Equinox. His declaration caused a significant schism in the church because Jewish converts in the East and South wanted to keep the day of the resurrection tied to the date of Passover. Because the day of Passover wanders through the weekly cycle, Christ's resurrection could be celebrated on a Tuesday or Friday, etc. The pope's method of determining Easter would eliminate any dependancy upon the Jewish calendar. At church counsels, Pope Pius I threatened those churches who stood in opposition with excommunication if they failed to accept his decision. This show of force splintered the early Christian community for many years. When Constantine became emperor, the controversy over the time for Easter was still ongoing because no one had enough authority over all of the Christian churches to silence opposition. Given this background information, consider the provocative words of Constantine in June, A.D. 325 when he defended and defined Christian doctrine. Especially notice his reasoning:

> When the question relative to the [timing of the] sacred festival of Easter arose, it was universally thought that it would be convenient that all should keep the feast on one day; for what could be more beautiful and more desirable, than to see this festival, through which we receive the hope of immortality, celebrated by all with one accord, and in the same manner? It was declared to be particularly unworthy for this, the holiest of all festivals, to follow the [dating] custom of the Jews, who had soiled their hands with the most fearful of crimes, and whose minds were blinded. In rejecting their custom [of determining the date for Passover], we may transmit to our descendants the legitimate mode of celebrating Easter, which we have observed from the time of the Savior's Passion to the present day. We ought not, therefore, to have anything in common with the Jews, for the Savior has shown us another way; our worship follows a more legitimate and more convenient course; and consequently, in unanimously adopting this mode, we desire, dearest brethren, to separate ourselves from the detestable company of the Jews, for it is truly shameful for us to hear them boast that without their direction we could not keep this

feast [at the proper time]. How can they be in the right, they who, after the death of the Savior, have no longer been led by reason but by wild violence, as their delusions may urge them? They do not possess the truth in this Easter question; for in their blindness and repugnance to all improvement, they frequently celebrate two Passovers in the same year.

We could not imitate those who are openly in error. How, then, could we follow these Jews, who are most certainly blinded by error? For to celebrate the Passover twice in one year is totally inadmissible. But even if this were not so, it would still be your duty not to tarnish your soul by communications with such wicked people. Besides, consider well, that in such an important matter, and on a subject of such great solemnity, there ought not to be any division. Our Savior has left us only one festal day of our redemption, that is to say, of his holy passion, and he desired [to establish] only one Catholic [universal] Church. Think, then how unseemly it is, that on the same day some should be fasting whilst others are seated at a banquet; and that after Easter, some should be rejoicing at feasts, whilst others are still observing a strict fast. For this reason, a Divine Providence wills that this custom should be rectified and regulated in a uniform way; and everyone, I hope, will agree upon this point. As, on the one hand, it is our duty not to have anything in common with the murderers of our Lord; and as, on the other, the custom now followed by the Churches of the West, of the South, and of the North, and by some of those of the East, is the most acceptable, it has appeared good to all; and I have been guaranteed for your consent, that you would accept it with joy, as it is followed at Rome . . . Make known to your brethren what has been decreed, keep this most holy day according to the prescribed mode; we can thus celebrate this holy Easter day at the same time, if it is granted me, as I desire, to unite myself with you; we can rejoice together; seeing that the divine power has made use of our instrumentality for destroying the evil designs of the devil . . . . (Eusebius, Vita Const., Lib iii., 18-20, insertions in brackets are mine.)

This quotation confirms three things. First, the importance of Easter observance and the dating of Easter are contrived issues. The Bible does not mandate an Easter observance and Constantine does not appeal to Scripture for authority. Second, any association with the "repugnant" Jews for dating Easter was unconscionable to Constantine. He plainly says so. Last, Constantine decreed that Easter be celebrated on the same Sunday for all Christians and he claims this is the will of "a Divine Providence." This last comment, no doubt, was designed to silence the argument. The formula for dating Easter advanced by Pope Pius I proved to be successful for four reasons. First, it eliminated any dependancy on "those repugnant Jews" for the timing of Easter. Second, it kept Easter Sunday as close as possible to the season when Jesus died and rose from the tomb (near the time of a full moon). Third, the celebration of Easter on Sunday supported the growing importance of Sunday sacredness among Roman Christians and last, Constantine liked the idea and simply resolved a theological problem by edict. In so doing, he affirmed the desires of the bishop of Rome. The bishop was happy and Constantine was happy. Problem solved.

Hopefully, after reading the past few pages, you can understand how some Christian doctrines and practice came to be. This background has been presented to demonstrate three things. First, anti-Semitism was a powerful influence in matters of theology and practice in early church history. A significant number of Christian traditions (like the observance of Easter) are responses born out of anti-Semitism instead of Scripture. Second, the answer to "What was nailed to the Cross?" is not as plainly stated in the Bible as the Ten Commandments, but every seeker for truth has enough information in the Bible to correctly answer the question. Last, the bishop of Rome came to a place where he presumed to have the authority to dictate the will of God for all other Christians. In essence, the church at Rome answered the question by concluding that *everything Jewish* was nailed to the cross.

There is a twist of irony in this story. The position of the Catholic Church on the question of what was nailed to the cross directly affects most Protestants. Whereas Catholics claim that the pope and church leaders have the authority to determine all matters regarding religious practice, Protestants claim the Bible is their only authority in matters of religious practice. Because Protestantism came out of the womb of Catholicism, Protestantism has a lot of Catholic baggage mixed into its theology. Ironically, those Protestants who defend the decisions of the church at Rome are left holding the bag. A Bible student cannot use Bible texts to justify a number of decisions which originated on the basis of anti-Semitism. We have seen in this chapter that the church at Rome dissociated Easter from the Passover *of the Jews* because the Romans had nothing but contempt for the Jews. Later in this book, it will be shown the same is also true for the Ten Commandments. The church at Rome declared the seventh day Sabbath to be null and void because it was the Sabbath *of the Jews* and in its place, Sunday was substituted.

Chapter 8
God's Covenants

For he himself is our peace, who has made the two [nations] one and has destroyed the barrier, the dividing wall of hostility, by abolishing in his flesh the law with its commandments and regulations. His purpose was to create in himself one new man out of the two, thus making peace, and in this one body to reconcile both of them to God through the cross, by which he put to death their hostility . . . Consequently, you [Gentiles] are no longer foreigners and aliens, but fellow citizens with God's people and members of God's household, built on the foundation of the apostles and prophets, with Christ Jesus himself as the chief cornerstone.

> — Ephesians 2:14-16,19
> (insertions mine)

The Bible Says . . .

Bible history reveals the Jews were not always faithful to God. Church history confirms the same is true of Christians. Human beings within any religious system are capable of adjusting or distorting their understanding of God's will for expedient social purposes. But, deviant theology has no effect on God's truth. God's truth is everlasting. Civilizations come and go, but God and His truth remain forever. So, what was nailed to the cross? In a sentence, two covenants were nailed to the cross. One covenant was given to Adam and Eve, the second was given to the biological descendants of Abraham. (Genesis 15:18; Exodus 24:1-8; Deuteronomy 31:16; Jeremiah 11:10; 31:31-34; Ephesians 2; Colossians 2:13-17). When these covenants became null and void at the cross, two things changed. Animal sacrifices were no longer necessary, and all distinction between Jews and Gentiles came to an end. Paul wrote, **"For there is no difference between Jew and Gentile – the same Lord is Lord of all and richly blesses all who call on him, for, 'Everyone who calls on the name of the Lord will be saved.' "** (Romans 10:12,13) After the cross, salvation comes through faith in Jesus Christ. **". . . Whosoever believes in Him shall not perish but have everlasting life."** (John 3:16)

To understand the two covenants that were made null and void at the cross, a person has to understand God's use of covenants in the Bible.

Unfortunately, many Christians do not concern themselves with the basics on this subject and this explains why there is so much confusion. It is not necessary to be confused on this topic, since the Bible provides the answer.

Unilateral and Bilateral Covenants

God has two types of covenants: unilateral and bilateral. A unilateral covenant is a *one-sided* covenant which God *imposes* upon Himself and/or man. A bilateral covenant is a *two-sided* covenant or a *mutually agreed* upon covenant between God and man. Both types of covenants require a continuous relationship between God and man. Both types of covenants have rules within them giving them the effect and the appearance of law. But, a covenant is more than a set of laws. A covenant requires an ongoing relationship between God and man whereas a law does not. For example, the law of gravity is not "a covenant" because there is no intelligent relationship between gravity and man. A "law" is an authoritative statement and a covenant may have certain laws or authoritative statements within it. The quality of a covenant relationship is determined by love and affection. When both parties are happy in a mutually agreed upon covenant, the covenant is wonderful. However, if disaffection should arise between the parties, the covenant becomes a terrible bondage for both parties! Have you ever noticed that some marriages begin so happily and end so miserably? Obviously, the marriage covenant did not change. There was a change in affection which brought about a change in the relationship. How long should a mutually binding covenant be honored when there is no love in the heart of one party?

Contrasting the Covenants

A unilateral covenant is one-sided and nonnegotiable. It *is not* a mutual agreement between God and man. God's unilateral covenants are imposed on Himself or man for as long as He deems necessary. This is why it is called unilateral or one-sided. On the other hand, a bilateral covenant is a *mutually agreed* covenant between God and man. A bilateral covenant has a set of rules or laws that are binding upon both parties. A bilateral covenant is drawn up and put into effect for mutually beneficial purposes and it remains in effect for as long as the covenant stipulates. The terms and conditions set forth in a bilateral covenant can transfer to succeeding generations. A bilateral covenant comes to an end when (a) either party is unfaithful to the agreement, or (b) when the object for which the covenant was created is fulfilled. Consider these examples: Marriage is a bilateral covenant – two people fall in love and they willingly *agree* to honor vows of moral fidelity and faithfulness "until death do us part." The exchange of vows constitutes a mutual agreement and the marriage covenant is put into effect before witnesses. At death, the marriage covenant is terminated because all that was promised has been fulfilled. Similarly, if a builder and a customer enter into an agreement to build a new house, the bilateral covenant between them ends when the house is finished – because the covenant is fulfilled. When the purpose of the covenant is fulfilled, the covenant expires. To be legal, bilateral covenants require witnesses. In ancient times, if third-party witnesses were not available when a bilateral covenant was made, inanimate objects such as stones were stacked into a large pile as a witness to the agreement. (See Genesis 31:44-48.)

Covenant Definitions

If a person enters into a contract with a realtor to sell his house, the realtor's contract will state certain matters (covenant laws) which the seller and the realtor are expected to honor (through obedience). The contract goes into effect when both parties sign (or ratify) the contract. We may use the word "contract" to describe this relationship, but in a biblical sense the contract between the seller and the realtor is a bilateral covenant because a relationship exists for the duration of the contract. Even though the contract has a number of covenant laws or performance specifications in it, we know that compliance with the terms of a covenant is something else. The realtor may not meet the expectations of the seller; he may not promote the property as specified or the realtor may not represent the seller's best interest in selling the property. Likewise, the seller may refuse to meet certain demands set forth in the contract. The point is that all bilateral covenants are performance-based covenants entered into on the basis of "good faith" from the moment they begin. A bilateral covenant becomes necessary when two parties need each other to accomplish something one party cannot do alone. The hope and expectation of both parties at the beginning of a bilateral covenant is superior performance out of each other.

Many people get married each year in the United States. The marriage covenant is a bilateral covenant. At last count, the number of people in the United States terminating the marriage covenant each year is about half of the number getting married. So, even though two people may enter into the marriage covenant, neither party loses its right to abandon the covenant if the performance of the other party does not meet the specifications of the covenant. Of course there can be serious consequences for choosing to violate the terms and conditions of a mutually agreed upon covenant.

A bilateral (two sided) covenant can be declared null and void if there is evidence affirming that one party violated the laws or stipulations within the covenant. But, unilateral covenants are not declared null and void if they are violated. For example, when Adam and Eve sinned, they came under the condemnation of a unilateral covenant which states: **"But you must not eat from the tree of the knowledge of good and evil, for when you eat of it you will surely die."** (Genesis 2:17) Because this covenant required their death, Jesus had to die. In other words, someone had to die to pay for the penalty for sin because this unilateral covenant could not be declared null and void. **"The wages of sin is death. . . ."** (Romans 6:23) This is a fundamental covenant of the universe and it cannot be altered. With these definitions in mind, let us consider five unilateral covenants that were put in place *before* Moses went up Mt. Sinai to see God.

1. Unilateral: "Do Not Eat of the Tree . . . ."

At the time of Creation, God commanded Adam not to eat of the Tree of the Knowledge of Good and Evil for if he did, he would be put to death. (Genesis 2:17) According to divine wisdom and sovereign authority, God *imposed* this unilateral (one-sided) covenant upon Adam and Eve *before* sin began and it was nonnegotiable. A unilateral covenant is not a mutual covenant. When God imposed this covenant upon Adam, He spoke to Adam as the father of the human race. Eve had not been created yet. In other words, this unilateral covenant rested upon Adam and all of Adam's offspring that were forthcoming. (In a sense, Eve is considered an offspring of Adam since she was made from Adam's rib.) When Eve was deceived and disobeyed this covenant she came under its condemnation even though God spoke the covenant to Adam. Adam, we know, willfully violated this covenant and God condemned him to death just like Eve, but Jesus spared their lives by stepping "in the way" of the executing angel when He offered to die in their place.

2. Unilateral: "I Will Put Enmity . . . ."

After Adam and Eve sinned, God announced another unilateral (one-sided) covenant to man. He declared that (a) He would put enmity between the offspring of the serpent and the offspring of the woman, and (b) that "He," the Messiah, would someday crush the head of the serpent even though the serpent would strike His heel. (Genesis 3:14,15) God imposed this covenant upon Himself. (Praise God!) Carefully notice that this covenant is not dependent upon the cooperation or agreement of man. This covenant declares the forthcoming actions of God. This covenant will be fulfilled when the serpent's head is finally crushed at the end of the one thousand years. (Revelation 20)

3. Unilateral: "Destroy Those Who Commit Murder . . . ."

Soon after the flood waters subsided, God declared a third unilateral covenant to Noah. **"And for your lifeblood I will surely demand an accounting. I will demand an accounting from every animal. And from each man, too, I will demand an accounting for the life of his fellow man. "Whoever sheds the blood of man, by man shall his blood be shed; for in the image of God has God made man."** (Genesis 9:5,6) This covenant was unilaterally imposed upon Noah and his offspring (there were only eight people living at the time) and it declares man's accountability to God. Notice that death by execution in the event of murder is a unilateral decree. God did not negotiate with Noah. (Compare Genesis 9:5,6 and Numbers 35:33.) God left no wiggle room on this subject. God has imposed accountability on every beast and on every person and He declares that murderers must be executed.

4. Unilateral: "Never Again . . . ."

A fourth unilateral covenant was also given to Noah right after the flood. God declared, **"Never again will all life be cut off by the waters of a flood . . . ."** (Genesis 9:9-17) Notice again that this covenant is one-sided. This covenant is binding upon God, not man, and God has faithfully honored this covenant for nearly 4,500 years!

5. The Fifth Unilateral Covenant

In Genesis 12 and 13, we find a compelling story of faith. God selected a man who was eager to follow Him and obey His commandments. Every time I review Abraham's life, I am impressed with his deep faith in God. I am not surprised that God gave a unilateral covenant to Abraham. Neither am I surprised that Abraham's humanness got the best of him at times. Abraham died without seeing the things that God promised him, but Abraham will live again and he will see everything God promised to him. God promised a childless Abraham three things:

(a) Through Abraham, all nations of the Earth would be blessed.

(b) Abraham's descendants will be more numerous than the stars in the sky.

(c) God would give Abraham and his heirs a specific section of land. (Genesis 13:14-17; 15:5)

The unilateral covenant God gave Abraham was not conditional nor was it based on mutual agreement. God honored Abraham's faith by granting a unilateral covenant to him! We find the same to be true for a few other people of faith in the Bible such as kings Hezekiah and David. God promised Hezekiah that he would live 15 more years and God promised David that his throne will remain forever. (1 Kings 2:4; 2 Kings 20:6; 2 Samuel 7:16) The unilateral covenant God gave Abraham was implemented because of sin. As the first man of the human race, Adam was to be the Great "grandfather" of billions of sinless beings, but he forfeited that honor when he sinned. After the flood, God started over by honoring Abraham's faith, declaring him to be the Great "grandfather" of all who would live by faith. However, the unilateral covenant which God gave to Abraham still awaits completion. Notice this text: **"If you belong to Christ, then you are Abraham's seed, and heirs according to the promise** [that still stands]." (Galatians 3:29, insertion mine.) This verse, written about 30 years after Jesus died on the cross, confirms three things. First, God reckons all people who put their faith in Christ to be children of Abraham (heirs). Second, the time and setting of this verse confirm that the covenant given to Abraham was in effect *after* the cross! Third, this text indicates that anyone can become Abraham's heir through faith in Jesus. (Ephesians 2; Romans 2:28,29; 9:6,7) So, the unilateral covenant God gave Abraham still stands and as far as God is concerned, the offspring of Abraham are those people who put their faith in Christ!

Actually, faith in God has always been the core issue for salvation from the beginning of sin, but the biological offspring of Israel stubbornly refused to comprehend this point. (Jeremiah 3:20; Hebrews 4) Rebellion is the opposite of obedient faith and because of rebellion, God finally destroyed Jerusalem. But, Abraham will receive everything that God promised to him because *God redefined Israel at the cross*! The Israel of God are believers in Christ. (Romans 9 - 11; Ephesians 2; Galatians 3 and 4; James 1:1)

At the end of the 1,000 years, the unilateral covenant God gave Abraham will be fulfilled. At that time everyone will see that all nations were blessed through Abraham for the Savior of the world came through the lineage of Abraham! Second, at that time the saints will be a numberless multitude, numbering more than the stars in the sky. Last, when the Holy City, New Jerusalem, descends from God out of Heaven, it will rest upon *the specific land* that Jesus promised to give to Abraham and his offspring! (Zechariah 14; Revelation 21) Abraham well understood the curse of sin. He knew

God's covenant included more than merely living in the land of Canaan. This is why the Bible says Abraham was looking for a city whose builder and maker was God. (Hebrews 11:10) By faith, Abraham could see beyond the curse of sin. He was looking for a new Heaven and a new Earth. So, be assured that the unilateral covenant God gave to Abraham will be fulfilled because God *always* keeps His word.

Five Unilateral Covenants

So far, we have examined five unilateral covenants. All of these covenants *predate* Mt. Sinai by hundreds of years. They are:

1. "Do not eat of the Tree of the Knowledge of Good and Evil."

2. "I will put enmity between the serpent and the woman and will one day send a Savior."

3. "I will demand an accounting for each man's life. Murderers are to be put to death."

4. "I will not destroy the world again with a flood."

5. To Abraham: "Through you, all nations will be blessed."
   "I will make you the father of many nations."
   "I will give you and your descendants this land."

Bilateral: If You Will Be My People . . . .

Now, we turn our attention to the first bilateral or mutual covenant offered to man the day sin began. Although Genesis 3 does not say this in the clearest of terms, God offered a bilateral covenant (a two-sided agreement) to fallen man before He evicted them from the Garden of Eden. The silver lining of that dark day is this: God offered man a way back home if he wanted to return. It may take God 7,000 years to restore man to his garden home, but returning home is possible! This covenant can be summarized with words that God has used in various places in the Bible: "*If* you will be *my* people and show faith in *me* by obeying *me*, I will be your Salvation." (See Exodus 6:7; 19:5,6; Jeremiah 7:23; Ezekiel 36:28; Revelation 21:7.) Because bilateral covenants are performance based, notice the conditional element in this bilateral covenant. "*If* you will be my people . . . ." It is apparent from Genesis 3 that Adam and Eve accepted the covenant. Jesus ratified this covenant by conducting the first animal sacrifice to demonstrate the price of sin. (Genesis 3:21) The killing of a flawless lamb was a shadow of the death of man's Creator. After slaying the lamb, I believe Jesus covered the nakedness of Adam and Eve with the skin of the lamb. This is a beautiful object lesson showing how God covers our sins through the righteousness of Christ. (Romans 3:21,22)

This bilateral covenant, which was offered in perpetuity to Adam and Eve and their descendants, is one of the two covenants that was nailed to the cross. When Jesus died, the requirement for animal sacrifices – established in the Garden of Eden – came to an end. This bilateral covenant between God and man was fulfilled and a fulfilled covenant is a finished covenant. A new bilateral covenant was implemented at the cross which is based on the blood of Jesus.

Abel's Sacrifice

Consider for a moment how the first bilateral covenant worked: Because the blood of Jesus would have to be spilled to bring about man's restoration, God mandated that animal blood be periodically shed until Christ's blood could be shed. (Genesis 4:4) Animal sacrifices served as a symbolic reminder of the price of salvation. We know this to be true because of Abel's "approved" offering and subsequent death. (Hebrews 11:4; 12:24; 1 John 3:12) Although Cain could actually see into the Garden of Eden, he was so rebellious that he would not submit to the terms and conditions that God required to return there! He refused to offer the prerequisite animal sacrifice and God refused to honor Cain's offering of fruit. As Abel obediently presented the prerequisite sacrifices, God commended him and Cain went deeper and deeper into a jealous rage. No doubt Cain thought, "How can God continue to embarrass me, the firstborn of mankind, in front of this lesser (younger) brother?" Finally, Cain vented his rage toward God and Abel by killing Abel. For 4,000 years, from Adam to the time of Christ, everyone wanting salvation had to submit to the requirements of the first bilateral covenant God gave to Adam and Eve. Noah obediently submitted to this requirement. (Genesis 8:20,21) Remember that everyone prior to the flood (with the exception of Enoch) who offered animal sacrifices went to their death without receiving what was promised. (Hebrews 11:39,40) Understand that salvation is granted to no one on the basis of obedience. Obedience can be the result of faith or obedience can be the result of conformity. In other words, a person can offer animal sacrifices because it is "the religious thing to do," but this is not faith. Faith is most clearly revealed when obedience comes with a penalty. In Abel's case, it cost him his life.

Bilateral Covenant Expanded at Sinai

The bilateral covenant which God offered to Adam and Eve was both perpetual (for 4,000 years) and temporary (until Jesus died). The slaying of animals was an act of faith for 40 centuries. The slaying of sacrificial animals, according to the requirements that God established, was an expression of faith. Faith renders obedience; presumption excuses transgression. At Mt. Sinai, God offered the descendants of Abraham a bilateral covenant. This covenant was an enhanced and expanded version of the bilateral covenant that He had offered to Adam and Eve. The covenant which God offered to the offspring of Abraham at Mt. Sinai was not entirely new nor was it entirely unique. Instead, it was a repetition and enlargement of certain issues that had been extended to the human race through Adam and Eve. The bilateral covenant offered to Israel included certain new features for Israel (such as the privilege of being a kingdom of priests to God), but it remained a conditional two-sided covenant, "*If* you will be my people, then I will be your God." (Leviticus 26; Deuteronomy 28-30)

Dispensationalism

A misunderstanding of God's covenants has led to the rise of a concept called dispensationalism. Proponents of dispensationalism teach that salvation is offered to man in different ways at different times. Dispensationalists have a point, but their balance and message is wrong. It is true that God has required people at different times to do different things. For example, prior to the death of Jesus, all who chose to accept the terms of the original bilateral covenant were required to offer animal sacrifices – from Adam down to the time of Christ. But, the offering of animal sacrifices did not provide salvation (Hebrews 10:4) nor do sacrificial animals change the means to salvation. (Ephesians 2:8,9) Faith in God has always been the prerequisite for salvation. Review the "Hall of Faith" in Hebrews 11 and notice: "By faith Abel . . . "; "By faith Enoch . . . "; "By faith Noah . . . "; "By faith Abraham . . . "; "By faith Moses . . . ." Dispensationalism teaches that God starts over from time to time by declaring a covenant obsolete and creating a new one. Again, dispensationalists have a point but their emphasis is wrong. As we shall see, it is true that God can declare a covenant void and create a new covenant. The problem with dispensationalism; however, is that it does not properly define the covenants that God created and discarded!

Basic Problem

The following comments may appear to be entirely out of context in this study on God's covenants. However, I would like to address the fundamental reason for dispensationalism at this point. Protestants are on the horns of a dilemma. They have a thorny problem with the fourth commandment that will not go away. The fourth commandment states: **"Remember the Sabbath day by keeping it holy. Six days you shall labor and do all your work, but the seventh day is a Sabbath to the Lord your God. On it you shall not do any work, neither you, nor your son or daughter, nor your manservant or maidservant, nor your animals, nor the alien within your gates. For in six days the Lord made the heavens and the earth, the sea, and all that is in them, but he rested on the seventh day. Therefore the Lord blessed the Sabbath day and made it holy."** (Exodus 20:8-11) If Protestants honored this commandment as they do the other nine, the behavior of millions of Christians would be vastly different each weekend. Saturday is God's holy day, the seventh day of the week. Sunday is the first day of the week. The Lord's Day (Mark 2:27,28) was changed from Saturday to Sunday by the church of Rome. This change came about because of two factors. First, Saturday was the Sabbath of the Jews and early Christians in Rome did not want any association with those "repugnant" Jews, especially after Jerusalem was destroyed in A.D. 70. (The theological impact of anti-Semitism upon early Christianity was mentioned in the previous chapter.) Second, about 100 years before Christianity arrived in Rome, the ancient pagan religion of Mithraism arrived in Rome and it quickly gained a very large following. Later on, the emperor Commodus (A.D. 180-192) even made Mithraism an imperial cult. Mithraism centers around the worship of the sun-god, Mithra, whose day of worship is Sunday, the day of the Sun. Priests of Mithraism were called "father" and they promoted a high moral code of conduct. In fact, the similarities between Mithraism and Christianity were so striking that Tertullian (A.D. 160-225) believed the devil had created a deliberate parallel of Christianity even before Christianity began. Converts from Mithraism to Christianity brought "the observance of Sunday" with them into Rome's version of Christianity. Remember, early Christians in Rome wanted to distance themselves from the hated Jews, and since Sunday worship was commonly practiced in Rome, why not worship Jesus on Sunday? The first Sunday keepers in Rome did not use a command from Scripture to support this transition, but they did attempt to justify their actions. About A.D. 150 Justin Martyr wrote:

> But Sunday is the day on which we all hold our common assembly because it is the first day on which God, having wrought a change in

the darkness and matter, made the world; and Jesus Christ our Savior on the same day rose from the dead. (Justin Martyr, *First Apology of Justin Martyr, Ante-Nicean Christian Library*, (Boston 1887) p. 187 Chap. 67)

Christian groups differed in theology and practice because of distance, the lack of communication, regional religious baggage and anti-Semitism. Sunday observance was a unique feature that began in Rome and spread to Alexandria. About the turn of the fourth century, Socrates, a church leader of that time observed:

Such is the difference in the churches on the subject of fasts. Nor is there less variation in regard to religious assemblies. For although almost all churches through the world celebrate the sacred mysteries on the Sabbath of every week, yet the Christians of Rome and Alexandria have ceased to do this. (Socrates, *Ecclesiastical History,* Book V, Chap. 22, *Ante-Nicean Christian Library*, Vol II, (Boston, 1887) p. 132)

These facts are presented because the Catholic Church does not historically defend the change from Sabbath to Sunday on the basis of Scripture, but on the basis of church authority. After Constantine came to power, the sacredness of Sunday for Christians was affirmed by law in A.D. 321. Eusebius, the trusted confidant and advisor to Constantine, defended this action saying:

And all things whatsoever that it was the duty to do on the Sabbath, these we have transferred to the Lord's Day, as more appropriately belong to it, because it has a precedence and is first in rank, and more honorable than the Jewish Sabbath. All things whatsoever that it was duty to do on the Sabbath, these we have transferred to the Lord's Day. (Eusebius's Commentary on the Psalms 92, quoted in Coxe's Sabbath literature, Vol I, p. 361, insertions mine.)

These references are presented because Protestants separated from Catholicism because of conflict between Bible truth and church authority. Protestants claim there is no authority on matters of faith and duty other than that what is found in Scripture. Catholics claim that authority is found in either the inerrant declarations of the pope or decisions reached by scholars and church leaders. So, the only way Protestants have found to void the fourth commandment which mandates the observance of Saturday as a holy day is to nail all Ten Commandments to the cross. This is the primary objective and function of dispensationalism. The scheme is elaborate and complex but the net effect is that millions of Christians have been misled into believing that the Sabbath commandment was nailed to the cross. However, if you ask most Christians about murder, adultery, stealing, etc., they will return to the Ten Commandments for authority to show that these behaviors are wrong. This is a great mystery. Somehow, the Ten Commandments were made void at the cross only to have nine command-ments immediately reinstated! This doctrine is one of the harmful contribu-tions of dispensationalism to Protestantism.

The Ten Commandments Are Called a Covenant

There is sufficient evidence in the Bible to conclude that the Ten Com-mandments are a unilateral covenant which God has imposed on all mankind for the duration of sin. Let us examine the evidence.

The Ten Commandments are called "the covenant" in the Bible. **"Moses was there with the Lord forty days and forty nights without eating bread or drinking water. And he wrote on the tablets the words of the covenant—the Ten Commandments."** (Exodus 34:28) The Israelites kept the two tablets of stone in a golden box that was called, "the ark of *the covenant.*" The Ten Commandments are not ten suggestions and contrary to what dispensationalists teach, they are not included in God's bilateral covenant with Israel. They are ten laws that were unilaterally imposed upon all of mankind by divine authority when sin began! We know that obeying the Ten Commandments will not bring salvation. They are not a shadow of good "things to come." They are not ceremonial. They say nothing about sacrifices, rituals or redemption. Instead, they are ten profound command-ments from man's Creator telling people on Earth how to live. The first four commandments define man's relationship to God. The last six define man's relationship to man. Even though God deposited them with Israel as trustees of His grace, He spoke them and wrote them down for the benefit of all mankind. There is nothing *Jewish* in the Ten Commandments.

Consider this thought question: When you study the *New* Testament, do you get the impression that obeying the Ten Commandments is harmful? If so, which commandment is harmful to Christian growth and development? Do you find any behavior forbidden in the Ten Commandments that is *permitted or sanctioned* in the New Testament? If you answer yes to either question, please send the Bible text to me. In my study of the Bible, I have found that there is only one new commandment in the whole New Testa-ment. Jesus said, **"A new command I give you: Love one another. As I have loved you, so you must love one another. By this all men will know that you are my disciples, if you love one another."** (John 13:34,35) Have you wondered why Jesus calls this a new command? What makes this commandment new and different from anything said before in the Old Testament? The answer is that divine love was demonstrated through the humanity of Jesus. Jesus gave man a new example of what it means to love one another. He gave His life for us, and we should love one another enough to do the same. Because we have a living example to follow, a model of perfection, we have one new command, we are to "love one another as Jesus has loved us."

The Ten Commandments Are a Unilateral Covenant

I am convinced the Ten Commandments are a unilateral covenant that God revealed to man *at the fall.* Prior to the fall, Adam and Eve were in perfect harmony with God's will. After all, they were created in His image. A written copy of the Ten Commandments was not necessary *before* sin occurred because Adam and Eve had the laws of God written in their hearts. Stealing or lying were foreign to Adam and Eve before the fall. We know from our study of the sealing in Chapter 6 that God will remove the carnal nature and write His laws in our hearts and minds as He originally wrote them in the hearts of Adam and Eve. (Hebrews 8:10-13) Although the Bible does not specifically mention the Ten Commandments prior to Mt. Sinai, this silence does not eliminate the presence or knowledge of God's law as dispensationalists claim. Moses says very little in Genesis about the extent of man's knowledge as it pertains to God's laws. But, Moses does explain how sin began and that God's patience with sin and rebellion reached its limit during the time of Noah. (Genesis 6:5,6) The silence of Moses does not prove the absence of the Ten Commandments. Moses says nothing about adultery prior to the flood. Does this mean adultery did not occur prior to the flood? No! It is inconceivable that God would wait 2,500 years after sin began to give humanity a basic understanding of right and wrong at Mt. Sinai. Did it suddenly become wrong to worship idols, profane God's name, violate His holy Sabbath, kill, steal, lie and commit adultery at Mt. Sinai? No! If so, were these sins unique to the Jews only? No! From the beginning, murder was a sinful act and Lucifer as well as Cain knew it. (John 8:44; 1 John 3:12) It was also a sin to steal, to commit adultery, to profane God's name, and to violate God's holy Sabbath day long before events at Mt. Sinai took place.

A knowledge of God's law existed prior to Mt. Sinai. Noah faithfully reminded the antediluvians about God's laws. Peter says that Noah was a preacher of righteousness for 120 years! (2 Peter 2:5) If there were no commandments defining sin and rebellion prior to the flood, righteousness and wickedness could not be defined. Paul argues, where there is no law, there is no sin. (Romans 4:15) If there is no law establishing a speed limit, there can be no speeding! The wholesale destruction of the world by a flood convinces me that millions of men and women had a generous opportunity to know God's will (His laws), but they rejected it. From Genesis to Revelation, rebellion is the only justification that God ever uses to destroy anyone! If humanity was almost obliterated from the face of Earth because every thought was "only evil continually," then humanity must have knowingly chosen a course of rebellion. (Genesis 6:5 [KJV]; 2 Peter 3) This is why Jesus compares the end of the age with days of Noah. When men and women refuse to walk according to the laws of the Almighty, He has no other option but total destruction. (Matthew 24:37)

Consider the words of Paul: **"Therefore, just as sin entered the world through one** [disobedient] **man, and death through sin, and in this way death came to all men, because all** [have] **sinned – for before the** [Mosaic] **law was given** [at Mt. Sinai], **sin was in the world. But sin is not taken into account when there is no** [knowledge of] **law. Nevertheless, death reigned** [because it is mandatory that sinners die] **from the time of Adam to the time of Moses, even over those who did not sin by breaking a** [known] **command, as did Adam, who was a pattern of the one to come."** (Romans 5:12-14, insertions mine.) Some people offer these three verses to prove that there was "no law" before God gave the Ten Commandments at Mt. Sinai. If there was no law, how could God condemn Adam or the antediluvians? What were they guilty of? They could not have been declared lawless if there was no law. We must be careful to understand what Paul is actually writing in Romans 5. Paul is making the point in Romans 5:12-14 that we cannot escape the consequences of sin. Even if a man does not know that he is a sinner, even if he knows nothing about God's law, death still reigns over him because the law of God demands death for all sinners. Paul is clear that before the law was given at Mt. Sinai, sin was in the world. What is sin? Sin is the transgression of God's law. (Romans 4:15; 1 John 3:4) Paul is making the point that God's law was present from Adam to Moses, but man's knowledge of God's law was limited in scope compared to what was known about sin after Mt. Sinai. Because man's knowledge was limited to the Ten Commandments, God overlooked certain sins because man had no knowledge. God did not destroy the antediluvians for their sinful ignorance. Instead, he sent "a preacher of righteousness" who spoke plainly about the authority and presence of God's law and its penalty. God destroyed the antediluvians because they willfully rejected His laws. God's Ten Commandments existed prior to the flood. In fact, the holiness of God's Sabbath is declared in Genesis 2!

God reduced "oral law" to written form at the time of Mt. Sinai. The Ten Commandments existed in oral form from the beginning. Adam and Eve instinctively knew the contents of the Ten Commandments for these laws were written in their minds and hearts! They knew it was wrong to lie or steal because their lives were in complete harmony with God's character. They knew of the holiness of the Sabbath because it was their first full day of life with their Creator. (Genesis 2:1-3) But the day sin entered their souls, rebellion clouded their hearts and darkened their minds. The off-spring of Adam and Eve became even more ignorant of God. This is why eventually, God wrote the law on tablets of stone and God required the reading of law every sabbatical year to make sure that each generation heard "the Word" with their own ears. (Deuteronomy 31:10,11)

Unilateral in Content

It makes no sense to include the Ten Commandments with the Mosaic covenant because the stipulations given in the Ten Commandments are universal and eternal. No born again Christian will say that worshiping other gods, committing adultery, murder, stealing and using God's name in vain was permissible *before* Mt. Sinai or *after* the death of Jesus. There-fore, scholars who abolish the Ten Commandments with the Mosaic cov-enant have to restore nine of the Ten Commandments by proposing these commandments are mentioned in the New Testament and stating that the Sabbath commandment is not. This is foolish reasoning. The authority of the Sabbath commandment is affirmed throughout the New Testament. The underlying purpose for this dispensational maneuver is to eliminate the obligation of the fourth commandment. Christians do not want to observe the seventh day Sabbath of the Jews – actually though, it is the seventh day Sabbath of man's Creator, Jesus Christ.

Thus far, we have examined six unilateral covenants and one bilateral covenant:

Unilateral

1. "Do not eat of the Tree of the Knowledge of Good and Evil."

2. The Ten Commandments.

3. "I will put enmity between the serpent and the woman and will one day send a Savior."

4. "I will demand an accounting for each man's life. Murderers are to be put to death."

5. "I will not destroy the world again with a flood."

6. To Abraham: "Through you, all nations will be blessed."
                  "I will make you the father of many nations."
                  "I will give you and your descendants this land."

Bilateral

1. To Adam and Eve: "If you will be my people, I will be your God."

We now turn our attention to the bilateral covenant offered to Israel. To understand the origin of this covenant, we must start with a visit between Jesus and Abraham.

A Bilateral Covenant for Abraham's Offspring

A few years after declaring His unilateral covenant to Abraham, Jesus visited again with Abraham and told him that He was going to offer a special covenant to his descendants after 400 years passed. This covenant would be a bilateral covenant, that is, based upon mutual agreement. (Genesis 15) There is a sharp distinction between the *unilateral* covenant given to Abraham and the *bilateral* covenant that would be offered to Abraham's descendants 400 years later. God intended to make Abraham's biological descendants a kingdom of priests, a holy nation. (Exodus 19:6) In other words, because of God's great love for Abraham, God wanted to exalt Abraham's offspring as "His finest sons" on Earth. The sons of Abraham would stand between God and the nations of Earth as priests, trustees of His grace. God intended the "Abrahamites" would be men of faith like their father. He wanted them to love Him with all their hearts and their neighbors as themselves – *just as Abraham, Isaac and Jacob did*! God wanted the Israelites to be a shining light to the Gentile nations in darkness. He wanted Israel to love the people of other nations and hate their sin. God wanted Israel to evangelize the world with a testimony about His love and gather a great harvest of souls for His coming kingdom. (Isaiah 49:6; Acts 13:47) Israel was to be a nation of "Jehovah's Witnesses," a literal "Salvation Army," a "World-wide Church of God."

At the time of this second visit, Abraham still had no offspring. So, Jesus did something that was customary in ancient times. He made an oath to Abraham assuring him that He would offer a bilateral covenant to his descendants. This oath was ratified by Jesus when He walked through animal parts that Abraham laid upon the ground. (See Genesis 15, also Jeremiah 34:19,20 on this practice.) This event served as a witness to the oath that Jesus made to Abraham. In other words, Abraham killed the necessary animals for this oath and Jesus passed through the animal parts signifying that He would offer His covenant to descendants of Abraham who were not yet present on Earth. Although Abraham knew he would not live long enough to see God's plans fulfilled, Abraham was satisfied that God would keep vigil and honor His oath. (Exodus 12:42) By requiring blood at the declaration of this oath, Jesus signified to Abraham that He, the Great I AM, an eternal member of the Godhead of the Universe, would keep His covenant with Abraham's offspring upon pain of death.

Ratification of the Abrahamic Covenant

Although Jesus gave Abraham an oath that He would offer a bilateral covenant with his offspring, the covenant with the heirs was not ratified (mutually agreed upon) for more than 400 years. (Exodus 12:41; Hebrews 9:18-21) In fact, the bilateral covenant was not ratified until *after* God gave all of the details to Moses on Mt. Sinai. (Exodus 24:1-8) Remember, a bilateral covenant is two-sided; based on performance. Unlike a unilateral covenant, both parties must agree and both parties must be faithful to the terms and conditions set forth in a bilateral covenant. So, when the time came to fulfill the oath that God had promised to Abraham, God directed Moses to come up the mountain and meet with Him. Moses was required to write down all the terms and conditions of a bilateral covenant. This covenant would be both perpetual (until Messiah appeared on Earth) and temporary (until Messiah should die for mankind). This covenant bound God and the seed of Abraham together for more than fourteen hundred years. When Moses had completed this task, he went down the mountain and read the words of this covenant to all of the people. Notice how the story unfolds in the Bible:

"Then he [Jesus] said to Moses, 'Come up to the Lord, you and Aaron, Nadab and Abihu, and seventy of the elders of Israel. You are to worship at a distance, but Moses alone is to approach the Lord; the others must not come near. And the people may not come up with him.' When Moses went and told the people all the Lord's words and laws, they responded with one voice, *'Everything the Lord has said we will do.'* Moses then wrote down everything the Lord had said. He got up early the next morning and built an altar at the foot of the mountain and set up twelve stone pillars representing the twelve tribes of Israel. Then he sent young Israelite men, and they offered

burnt offerings and sacrificed young bulls as fellowship offerings to the Lord. Moses took half of the blood and put it in bowls, and the other half he sprinkled on the altar. Then he took the Book of the Covenant and read it to the people. They responded, *'We will do everything the Lord has said; we will obey.'* Moses then *took the blood, sprinkled it on the people* and said, 'This is the blood of the covenant that the Lord has made with you in accordance with all these words.' " (Exodus 24:1-8, insertion and italics mine.)

The bilateral covenant between God and the descendants of Abraham was ratified with the sprinkling of blood. After hearing the terms and conditions of the covenant, the people voiced their agreement twice. Since third party witnesses were not present, Moses stacked twelve huge stones (one for each tribe) in a pile as a witness to this event, signifying Israel's corporate agreement. The shedding of blood put this covenant into effect. (See Hebrews 9:18-22.) The significance of the blood is very important. A blood covenant in ancient times was a life or death issue for both parties. For God, the only way out of this covenant was through His own death. For Israel, the only way out was their destruction. (Leviticus 26; Deuteronomy 28) If one party proved to be unfaithful, then the faithful partner had the right to demand the blood (death) of the unfaithful party.

Sunset Clause

The bilateral covenant (or Mosaic covenant) between God and Abraham's offspring was temporary from its inception. It had a sunset clause in it. (Matthew 26:28; Colossians 2:17; Hebrews 9:15-10:4) Jesus offered a covenant to the descendants of Abraham because He needed a special job done. Basically, He needed a group of informed people to reveal what He was all about to an uninformed world. (Acts 13:47; 26:22,23) As with any covenant, the special covenant that Jesus offered Israel contained a number of laws. The Mosaic covenant included laws regarding food (clean and unclean), tithing, animal sacrifices, purification ceremonies, the obser-vance of annual feast days, new moon celebrations, the observance of sabbatical years, circumcision, the priesthood of Aaron, and many civil laws. All of these laws served as illustrations of Jesus as King and High Priest, His coming kingdom and shadows of His death and ministry. When "The Light of the World" came to Earth, the shadows expired. (Colossians 2; Galatians 3) After the covenant between Israel and God was nailed to the cross, all believers in Christ stand before God as one flesh.

Israel's Prophetic Destiny

Because of dispensational theology, many Christians disagree with the previous paragraph. Christians widely believe that God's covenant promises given to ancient Israel must last forever. This doctrine is affirmed by many popular end-time scenarios promoted by Christians. But, all of the terms and conditions put forth in the Mosaic covenant *were conditional.* A bilateral covenant is based on good faith and the performance of the parties involved. It is a distortion of Scripture to teach that God is still obligated to fulfill promises He gave to ancient Israel during a future 70th week. God did offer many promises to Israel, but they were based on terms and conditions. If Israel had "kept faith" with the Lord, loved Him whole-heartedly, and walked according to His commandments and statutes, **then** God would have fulfilled all of His promises. (Deuteronomy 6:5; Ezekiel 20) "If" is the key word on this topic because God *is not* obligated to keep a mutual covenant with any party that persists in rebellion. (See Leviticus 26; Deuteronomy 28, 31:16-32:52; Romans 9-11; Galatians 4.) Bible history underscores God's behavior regarding this fact repeatedly. For example, "the Israel" who experienced a jubilant Exodus from Egypt entered into a covenant with God at Mt. Sinai (Exodus 19:4-8), but they all perished in the wilderness because of rebellion (except Joshua and Caleb). (Psalms 95:10,11; Hebrews 3:7-4:1) God's plan for leading Israel into the Promised Land was ultimately fulfilled, but not for *those people* to whom the opportunity was first given! (Hebrews 3:16-19) Furthermore, honest Bible students cannot overlook God's subsequent actions during 1,500 years of Jewish history. Israel rebelled and God sent the king of Assyria to destroy the northern ten tribes of Israel in 722 B.C. Then, in 586 B.C., God sent King Nebuchadnezzar to finally destroy Jerusalem and the two remaining southern tribes.

A Fulfilled Covenant is a Finished Covenant

At the cross, the covenant between God and Israel was declared void. Jesus declared the bilateral covenant between God and Israel, with all its commandments and regulations, null and void. Consequently, God abandoned the nation of Israel because of their persistent unfaithfulness. This is why Jesus pronounced this final benediction upon Israel, **"Behold, your house is left unto you desolate."** (Matthew 23:38, [KJV]) What did He mean with these solemn words? The Jews regarded the temple at Jerusalem as God's dwelling place. They believed they were (a) the apple of God's eye, and (b) safe from the threat of any nation. (Deuteronomy 28; Jeremiah 7:4; Luke 21:5,6) Israel did have an opportunity to be the apple of

God's eye, but they forfeited this great opportunity by rebellion. They could have been safe from the threat of other nations, but they chose to rebel. "The Great I Am" came and lived in their midst, but they rejected Him. So, what did Jesus mean when He said, "Your house if left unto you desolate?" He meant that "never again" would His Presence enter that temple. Their house of worship (the centerpiece of their religion) was declared an empty hollow building. A desolate house is an empty house and the Shekinah would never return to it. John says, **"He came unto His own and His own received Him not."** (John 1:11, [KJV]) In A.D. 70, Jesus sent the Roman army to destroy Jerusalem. He fulfilled the terms and conditions set forth in the blood covenant through His death on the cross. Not only did He shed His blood to fulfill the covenant, He demanded their blood for unfaithfulness. (See Deuteronomy 28:44,45 and Daniel 9:26,27) When the Roman army burned Jerusalem, no two stones of the temple were left standing together. (Matthew 24:2) The Romans pulled the temple stone apart looking for the gold that melted in the great calamity. Jesus decreed an end to the temple that bore His Name and contrary to what many Christians believe, it will not be built again. To ensure His decree remains perpetual, Jesus moved the Moslems to build the Dome of the Rock on that site.

Two Covenants Fulfilled

The blood Jesus shed at Calvary *fulfilled* the unilateral covenant given to Adam and Eve, as well as the bilateral covenant between God and the nation of Israel. A fulfilled covenant is a *finished* covenant. The animal offerings required under the blood covenant pointed forward to Jesus' death. When He died, the covenant ended because Jesus' blood had been shed – the shadow was replaced with reality! (Colossians 2:17) God designed the blood covenant (the Mosaic covenant) from the beginning to be a "tutor" or schoolmaster to explain the wonderful dimensions of the Plan of Salvation. If Israel had properly understood the object lessons of salvation, it would have had an endless supply of wonderful themes to share with the whole world. (Galatians 3:24-26, [KJV]) Incidentally, the Mosaic covenant was not designed as something that belonged exclusively to Israel. While they were the trustees of salvation and the first in line to benefit from it, God promised to bless *all nations* through Abraham by allowing Gentiles to partake of the wonderful provisions of this covenant. (See Isaiah 2 and 56.) This is why God called Abraham the father of *many* nations! (Genesis 17:4)

The New Covenant in the New Testament

Because the bilateral covenant with Adam and Eve and the Mosaic covenant were coming to an end, Jesus initiated a new covenant just before His death. Luke writes, **"In the same way, after the supper He took the cup, saying, 'This cup is the new covenant in my blood, which is poured out for you.' "** (Luke 22:20) When Jesus said to His disciples, **"This cup is the new covenant in my blood, which is poured out for you,"** He initiated a new bilateral covenant, a better covenant than what He had offered to Israel at Mt. Sinai. (2 Corinthians 3:6; Hebrews 7:22; 9:15) A new blood covenant became necessary because the Kingdom of God could not be established as originally planned. Israel had rejected God for the last time. Consequently, God opened the door of opportunity to the Gentiles. (Luke 21:24) "Whosoever will," let him come and be my people. (John 3:16; Revelation 22:17) Jesus offered a new bilateral covenant to everyone who would believe He was the Messiah. *There are two essential differences between the new covenant based on Christ's blood and the old covenants based on animal blood:* First, the old covenant required the use of teaching aides (such as sacrificial lambs, ceremonies, etc.), whereas the new covenant is based on a study of the life of Christ. Second, God gave the old covenant to the biological offspring of Abraham whereas He extends the new covenant to anyone in any nation or race who puts his or her faith in Jesus! In both covenants, the means to salvation is the same, namely, obedient submission to the will of God – an experience known as "living by faith."

God entered into the old covenant with a nation of people who were carnal and rebellious from the start. God enters into the new covenant with people of all nations who are willing to be "born again." Israel was initially awed into submission at the display of His glory and power at Mt. Sinai (Exodus 19; Galatians 4:24,25), but their hearts remained unconverted. Bible history faithfully records their failures beginning with the golden calf at the base of the Mt. Sinai! In every case, Israel's hard heart led to failure. (Ezekiel 2,3) The Israel that entered into the Mosaic covenant at Mt. Sinai was the Israel that died in the desert because of rebellion. (Hebrews 3:16)

No Anti-Semitism

I am not bashing the Jews for their failures. Instead, I am reporting the contents of Scripture. I am very confident that if God had chosen any other race of people, the same results would have occurred. The story would be the same, only the names would change. The story of Israel is the story of human nature. Israel's rebellion at the corporate level is no different from all nations who have come and gone. Israel's rebellion at the individual level is no different from our personal rebellion against God. The problem with Israel and the problem with all nations is the power of sin!

New Covenant

Unlike the old covenant, the new covenant exists only between God and a self-selecting group of people who receive Jesus as their Savior. No longer does God favor one nation as trustees of the Plan of Salvation. Both the old and new covenants are similar in one way; both are based on faith. This faith means a complete surrender to God's will. However, the second covenant is based on the life and death of Jesus – a much better blood covenant than that of animals. (Hebrews 8:6; Romans 5:10) His offer of salvation is extended to everyone, first to the Jew and then to the Gentile, on the basis of spiritual rebirth and regeneration. (John 3:3-16; Romans 8:3,4; 11:19-23) Paul says the new covenant is available to the Jew first, then the Gentile. He makes this distinction because He thought the Jews would be quick to grasp the significance of this better covenant. The Jews were much better acquainted with God's ways. Paul knew the Gentiles would have to start from the beginning to understand the big picture. The bottom line for Jew and Gentile though, is the same. Instead of entering into a blood covenant with a nation of carnal-hearted people who would not understand God nor live according to His ways, God now offers a new covenant to a self-selecting group of people. These are the people who will receive Jesus as Lord and Master and choose to live by faith in Him. Anyone who wants salvation on God's terms can have it! This is good news!

What Obligations Carry Over?

People often ask me if Christians are under any obligations stemming from the Mosaic covenant – including tithing, abstaining from unclean foods, the observance of feast days, etc. My response in general, and about feast days in particular, is this: *How can the specifications regarding the feast days be satisfied without doing the things required on the feast days?* In other words, how can a person observe Passover and not kill the paschal lamb? I have heard the response that observing the *date* of Passover is not to be confused with the Mosaic ceremonies required at Passover. I dis-agree. This is similar to the idea of observing Sunday by doing the things required on Sabbath. In the Mosaic covenant, the sacrificial ceremony and the appointed time to observe the feast were inseparable parts of the package. The Passover, the Feast of Unleavened Bread, the Feast of Weeks or Pentecost, the Feast of Trumpets, the Day of Atonement and the Feast of Tabernacles were services conducted under the auspices of the Aaronic priesthood. Ever since the cross, we do not live under the laws of that priesthood. Those laws have been declared null and void. Our High Priest comes from the tribe of Judah, not Levi! Jesus does not preside over any of the Aaronic feasts. This would be illegal. Paul makes it very clear in Hebrews 7 that with a change in the priesthood, also comes a change of law (a different bilateral covenant). Paul says that since the descendants of Aaron can no longer be high priests, Levitical laws (including requirements such as tithing) are no longer valid. (See Hebrews 7.) Therefore, we are no longer *obligated* to keep any of the requirements of the Mosaic covenant.

In Paul's day, many of the Jewish believers could not let go of their Mosaic baggage. They diligently tried to enforce feast observances on new Gentile converts in Galatia. Paul wrote a strong denunciation to the Gentiles who were following in the footsteps of Jewish converts saying, **"Formerly, when you did not know God, you were slaves to those who by nature are not gods. But now that you know God – or rather are known by God – how is it that you are turning back to those weak and miserable principles? Do you wish to be enslaved by them all over again? You are observing special days and months and seasons and years! I fear for you, that somehow I have wasted my efforts on you."** (Galatians 4:8-11)

To underscore the transition from the Mosaic covenant to the "new covenant with Jesus," Paul used the illustration of tithing (verses 5-10). He wrote, **"For when there is a change of the priesthood, *there must also be a change of the law.* He [Jesus] of whom these things are said belonged to a different tribe, and no one from that tribe has ever served at the altar. For it is clear that our Lord descended from Judah, and in regard to that tribe Moses said nothing about priests."** (Hebrews 7:12-14, emphasis mine.) The significance of Paul's statement is profound. How could the Levites demand tithe when the law that gave them authority to collect the tithe has been abolished? How could the old order under the animal blood covenant be intact if Jesus, from the tribe of Judah, is now our High Priest?

Before you jump to the conclusion that God wants us to keep *all* of our money for personal use, we need to consider the next point. Even though the Levitical code and its commands have been made null and void, there is divine wisdom and great beauty in the Mosaic covenant which God presented through Moses at Mt. Sinai. God did not offer Israel a shabby covenant. It is one of the most interesting and valuable illustrations of the ministry of Jesus that has ever existed. If Israel had *combined* the Mosaic covenant with faith in God, they would have received more blessings than they could count! (Malachi 3:10,11) The world would have been astounded by the nation of Israel, for it would have been the head, and not the tail! Instead of anti-Semitism, there would have been pro-Semitism! (Deuteronomy 28:13) Remember, it is God's desire that we mature in the faith experience. God wants carnal, self-centered people (the human race) to have a change of heart. He wants us to step out in faith and obey Him. In this light, the Ten Commandments represent a starting place for spiritual growth. The content of the Ten Commandments is simple and direct. The fourth commandment is a testing commandment. To the carnal mind, the Sabbath is a big waste of time. To the spiritual mind, it represents a wonderful rest. It all depends on our perspective of God and our attitude toward His laws. The Sabbath commandment challenges our faith by telling us to "let go and let God" every seventh day. It challenges us to stand still and see God's salvation. "The Sabbath was made for man," but the devil has led the people of the world to consider it with contempt by making it appear to be Jewish or legalistic. It is interesting that the fourth commandment is the *only* commandment of the ten that requires us to do nothing! To honor God, we just have to rest at the right time each week.

God's standard of righteousness is not less today than it was yesterday. God has not changed nor have the Ten Commandments been made void. What has changed is God's approach. Israel's example has proven that righteous laws do not make people righteous. Rather, people become righteous when they inwardly submit to God's Word and obediently follow the leading of the Spirit. (John 14:16,17; Hebrews 12:14) Under the current "new covenant" that Jesus established, God has not imposed the rules and obligations of the Levitical covenant. However, the requirements for faith and the struggle to do God's will *remains the same*. This suggests to me that God certainly expects a high level of character development from all who claim to be Christian!

Some people claim that tithing is still obligatory even though they agree the Levitical covenant was nailed to the cross. My response is this: Where does the obligation of tithing originate? Is it through law? No! Abraham tithed long before there was a Levitical requirement to do so. Furthermore, there is no record that God commanded Abraham or anyone else prior to the Mosaic covenant to tithe. Abraham tithed because he came to the place in his personal experience with God where he realized that everything he owned was a gift from God. So, through faith, Abraham voluntarily gave 10 percent of his income to God in recognition of God's ownership of everything that he had. He acted, not according to law, but according to the Spirit. In fact, when a person obeys the Spirit, he or she will conform to God's law because that law is written in the heart.

Holy Spirit Conviction

As the Holy Spirit convicts us of God's will and truth, we must obediently follow just like Abraham. If the Holy Spirit convicts you to tithe, then follow the Spirit's leading. You will be blessed – not because of the money you gave – but for the faith you exercised. God's eternal wisdom and limitless love is wonderfully illustrated in the Mosaic covenant that He made with ancient Israel. Many Christians want nothing to do with the Old Testament for fear they will lose their freedom. This is not true. God gave Israel many principles that are incredibly brilliant and few people appreciate the wisdom which God has revealed. Surely, by reviewing the laws God gave to Moses, we can learn much about the principles of life, as well as the ways and blessings of God. The key is to allow the Spirit to lead you into a deeper understanding and application of God's principles in your life and you will be richly blessed. God's wisdom is always beneficial to His creatures.

One note of caution regarding the freedom that God grants under the new "believers covenant." God gives us the freedom to follow a Spirit-led conscience. He gave **no one** the authority to impose their convictions upon you or condemn you because you disagree with them. (Romans 14) The exception to this is promiscuous or immoral behavior and its destructive effect within the corporate body of Christ. In such situations, the body of Christ is required to pass judgment because of the harmful impact that sexual misconduct produces. (See 1 Corinthians 5 and 6.) Remember, in matters of diet, dress, culture and lifestyle, some people may not agree or have the same level of conviction you may have in these areas. (Romans 14:1-10) The Holy Spirit knows our heart and tests each of us in different ways and at different times. Each person matures spiritually at their own rate and we are on different rungs of the spiritual ladder. Some people are babes in the Lord, while some may have had ten years of spiritual maturity. (Unfortunately, some are still babes, even in their tenth year!) However, remember this truth. Although Israel voluntarily entered into the Mosaic covenant, the results were a dismal failure because they were unwilling to surrender their hearts to the Holy Spirit. When the apostles finally under-stood that the Mosaic covenant had been nailed to the cross, their joy knew no bounds. (Romans 8:2; 2 Corinthians 3:6) At last, Paul concluded, everything is permissible, even if it is not beneficial. (1 Corinthians 6:12)

The disciples were free from the guilt and condemnation of the Pharisees! Free to listen to God's Spirit! They were free to grow up in Christ rather than being watched and criticized by people who had a legalistic mentality. They were free to respond to God out of love, receiving Christ's righteousness that satisfied God's requirements for man's salvation. The truth will set you free, but it may also set you free from your family, friends, church and possibly, your job. Remember the illustration about Benjamin at the beginning of this chapter?

It is imperative that we submit to the conviction of the Holy Spirit. Failure to surrender can lead to the unpardonable sin. (Matthew 12:31) Paul wrote, **"If we *deliberately keep on* sinning after we have received the knowledge of the truth, no sacrifice for sins is left, but only a fearful expectation of judgment and of raging fire that will consume the enemies of God."** (Hebrews 10:26,27, emphasis mine.) In fact, failure to surrender will ultimately cause us to rebel against God! Do not forget, when the Holy Spirit speaks to you, He speaks with the authority of God. To refuse Him is to refuse God.

One Last Covenant

Thus far, we have examined six unilateral and three bilateral covenants:

Unilateral

1. "Do not eat of the Tree of the Knowledge of Good and Evil."

2. The Ten Commandments.

3. "I will put enmity between the serpent and the woman and will one day send a Savior."

4. "I will demand an accounting for each man's life. Murderers are to be put to death."

5. "I will not destroy the world again with a flood."

6. To Abraham: "Through you, all nations will be blessed."
                 "I will make you the father of many nations."
                 "I will give you and your descendants this land."

Bilateral

1. "If you will be my people, I will be your God."

2. "If you will be my people, you will be a kingdom and nation of priests . . . ."

3. New: "This is the new covenant in my blood . . . ."

For reasons stated earlier in this chapter, the first two bilateral covenants were nailed to the cross. The good news is that a time is coming when all of these covenants will be made null and void as well! At the end of sin, Jesus is going to declare one final unilateral covenant. Paul knew it was coming. Notice, " **'This is the covenant I will make with the house of Israel after that time,' declares the Lord. 'I will put my laws in their minds and write them on their hearts. I will be their God, and they will be my people.** *No longer will a man teach his neighbor,* **or a man his brother, saying, "Know the Lord," because** *they will all know me,* **from the least of them to the greatest. For I will forgive their wickedness and will remember their sins no more.' By calling this covenant 'new,' he has made the first one obsolete; and what is obsolete and aging will soon disappear."** (Hebrews 8:10-13, italics mine.)

When this covenant is put into effect, there will have been a total of seven unilateral and three bilateral covenants. The seventh unilateral covenant will sustain the redeemed throughout eternity. Notice how this covenant is stated near the close of Revelation: **"He said to me: 'It is done. I am the Alpha and the Omega, the Beginning and the End. To him who is thirsty I will give to drink without cost from the spring of the water of life. He who overcomes will inherit all this, and I will be his God and he will be my son.' "** (Revelation 21:6,7) This is the final covenant. It brings all others to an end. I long to hear these words with my own ears!

Summary

I hope this study has brought you a new appreciation for what was nailed to the cross. In a sentence we can say the bilateral covenant given to Adam and Eve and the Mosaic system was nailed to the cross. The Levitical laws are part of a covenant that was temporary and the authority given to the descendants of Aaron, the high priests, has been made null and void. Ever since the death of Jesus on the cross, we have the privilege of accepting a covenant based on the blood of Jesus, our High Priest, who sits at the right hand of the Father. The Ten Commandments remain intact; they are a unilateral covenant. They were not nailed to the cross. The Ten Commandments are eternal, timeless and universal. Even if we do not understand everything about God's covenants, we can know we are on the right track if we can say to Jesus, **"I desire to do your will, O my God; your law is within my heart."** (Psalm 40:8) This is an attitude that pleases God, because the last unilateral covenant given in the Bible contains this promise: **"This is the covenant I will make with the house of Israel after that time, declares the Lord. I will put my laws in their minds and write them on their hearts. I will be their God, and they will be my people."** (Hebrews 8:10)

Chapter 9
What Happened to the Lord's Day?

I said to their children in the desert, "Do not follow the
statutes of your fathers or keep their laws or defile your-
selves with their idols. I am the Lord your God; follow my
decrees and be careful to keep my laws. Keep my Sabbaths holy, that they may be a sign between us. Then you
will know that I am the Lord your God." But the children
rebelled against me: They did not follow my decrees, they
were not careful to keep my laws – although the man who
obeys them will live by them – and they desecrated my
Sabbaths. So I said I would pour out my wrath on them
and spend my anger against them in the desert.

– Ezekiel 20:18-21

Most Christians believe that Sunday is the Lord's Day, the day appointed to
worship God. However, since World War II, the observance of Sunday as a
holy day in the United States has changed significantly. Yes, church bells
still ring and people still go to church on Sunday morning, but Sunday
afternoon has become a different story. If Sunday is the Lord's Day, why
doesn't the observance of the Lord's Day last *all day?* For many people,
Sunday has become a holiday instead of a holy day. Does God really care
what we do on His holy day? Does He care if we work, go shopping,
conduct business, wash the car, watch TV, mow the lawn, clean out the
garage, attend ball games or go skiing? The answer to these and other
questions about the Lord's Day are found in the Bible. So, let us take a look.

The First Lord's Day

After six days of work, Jesus created something very special. He created the
seventh day. His crowning act at Creation was a gift to man. (Mark 2:27,28)
Jesus gave the Sabbath to man and He made it a sign of allegiance
between man and God. (Exodus 31:16-17) His action, of course, makes
the Sabbath as old as the world itself. **"By the seventh day God had
finished the work he had been doing; so on the seventh day he rested
from all his work. And God blessed the seventh day and made it holy,
because on it he rested from all the work of creating that he had
done."** (Genesis 2:2-3) Contrary to what many people say, God did not
make all seven days of the week holy. According to the Bible, the Lord

made one day of the week holy. Webster says the word *holy* means *to set apart* or to make unique. For example, when a couple gets married, their union becomes holy and they are "set apart" from the dating crowd. In like manner, at the time of creation, God "set apart" the seventh day of the week and made it unique from the other six days. The Bible says that God rested on the seventh day from His work of creating, blessed the seventh day and made it holy. If Jesus made the seventh day holy by resting from His labors on the seventh day, what do you think Adam and Eve did on the Sabbath? Consider this statement: There is a direct link between observing the Lord's Day and exalting the Lord. If the Lord's Day is not faithfully observed, subsequent generations will soon forget the authority of God. Review the opening text for this chapter and you will understand this important point: *When the worship of God is compromised, the authority of God is lost.* This point is easily demonstrated throughout the Bible. Both the antediluvians and Israel refused to worship God according to His commandments and they ended up in total rebellion against their Maker. (See 2 Peter 2 and 3; Jeremiah 25 and Ezekiel 20.) If history proves anything, it proves how quickly respect for God is lost. For example, there are ten generations between Adam's creation and the flood. Do you think the tenth generation antediluvians doubted Noah when he told them God was going to destroy the world with a flood?

Is the Lord's Day Optional?

In the United States, Christians overlook the sacredness of the Lord's Day. This is a mystery since God elevated the significance of the seventh day to the same level as nine other commandments. Think about it. The Sabbath commandment is one of the Ten Commandments. In God's sight, the Sabbath commandment is just as moral, just as binding and obligatory as the sixth commandment which says, "Thou shalt not kill." It is ironic that men will put a murderer to death, but think nothing of breaking the fourth commandment. This phenomenon occurs because God has given man the concept of government. (Romans 13:1-4) Man governs man. Is murder a serious crime because it violates the right of another person to live or because it is a violation of the sixth commandment? The answer is "yes" to both questions. Then the next question to be asked is, what about the Sabbath? Is the fourth commandment optional? Is the sixth commandment optional? Israel's history confirms the fact that when His chosen people forgot to observe the Lord's Day, it was only a matter of time until the nation was in complete rebellion regarding God's supreme authority! Jesus spoke the words found in Ezekiel 20 while the nation of Israel remained in rebellion and consequently, in Babylonian captivity.

The Sabbath Brought into Focus

About eight hundred years after the flood, God sent Moses back to Egypt to lead Abraham's descendants out of slavery. As a condition for deliverance from slavery, God required the slaves to rest from their weekly labor on the seventh day of the week. God's demand was bittersweet. Naturally, every slave welcomed a day of rest. Even more, every Hebrew in Goshen wanted to be delivered from Egyptian bondage. But after Israel kept their first Sabbath, Pharaoh realized that he was losing control over the Hebrews. To regain the upper hand, Pharaoh required the slaves to produce the same quota of bricks in six days that they had been producing in seven. On top of this, Pharaoh increased their workload and required them to gather all the necessary straw as well! This unreasonable demand pushed the Hebrews beyond their physical ability. Failure to meet the quota provided Pharaoh the "license" he wanted to beat the Hebrew slaves into submission. The consequence for obeying God caused the Hebrews to suffer unmercifully since it was not possible to meet Pharaoh's demand for bricks. This Sabbath "rest test" put the Hebrews in a very difficult position.

A Rest on the Seventh Day?

Some scholars have proposed that the work stoppage prompted by Moses and Aaron was to observe God's seventh day Sabbath. Although the Bible does not specifically say that the slaves were required to observe the *seventh day* Sabbath, I believe this issue can be resolved by reviewing four texts:

1. From the Creation of the world to the time of the Exodus, the Bible identifies one day of rest, the seventh day of the week. (Genesis 2:2,3) By divine decree, the seventh day Sabbath enjoys preeminence above all other days of the week. Jesus did not complete creating the world until the seventh day Sabbath was established and "set apart." The continued presence of the seventh day (causing a weekly cycle of seven days) confirms this point.

2. The language Pharaoh uses indicates that Moses and Aaron had called on Israel to *rest* from their labor. The words of Pharaoh in Exodus 5:5, **"You make them rest from their labor"** (KJV) or **"You are stopping them from working"** (NIV) reveals two points. First, Pharaoh blames Moses and Aaron for causing the slaves to "rest" from labor by emphasizing "*You* . . ." Second, the word Pharaoh used for rest is *shabath* (Strong's #7673). This is the same word and idea expressed in Genesis 2:2 when God "rested" or ceased from His creative works on the

seventh day. To suggest that Moses and Aaron required the Hebrews to rest from their labor on any other day of the week other than God's holy day would be inconsistent with God's declaration about the seventh day at Creation and the Sabbath day "manna test" that transpired shortly after the Exodus. (Exodus 16)

3. The Bible indicates that God tested Israel with the observance of His seventh day rest *before* He spoke the Ten Commandments from Mt. Sinai. (See Exodus 16.) This proves two interesting concepts: First, Israel knew about God's seventh day rest *before* Jesus spoke the Ten Commandments from Mt. Sinai; and second, by withholding manna on the Sabbath, Jesus confirmed which day of the week was the seventh – just in case there was any question. The absence of manna on the Sabbath further confirmed the importance and holiness of the seventh day *before* Jesus spoke the Ten Commandments from Mt. Sinai. Given God's consistent behavior, we can conclude that God's regard for the holiness of the seventh day did not change between Creation and the Exodus, a period of about 2,500 years.

4. When the Lord spoke the Ten Commandments from Mt. Sinai, He expressly commanded a cessation from work on the seventh day of the week. The fourth commandment begins with, **"Remember the Sabbath day to keep it holy . . . ."** (Exodus 20:8) If the observance of the seventh day Sabbath was a new concept codified in the Ten Commandments at Mt. Sinai as some scholars argue, why does the fourth commandment refer back to the original Sabbath day that took place at the creation of the world? The fourth commandment emphasizes the holiness placed upon the seventh day of the week at the time of Creation! Notice: **". . . For in six days the Lord made the heavens and the earth, the sea, and all that is in them, but he rested on the seventh day. Therefore the Lord blessed the Sabbath day and made it holy."** (Exodus 20:11)

When these four texts are aligned, we can be safe in saying that Moses and Aaron caused the Hebrews to stop working on the seventh day. The Sabbath rest infuriated Pharaoh and he began persecuting the Hebrews. The actions of the Israelites and Pharaoh confirm the thorny presence of a Sabbath rest test before the Exodus. The holiness of the seventh day of the week did not begin at Mt. Sinai as many people claim. Instead, the holiness of God's seventh day began at Creation and the patriarchs and elders who *walked* and *talked* with God honored the Creator's holy day.

Evidently, Moses and Aaron told the Hebrew elders that deliverance from Egyptian bondage would only be possible if they put complete faith in God.

Abraham's offspring were required to live by faith. They had to obey the higher laws of God in order to receive His deliverance. Israel's faith was to be tested and the test centered on observing God's Sabbath. Would Israel recognize the higher authority of His law by disobeying the laws of Pharaoh? A person's faith in God is revealed when there is both an obedience and disobedience penalty. If the Hebrews obeyed God, they received the wrath of Pharaoh. If the Hebrews obeyed Pharaoh, they would receive the wrath of God. The elders of Israel were afraid of God's wrath and begged Pharaoh to let them go out into the desert and obtain reconciliation with God saying, " ' . . . or He,' they said, 'may strike us with plagues or with the sword.' " (Exodus 5:3)

Observing the Lord's Day

If the Holy Spirit brings conviction to a person's heart about the seventh day Sabbath and that it should be honored, a common question arises, "How do I observe the Sabbath?" The answer to this question is determined by examining the fourth commandment and investigating *the intent* of the law. Fortunately, the Bible offers some very good insight on observing the Lord's Day.

Since sin began, the fourth commandment has stood in direct opposition to the ways of the world. For young and old people alike, observing God's Sabbath produces conflicts with family, friends, work, entertainment, recreation and shopping. However, the beauty of the fourth commandment can be observed through the act of obeying God, when man exalts the demands of God above the demands of this world. The world runs 24 hours a day, seven days a week without any rest. This was not God's intention for His created beings. God created the Sabbath and He commanded rest on the seventh day each week for man's benefit! When we rest according to the commandment, we admit and submit to the authority of our Creator. When we choose to obey Jesus, we are making a statement. We say to the world, "I love God's law more than anything the world has to offer." The commandment says: **"Remember the Sabbath day by keeping it holy. Six days you shall labor and do all your work, but the seventh day is a Sabbath to the Lord your God. On it you shall not do any work, neither you, nor your son or daughter, nor your manservant or maidservant, nor your animals, nor the alien within your gates. For in six days the Lord made the heavens and the earth, the sea, and all that is in them, but he rested on the seventh day. Therefore the Lord blessed the Sabbath day and made it holy."** (Exodus 20:8-11)

The fourth commandment makes four statements to be considered:

1. Do not regard the seventh day of the week like the other six, for it was set apart.

2. Do no work on the seventh day, it is holy.

3. Do not allow others under your dominion, whether man or animal, to work on the seventh day.

4. The seventh day is not a holiday. These hours belong to God; it is "the Lord's Day." He rested on the seventh day from His labors, blessed it and made it holy. He wants us to enjoy it as He enjoyed it!

The Sabbath was Set Apart

The first statement, "Do not regard the seventh day of the week like the other six, for it was set apart," eliminates several arguments. Most Christians are convinced that it does not matter which day of the week they worship on as long as God is worshiped. (Among Christians, this argument was first advanced in Rome around A.D. 150.) But God disagrees, because His commandment states that the seventh day of the week, Saturday, is His holy day. Some people say, "I worship God seven days a week." While there is nothing wrong with worshiping God every day, the fourth commandment is not about daily devotion. It is about submission to God's will which is demonstrated by ceasing from work on the seventh day of the week. The argument, "I worship God seven days a week," was used to profane the Sabbath in Israel before King Nebuchadnezzar destroyed Jerusalem. Notice what God says about Israel's apostate priests: **"Her priests do violence to my law and profane my holy things; they do not distinguish between the holy and the common; they teach that there is no difference between the unclean and the clean; and they shut their eyes to the keeping of my Sabbaths, so that I am profaned among them."** (Ezekiel 22:26)

Do No Work

The second statement, "Do no work on the seventh day, it is holy," raises several questions. What is work? Work is defined as something we do for gain, something we do for survival, something that we *have* to do to sustain life. The fourth commandment does not mean that we have to stay in bed on the Lord's Day. It means that we should not do things on the Sabbath that we do during the week.

What about the dairy farmer? Should he forego milking his cows on Sabbath? How does a nurse keep the Lord's Day when patients need care in the hospital? How does a policeman keep the Lord's Day when criminals are at work seven days a week? How can the mechanic or electrician, who services the generators that provide electricity to thousands of homes, take the Lord's Day off? How can cooks in nursing homes observe the Lord's Day when the elderly need food seven days a week? When God gave the fourth commandment, did He anticipate the problems that we would face today? Yes, of course. Then, how are these needs reconciled with the fourth commandment?

Before answering these questions, we need to observe how Jesus interpreted the intent of the Lord's Day. The following text is the first of three important texts: **"At that time Jesus went through the grainfields on the Sabbath. His disciples were hungry and began to pick some heads of grain and eat them. When the Pharisees saw this, they said to him, 'Look! Your disciples are doing what is unlawful on the Sabbath.' He answered, 'Haven't you read what David did when he and his companions were hungry? He entered the house of God, and he and his companions ate the consecrated bread – which was not lawful for them to do, but only for the priests. Or haven't you read in the Law that on the Sabbath the priests in the temple desecrate the day and yet are innocent? I tell you that one greater than the temple is here. If you had known what these words mean, 'I desire mercy, not sacrifice,' you would not have condemned the innocent. For the Son of Man is Lord of the Sabbath.' "** (Matthew 12:1-8)

Jesus makes four points within this text. First, gathering food to eat "on the way" through the field that day was not a violation of the Sabbath *as God interprets* the law. (See Exodus 16:23,24 for the basis of the Pharisee's complaint.) Second, Jesus pointed out that when it comes to survival, David and his men ate the holy bread that was in the tabernacle without incurring guilt. The bread they ate was reserved for priests only. So, there are instances where the immediate preservation of life *momentarily* overrides the letter of the law. Third, Jesus pointed out that the temple priests worked on the Sabbath (desecrated the day) without incurring guilt. Even though the Sabbath was a heavy work day for them, they were not guilty of contempt for God's law. (Note: The priests rotated assignments so that no priest was continuously desecrating the Sabbath. See Luke 1:8.) Last, the "Lord of the Sabbath," rebuked the Pharisees for abusing the purpose and intent of the Sabbath. As scholars and leaders of the people, they should have known better. When Jesus told them that He was the "Lord of the Sabbath," He applied a title to Himself that shows ownership and sovereign authority. For example, a person is called a "landlord" because he or she owns property and has control over the use of that property. When Jesus declared Himself to be the "Lord of the Sabbath," He indicated that He – not the Pharisees – had the authority to interpret how the Sabbath should be observed. Jesus Himself made the Sabbath and He alone has the necessary authority to define proper Sabbath conduct. The Pharisees did not understand the law or its intent and in their perverted, sanctimonious judgment, the Creator of the universe and His disciples continually broke the Sabbath. (John 5:18) How amazing that created beings would condemn their Creator!

The second text brings even more understanding to the subject of Sabbath observance: **"Going on from that place, he went into their synagogue, and a man with a shriveled hand was there. Looking for a reason to accuse Jesus, they asked him, 'Is it lawful to heal on the Sabbath?' He said to them, 'If any of you has a sheep and it falls into a pit on the Sabbath, will you not take hold of it and lift it out? How much more valuable is a man than a sheep! Therefore it is lawful to do good on the Sabbath.' Then he said to the man, 'Stretch out your hand.' So he stretched it out and it was completely restored, just as sound as the other. But the Pharisees went out and plotted how they might kill Jesus. Aware of this, Jesus withdrew from that place. Many followed him, and he healed all their sick, warning them not to tell who he was."** (Matthew 12:9-16)

From Jesus' statement we glean two important points: First, Jesus went about doing good for others on the Sabbath. He did not sleep the Sabbath away. He did not pass the Lord's Day in a mindless state of exhaustion because He had overworked during the previous six days. Instead, He used the Sabbath day to minister to others. Second, Jesus affirmed again that there are certain acts that do not violate the *intent* of the Sabbath. If rescuing an animal is not a violation of the intent of the law, then rescuing a human being from sin or suffering does not violate the fourth commandment.

This last text reveals two key issues on observing the Lord's Day. Notice the setting. Jerusalem was being rebuilt under Nehemiah's leadership. He writes, **"In those days I saw men in Judah treading winepresses on the Sabbath and bringing in grain and loading it on donkeys, together with wine, grapes, figs and all other kinds of loads. And they were bringing all this into Jerusalem on the Sabbath. Therefore I warned them against selling food on that day. Men from Tyre who lived in Jerusalem were bringing in fish and all kinds of merchandise and**

selling them in Jerusalem on the Sabbath to the people of Judah.
I rebuked the nobles of Judah and said to them, 'What is this wicked
thing you are doing – desecrating the Sabbath day? Didn't your
forefathers do the same things, so that our God brought all this
calamity upon us and upon this city? Now you are stirring up more
wrath against Israel by desecrating the Sabbath.' When evening
shadows fell on the gates of Jerusalem before the Sabbath, I ordered
the doors to be shut and not opened until the Sabbath was over.
I stationed some of my own men at the gates so that no load could be
brought in on the Sabbath day. Once or twice the merchants and
sellers of all kinds of goods spent the night outside Jerusalem. But I
warned them and said, 'Why do you spend the night by the wall? If
you do this again, I will lay hands on you.' From that time on they no
longer came on the Sabbath. Then I commanded the Levites to purify
themselves and go and guard the gates in order to keep the Sabbath
day holy. Remember me for this also, O my God, and show mercy to
me according to your great love."** (Nehemiah 13:15-22)

It is obvious from these verses that conducting business on the Lord's Day
is offensive to God – whether it is for food or merchandise is immaterial.
Second, like the Levites of old, we should "guard" the gates of our house in
order to keep the Sabbath day holy. Did you notice that Nehemiah associ-
ates God's wrath (the destruction of Jerusalem in 586 B.C.) with desecrating the Sabbath? Like Nehemiah, I believe the basis for God's coming
wrath upon the world is due in part to the fact that mankind does not have
respect for God or His holy day. When the Great Tribulation rumbles across
the face of the Earth, God's authority and His Sabbath will be put into
proper perspective. The strength and authority of His law will be plainly
seen. Until this occurs, this topic remains a matter of prophetic faith.

If we honor the Sabbath hours by resting from our work and labor, we
honor God. If we honor God, He will bless us. The Lord told Isaiah, "**"If you
keep your feet from breaking the Sabbath and from doing as you
please on my holy day, if you call the Sabbath a delight and the Lord's
holy day honorable, and if you honor it by not going your own way
and not doing as you please or speaking idle words, then you will find
your joy in the Lord, and I will cause you to ride on the heights of the
land and to feast on the inheritance of your father Jacob.' The mouth
of the Lord has spoken."** (Isaiah 58:13,14)

Sabbath Observance

What principles do we apply to the dairy farmer, the nurse, the cook, the policeman, etc.? Here is my personal view of the matter: The Lord's Day is the Lord's *Day* – all day long – from sunset to sunset. (Genesis 1; Leviticus 23:32) The Sabbath was made for man to be a rest, both physically and spiritually, or a day of renewal each week. God wants us to prepare all week for the Sabbath. Jesus wants us to enjoy the Lord's Day and call it a delight. The weekly Sabbath is not for God's benefit, but ours! When we honor the Sabbath commandment, we exalt the "Lord of the Sabbath!"

Preparation for the Lord's Day is important. In ancient times, the Jews did not have names for the days of the week. They used numbers such as the "the first of seven" for Sunday, or "the third day of the week" for Tuesday, etc. After the Babylonian captivity, the sixth day of the week became known as "The Preparation" or "the day of preparation." This title summarized the importance of being *prepared* for the Lord's Day. (Matthew 27:62; Mark 15:42; Luke 23:54)

As I understand it, actions that bring the blessing of Sabbath rest to others are permissible on Sabbath. Whether you prepare a good meal for a patient or help victims from a tornado, the Sabbath was made for man. Yes, the dairy farmer has to milk his cows. Yes, the doctor may be called for an emergency. Yes, the nurse may need to render care and the preacher may have to work harder on Sabbath than any other day. BUT, the first consideration that people need to address when trying to resolve this matter for themselves is this: How can I submit to the demands of the fourth commandment and still honor the Lord on His holy day with deeds of compassion?

Imposing Work on Others

The fourth commandment says that we are not to impose work upon others under our dominion, whether man or animal, on the Sabbath. This issue raises some interesting questions. Would it be appropriate for God to create the Sabbath and then force humanity to work on the Lord's Day while He rests? No, of course not. God is fair and just and He wants us to follow His lead. If the Ruler of the Universe gives rest to His servants each week, then each of us, as God's servants, must give our dominion (those under our management) rest as well.

A Holy Day Not a Holiday

The Bible says the world and all that is in it belongs to God. (Psalm 24:1) This means that human beings are stewards of "God's property." (Matthew 25:14; Leviticus 25:23) Jesus is the Landlord of Earth. Jesus is also the owner or "the Lord of the Sabbath." (Mark 2:27, 28) Observing the seventh day reminds humankind each week that we are not the owners of time or possessions. Notice how this works: Observing the Lord's Day *always* puts a person at odds with the pace and activities of this world. (This is a world in rebellion against God's will and His ways.) From the beginning of time, antagonism between God's Sabbath and the world has existed. God set apart a day for Himself and His children which not only offers physical rest, but also offers a time to spiritually reconnect with God each week. To the carnal mind, the Sabbath conflicts with our use of time or our pursuit of wealth and pleasure. To the spiritual mind, the Sabbath is a "time-out" from managing the assets God has given to us. (Matthew 6:33) The command to rest on the seventh day may sound easy to do, but in fact, "resting" according to God's commandment has financial and social consequences in a world that has no respect for God. Keeping the Sabbath holy can mean the loss of income, job or even a career. Yet, we need to remember that we really do not own these things in the first place. For some people, keeping the Lord's Day holy means rejection and ridicule by family members and friends. The devil has done and will do everything possible to make sure that the world forgets or rejects God's Sabbath. But, we can be sure of one thing: If we are willing to honor the Creator by resting on His holy day, we will find a faith experience. God sustains whatever we lay down so that when we resume our management of His assets after Sabbath, nothing will be lost or hurt. The devil is able to bring ruin and loss, but God owns everything and He will recover His losses if we are faithful. This may seem scary, but it is also the exciting part of living by faith. Observing God's Sabbath involves risk and the presence of risk proves the necessity for faith. If we are faith-full with all that God has given us to manage, we can be sure that Jesus will reward in full every faithful steward at the Second Coming. (Matthew 25:23)

The faith-full people who honor the Lord by keeping His Sabbath holy will come to know the "Lord of the Sabbath" more intimately. God will bless the people who look forward to entering into God's rest each week by giving them His eternal rest. (Hebrews 4) This is why God said: **"The Israelites are to observe the Sabbath, celebrating it for the generations to come as a lasting covenant. It will be a sign between me and the Israelites forever, for in six days the Lord made the heavens and the earth, and**

on the seventh day he abstained from work and rested." (Exodus 31:16,17)

Summary

The blessing surrounding the fourth commandment is both timeless and universal. Unfortunately, the corporate race to make more money and capture market share has become a powerful economic force that has pushed God's command to rest out of the weekly cycle. Jesus said, **"You cannot serve both God and money."** (Matthew 6:24) These entities are diametrically opposed. The pursuit of money never ends and opportunities to compromise God's Sabbath are limitless. Therefore, we have to be vigilant to "Remember the Sabbath day. . . ." If we plan to live in God's eternal kingdom, then the principles of God's kingdom need to be a priority in our lives. Honoring God's Sabbath is a faith exercise that Jesus invites us to experience with Him each week. Obeying God when something important is at stake is the experiential meaning of living by faith. I believe that if we forget the Sabbath, we will forget God. "If I were called upon to identify the principal trait of the entire 20th century, I would be unable to find anything more precise than to reflect once again on how we have lost touch with our Creator . . . Men have forgotten God." (Aleksandr Solzhenitsyn, *Reader's Digest,* September 1986).

Chapter 10
From Sabbath to Sunday

Her priests do violence to my law and profane my holy things; they do not distinguish between the holy and the common; they teach that there is no difference between the unclean and the clean; and they shut their eyes to the keeping of my Sabbaths, so that I am profaned among them.

– Ezekiel 22:26

Most Christians believe that Sunday is the Lord's Day. They believe that Jesus transferred the sacredness of the seventh day Sabbath to Sunday, the first day of the week, at the time of His resurrection. If Jesus made such a change, there should be sufficient evidence in the Bible to support this claim.

Bible Review

Eight texts in the New Testament mention the first day of the week. Biblical support for the sacredness of Sunday, if it exists, has to come from these verses. Here are the texts:

Matthew 28:1	Mark 16:2
Mark 16:9	Luke 24:1
John 20:1	John 20:19
Acts 20:7	1 Corinthians 16:2

Six of these texts refer to Jesus being resurrected on the first day of the week – a well-known fact. However, none of these texts indicate anything about Sunday sacredness. In fact, Luke 23:56 points out that a group of women delayed preparation of Christ's body for burial on Friday evening because of the nearness of the Sabbath. They rested on the Sabbath "according to the [fourth] commandment." Therefore, it would be fair to say that the women had no prior knowledge that the fourth commandment was voided that Friday afternoon.

Since the first six texts simply date the resurrection of Jesus on the first day of the week and say nothing about Sunday being sacred, we will investigate the remaining two verses.

Acts 20:7

Some people use Acts 20 as evidence to support that Sunday worship was practiced by the apostles. **"On the first day of the week we came together to break bread. Paul spoke to the people and, because he intended to leave the next day, kept on talking until midnight."** (Acts 20:7) Let us consider the details surrounding this verse.

The event recorded in Acts 20:7 took place about 30 years after Jesus ascended. During this 30-year interval, there is not one text in the Bible that describes how Sunday had become the day of worship or that the disciples worshiped on Sunday. Surely, if Jesus' death on the cross had made such a profound change concerning the day of worship, this would have been a very controversial issue. All of the disciples, including Paul, were Jews and as such, were Sabbath keepers! Paul's writings leave no doubt that the question of *what* was nailed to the cross was a matter of intense discussion for early believers. I find it interesting that nothing is written in Acts or the New Testament about the sudden sacredness of Sunday or the sudden obsolescence of the Ten Commandments.

The Apostle Paul stayed in Athens some length of time preaching the gospel. (Acts 17) When Paul finally left Athens, he went to Corinth. There he lived with Jewish believers, Aquila and Priscilla, who had been evicted from Rome by Claudius because they were Jews. (Acts 18) Actually, Aquila and Priscilla were converts to Christ, but Emperor Claudius could not distinguish between a Christian and the "repugnant" Jews, so the Romans evicted all Christians and Jews from Rome at this time. For a period of 18 months, Paul sustained himself in Corinth by making tents and he preached in the synagogue "every Sabbath" attempting to make believers of Jews and Gentiles alike. (See Acts18.) If the seventh day Sabbath had been nailed to the cross, and if Sunday was God's holy day, why is there no record of Paul teaching this new doctrine? Paul wrote 14 of the 27 books in the New Testament and he says nothing about the sacredness of Sunday! (Luke wrote the book of Acts.)

In Bible times, a day began at sunset and ended the following evening. Since Creation, Earth's rotation has produced this great clock. (See Genesis 1.) The Jews in Christ's time regarded a day from "evening to evening" and observed Sabbath from sundown Friday to sundown Saturday. Compare Luke 23:50-56 with Leviticus 23:32. So, the actual timing described in Acts 20:7 is as follows: Paul stayed with the believers in Troas for seven days. (Acts 20:6) At the beginning of the first day of the week, at supper time, the believers came together to eat supper with Paul and say good-bye to their dear friend. The first day of the week for Paul began at sundown, or what we call Saturday evening. Therefore, according to Scripture, Paul preached Saturday night until midnight. A few hours later, what we call Sunday morning, the first day of the week, Paul departed Troas for Assos. If Sunday had been a sacred day, Paul would not have departed for Troas. (See Acts 1:12)

Paul met with believers for supper and preached to them until midnight, Saturday night. A farewell supper and a Saturday night Bible study do not change or abrogate God's fourth commandment. Even if Paul chose to worship on Tuesday night, his actions could not make God's law void. Only God can make His law void. Some people claim that the term the "breaking of bread" indicates Paul's visit was a communion or worship service. This is not true! The disciples broke bread every day! (Acts 2:46,47 [KJV]) In Luke 24:13-31, Jesus "broke bread" at supper time with two of His disciples after walking with them more than seven miles to Emmaus. To this day, *breaking* bread is a custom in the Orient because bread is often baked so firm that it has to be literally *broken* in order to eat it. As was the custom at Passover, Jesus "broke bread" with His disciples on Thursday night during His last Passover and it was there that He instituted the "Lord's Supper." (John 13) Jesus' actions on Thursday night did not make Thursday a holy day. If this is true, Paul's actions in Troas could not make Sunday holy!

Paul did not confirm or authorize "Sunday sacredness" in Troas. Actually, he held a farewell meeting on Saturday night because he was leaving the following morning. The point here is that if Christians wish to exalt Paul's farewell at Troas as proof of Sunday sacredness, they should follow Paul's example and worship on Saturday night (between sundown and midnight).

1 Corinthians 16:2

Some people insist that Paul required offerings for the poor be collected on the first day of the week (as in a church service). Notice: **"Now about the collection for God's people: Do what I told the Galatian churches to do. On the first day of every week, each one of you should set aside a sum of money in keeping with his income, saving it up, so that when I come no collections will have to be made. Then, when I arrive, I will give letters of introduction to the men you approve and send them with your gift to Jerusalem."** (1 Corinthians 16:1-3)

When this text was written, Rome was severely persecuting Jews and Christians. (Jerusalem's destruction in A.D. 70 occurred about 10 years after this appeal was written.) Paul appeals to the believers in Corinth, where he had lived for 18 months, to help fellow Christians suffering in

Jerusalem. Paul does not hesitate to make this request because it was customary among Jews to use a portion of their tithe to help those in financial need. (Deuteronomy 26:12) Further, it was customary among the Jews to convert the tithe of their herds, flocks and harvest into money. Money was much easier to carry to distant places like Jerusalem. (Deuteronomy 14:24-26)

In Paul's day, money was not a common medium of exchange like it is today. The exchange of goods and services was done with barter; that is, a person might trade a chicken or something for cloth or pottery. Since Paul would not be able to travel to Jerusalem with a menagerie of roosters, goats, pottery and other things of value, he asked the believers in Corinth to convert their gifts into cash, "first thing after the Sabbath has passed." Paul suggested they begin each week by selling something at the bazaar so that he might be able to gather up a sum of currency. Paul indicated that "the first day of the week" was the appropriate day for conducting this business. Paul did not suggest doing this on Sabbath because it would have been inappropriate. (See Nehemiah 13:15.) Obviously, Paul's instruction did not change or make the fourth commandment void.

Thoughts on Romans 6

Some people suggest that Sunday worship is proper because Jesus arose from the dead on Sunday morning, the first day of the week. Yes, the resurrection is important, and the Bible does provide a celebration of the resurrection! It is called baptism. Notice what Paul says, **"What shall we say, then? Shall we go on sinning so that grace may increase? By no means! We died to sin; how can we live in it any longer? Or don't you know that all of us who were baptized into Christ Jesus were baptized into his death? We were therefore buried with him through baptism into death in order that, just as Christ was raised from the dead through the glory of the Father, we too may live a new life."** (Romans 6:1-4) Baptism absolutely does not make the fourth commandment null and void. Jesus was baptized at the beginning of His ministry and He faithfully observed the Sabbath afterwards! (Luke 4:16; Mark 2:27,28)

What was Nailed to the Cross?

It is a common, but not substantiated argument that the Ten Commandments were nailed to the cross. However, if this is true, then whatever happens to the fourth commandment, also happens to the other nine! **"For whoever keeps the whole law and yet stumbles at just one point is**

guilty of breaking all of it. For he who said, 'Do not commit adultery,' also said, 'Do not murder.' If you do not commit adultery but do commit murder, you have become a lawbreaker." (James 2:10,11) If we do away with the fourth commandment that declares the seventh day to be a holy day, then the seventh commandment that says adultery is wrong must be void as well. Paul wrote, **"What shall we say, then? Is the law sin? Certainly not! Indeed I would not have known what sin was except through the law. For I would not have known what coveting really was if the law had not said, 'Do not covet.' "** (Romans 7:7)

Many people are surprised to learn that the ceremonies of the sanctuary services, which were a shadow or explanation of the Plan of Salvation, were nailed to the cross. The key word here is shadow. Notice what Paul said, **"For in Christ all the fullness of the Deity lives in bodily form, and you have been given fullness in Christ, who is the head over every power and authority . . . When you were dead in your sins and in the uncircumcision of your sinful nature, God made you alive with Christ. He forgave us all our sins, having canceled the written code, with its regulations, that was against us and that stood opposed to us; he took it away, nailing it to the cross . . . Therefore do not let anyone judge you by what you eat or drink, or with regard to a religious festival, a New Moon celebration or a Sabbath day. These are a shadow of the things that were to come; the reality, however, is found in Christ. Do not let anyone who delights in false humility and the worship of angels disqualify you for the prize . . . ."** (Colossians 2:9-18)

If we look at these verses carefully, we see that Paul is writing about the regulations regarding *religious feasts, New Moon observances and Sabbath days.* The Sabbath days that Paul is talking about is not the seventh day Sabbath of the fourth commandment. Rather, the term "Sabbath days" in this context applies to Sabbath "feast days," such as the Feast of Unleavened Bread, or the Day of Atonement. (Exodus 12:16; Leviticus 16:31) The feast days of the Jews fell on different days of the week (like our birthday). These feast days were declared to be "special sabbaths" because they pointed forward to different aspects of the death and ministry of Jesus. For example, the Passover not only reminded the Jews of their deliverance from Egypt, but it also pointed forward to the time when the Passover Lamb – Jesus Christ – would die and all who put their faith in Him could be delivered from the bondage of sin!

The Jews confused the Ten Commandment law of God with the laws of Moses, much like Christians do today. Even though one set of laws was written with God's finger on two tablets of stone, and the other penned by the hand of Moses, the Jews did not understand the relationship between the moral law (written by the finger of God) and the ceremonial laws (written by the hand of Moses). One law is permanent and enduring while the other was temporary.

Understanding Shadows

Paul speaks plainly in Colossians 2 and Ephesians 2 disclosing that the laws nailed to the cross were those laws that were *shadows* of the real thing. Laws that governed the constitution of Israel ended at the cross. Since the shadows have been voided, there is neither Jew nor Gentile in Christ. The ceremonial laws requiring the observance of new moons, feast days and the sacrifice of lambs became unnecessary because the Lamb of God had died and the shadow of salvation's process was now fully disclosed. In other words, ceremonial laws were temporary until Jesus revealed their meaning. Moral laws are not temporary, because love never ends. One set of laws was written on paper; the other on stone. One law was penned by man; the other, by God. Surely this reveals something about their enduring nature. A time is coming during the Great Tribulation when everyone living on Earth will see the ark that contains the covenant, the Ten Commandments. In Revelation 11, the Bible says that God's temple in Heaven was opened and everyone saw the ark of the covenant. (Revelation 11:19; Deuteronomy 4:13)

Which is the Greatest Law?

As you might expect of a legalistic society, the Jews loved to argue about their laws. An expert lawyer challenged Jesus asking which law was the greatest. (Matthew 22:34-40) Of course, Jesus answered wisely saying that "loving God" with all of our heart, mind and soul is the greatest commandment, and the second is like the first, we are to "love our neighbors as ourselves." The Ten Commandments actually define the reciprocal of love. If we love God, we will want to comply with the first four commandments and more! The first four commandments define what love for God produces. Likewise, if we love our neighbor, we will want to comply with the last six commandments and more. When we love our neighbors, we will not want to steal from them because we will want the best for them. Love is expressed in giving, not taking.

If we become self-centered and love ourselves more than God or our neighbor, our relationship with God's law changes 180 degrees. Instead of loving God's law, it becomes a legal standard for behavior rather than love serving as the standard for righteousness. Self-righteousness *focuses* on conformity to the law, whereas a life of love and faith focuses on fulfilling the principles of love. When the widow gave her mite, Jesus said she had given more than anyone else present. She responded out of love and she gave all that she had while the others had given out of obligation. (Luke 21:3,4) Because of their carnal hearts, the religion of the Jews degenerated into a great legal system of darkness. When God's law is imposed on the carnal heart, the response is either defiant rebellion or the religious experience that follows is miserable and unbearable. (Matthew 23:2-15)

What About Romans 14?

Romans 14 is also used to prove that it does not matter which day of the week we worship God. Notice the text: **"Accept him whose faith is weak, without passing judgment on disputable matters. One man's faith allows him to eat everything, but another man, whose faith is weak, eats only vegetables. The man who eats everything must not look down on him who does not, and the man who does not eat everything must not condemn the man who does, for God has accepted him. Who are you to judge someone else's servant? To his own master he stands or falls. And he will stand, for the Lord is able to make him stand. One man considers one day more sacred than another; another man considers every day alike. Each one should be fully convinced in his own mind. He who regards one day as special, does so to the Lord. He who eats meat, eats to the Lord, for he gives thanks to God; and he who abstains, does so to the Lord and gives thanks to God. For none of us lives to himself alone and none of us dies to himself alone. If we live, we live to the Lord; and if we die, we die to the Lord. So, whether we live or die, we belong to the Lord. For this very reason, Christ died and returned to life so that he might be the Lord of both the dead and the living. You, then, why do you judge your brother? Or why do you look down on your brother? For we will all stand before God's judgment seat."** (Romans 14:1-10)

The context of these verses does not imply that a person can worship God whenever he or she feels like it. Instead, it is addressing specific problems that early Roman believers had to deal with; namely, the numerous customs of the Jews that have nothing to do with salvation through faith in Christ. In other words, if a Jewish believer felt the need to continue observing Passover, Paul did not condemn him except to say that his faith was weak. Also, if a new believer could not consciously eat meat purchased in the marketplace for fear it had not been killed correctly or that it may have been offered before idols, Paul said to leave him alone! (The Jews would not purchase or eat meat unless it was killed according to Mosaic code. Leviticus 19:26) The point here is that Paul is not condoning lawlessness. Paul does not declare the fourth commandment null and void. Paul is advocating tolerance because he knew that the more a person understands Jesus, the greater will be his religious experience.

Pentecost on Sunday

Another argument used to support Sunday worship is that Pentecost came on Sunday during the year that Christ died. Somehow, this is supposed to prove that Sunday is God's holy day. Interestingly enough, Pentecost always falls on Sunday! The wave sheaf offering was made on the first Sunday after Passover and after seven full weeks or seven Sabbaths had passed, Pentecost occurred on the 50th day (counting inclusively). This means that Pentecost *always* occurred on a Sunday. (Leviticus 23). The annual Feast of Weeks occurred on Sunday for more than a millennium before Jesus came to Earth. The fact that the Feast of Weeks was regularly celebrated on Sunday cannot make the fourth commandment void.

One last point. Some people claim that nine of the Ten Commandments are mentioned in the New Testament, but the fourth commandment is missing. This statement is not true. Even if it were true, does the absence of the fourth commandment in the New Testament prove that the commandment is void. A more reasonable explanation of this absence is that New Testament writers never doubted the continuing presence of the seventh day Sabbath. Paul removes any doubt for us when he wrote in A.D. 63, **"There remains, then, a Sabbath-rest for the people of God; for anyone who enters God's rest also rests from his own work, just as God did from his."** (Hebrews 4:9,10)

Grace and Faith Versus Law?

Many Christians think that faith and grace make the law unnecessary. The love between husband and wife does not eliminate the necessity for fidelity nor does living together make two people married. The relationship between love and obedience is simple. God grants salvation to everyone who becomes willing to do His will. He does not grant salvation to us based on our ability to do His will. We demonstrate our willingness by receiving strength from God to do what He wants. Paul understood this process. (See Romans 7.) All through his life, Paul faithfully observed the seventh day

Sabbath. (See Acts 13:44; 16:13; 17:2; 18:4,11.) Even more, when Jesus predicted the destruction of Jerusalem (which occurred in A.D. 70), He indicated the Sabbath would still be sacred at that time! (Matthew 24:20)

Cannot Break Just One Commandment

If we take the position that Jesus nailed the fourth commandment to the cross, then we must conclude that He also nailed the remaining nine as well. Whatever we do with the fourth commandment, we must also do with the other nine. This issue will become the all-important distinction between those people who love God and those who rebel against Him during the outpouring of God's judgments. The Ten Commandments are nonnegotiable. They stand as one unit representing the will of God. The Ten Commandments were written on two tables of stone because they are based on two enduring principles: love to God and love to man. The first four commandments explain how we are to love God. The last six commandments explain how we are to love our neighbor. One more point: Maturity in Christ begins when we acknowledge the binding claims of God's law, and realizing our great weaknesses, we place our faith in Jesus so that we can fulfill His law through His indwelling power.

Paul knew that all Ten Commandments were intact. He said, **"For I would not have known what it was to covet if the law had not said, 'Do not covet.' "** (Romans 7:7) James wrote, **"If you really keep the royal law found in Scripture, 'Love your neighbor as yourself,' you are doing right! But if you show favoritism, you sin and are convicted by the law as lawbreakers. For whoever keeps the whole law and yet stumbles at just one point is guilty of breaking all of it. For he who said, 'Do not commit adultery,' also said, 'Do not murder.' If you do not commit adultery but do commit murder, you have become a lawbreaker."** (James 2:8-11)

James brings us to an important and fundamental conclusion regarding the royal law, or the King's law. He says we must obey all the commandments. If we break any one of them, we are guilty of breaking them all, because the King's law is only fulfilled by love. We must first love God with all our heart, mind and soul and then our neighbor as ourselves. Jesus shared how we should express our love for God by saying, **"If you love me, you will obey what I command."** (John 14:15)

Submissive Loyalty

I have said many times, "keeping the seventh day Sabbath holy cannot save anyone" because salvation comes before works. When a person becomes *willing* to submit his or her life to God's sovereign authority, salvation is granted, full and free to that individual *before* he or she can do anything! The thief on the cross is an excellent example of this. The works of every person reveal faith or rebellion! This is why God designed the human race's final exam to test our faith in Jesus: The basis of salvation is faith. Faith produces submissive loyalty; doing what God requires at any cost. Ask Noah as he stands in the doorway of the ark. Ask Abraham as he is about to slay his son. Ask Moses as he stands at the Red Sea. Faith produces submissive loyalty. Because eternal life only comes by faith, and since every means of human survival will be cut off in days to come, you and I must have faith in God to remain loyal to Him! If it is hard to obey God now, what will it be like when our lives are at stake? Faith is like a mustard seed. It can grow. It can develop. Although it is tiny at the beginning, it can become great! (Matthew 13:31)

The Seventh Day of Creation was Saturday

God has expressed in the Bible how His subjects are to worship Him. This is not a matter left to human design. Unfortunately, the devil, during the past 6,000 years, has obscured God's truth, infiltrated every religion, and implemented many false ideas, concepts, and doctrines throughout the world. For example, Moslems regard Friday, Jews regard Saturday, and Christians regard Sunday as a holy day! These three religious bodies represent 50% of Earth's inhabitants, and each religious body claims to have the truth about God. Each religious system also declares that the other two religious systems are false – and yet, all together they unwittingly confirm a simple truth. Their diversity confirms that the weekly cycle is intact. Let me explain.

The sixth day of the week is adjacent to the seventh day, which is also adjacent to the first day of the week. In other words, each religious system worships on unique days that are adjacent to each other. This fact confirms the perpetuity of Creation's week ever since Jesus was on Earth and it shows that the weekly cycle has not been altered. Furthermore, God confirmed which day of the week was the seventh day to the children of Israel in the wilderness by the cessation of manna (no manna fell on the seventh day). Thus, the Israelites have formally worshiped on the seventh day ever since the Exodus in 1437 B.C. Christians in Rome, according to

Justin Martyr, have formally worshiped on the first day of the week since A.D. 150, and Moslems have formally worshiped on the sixth day of the week since the sixth century A.D. If the weekly cycle had been altered, the holy days of worship would not be adjacent to each other! This diversity proves the weekly cycle has not been altered. The seventh day (Saturday) is still God's holy day just as it was at creation.

So, What Happened?

So, how did Sunday become the Lord's Day? Who made the change and when did it occur? Material containing the history of Christianity during the first century is meager and imperfect. The best records for this time period have been collected and are known as the writings of the Apostolic Fathers. These records are not part of the Bible, nor do they have the authority of the Bible. However, they do offer a glimpse into the religious thinking of that era.

Apostolic Age

Several ancient references are included in this chapter for you to consider because a great number of scholars have used these ancient writings to show that Sunday observance was widely practiced by those living during the Apostolic Age (A.D. 30 - A.D. 100). The writings of early Christians, however, reveal a sinister process. They reveal how the Word of God soon became corrupt, even in the hands of well-intentioned people. You can study these references and draw your own conclusions.

The first mention of worship by the Apostolic Fathers occurs around A.D. 97. Clement of Rome wrote to the believers in Corinth:

> These things therefore being manifest to us, and since we look into the depths of the divine knowledge, it behooves us to do all things in [their proper] order, which the Lord has commanded us to perform at stated times. He has enjoined offerings [to be presented] and service to be performed [to Him], and that no thoughtlessly or irregularly, but at the appointed times and hours. (*Clement of Rome, Epistles to Corinthians, Vol I Ante-Nicean Library*, (Buffalo, 1887) p. 16, insertions mine.)

As you can see, Clement does not specifically endorse any particular day of week. This early quote, however, is included because some scholars claim that Clement of Rome openly defends Sunday observance in A.D. 97.

Another early reference often used to support Sunday observance in the early Christian Church was written by Pliny the Younger about A.D. 107. Pliny the Younger was the pagan governor of Bythinia at the time. He wrote to Emperor Trajan asking advice about Christian assemblies in his province. At that time, civil revolt was anticipated in a number of provinces by Roman leaders and Pliny was especially cautious of a new sect of Jewish people called Christians. He wrote:

> They [the Christians] affirmed that the whole of their guilt or error was that they met on a certain stated day before it was light and addressed themselves in a form of prayer to Christ as to some God . . . . (*Pliny the Younger, Pliny's Letter to Trajan, Harvard Classics*, Vol 9, (New York, 1937) p. 404, insertions mine.)

Pliny does not say which day of the week the Christians were meeting. All that we can learn from this quotation is that they were meeting for prayer before it was light. Regardless of the day he refers to, whether the Christians were secretly meeting to pray on Sabbath, Sunday or Monday makes no difference.

Post Apostolic Age

As Christianity spread throughout the Roman Empire, certain compromises and transformations were made within Christianity for a variety of reasons. In Rome, Christians were regarded as a dangerous sect since they were considered to be offshoots from the Jews and second, they refused to regard Caesar as a divine god. As time passed, however, Christianity began to appeal to the educated and wealthy people who lived in Rome. These people could afford manuscripts containing copies of Scripture and even more importantly, they also had influence within the government of Rome. By A.D. 150, Christians and converts of Mithraism (a small pagan sect) had some areas of compromise and mutual respect. About this time, a well-educated man by the name of Justin Martyr became a Christian. As a Christian, he tried to soften the hostility that existed between Romans and Christians. One area of compromise concerned the issue of religious meetings on Sunday. The followers of Mithra regarded Sunday as a holiday. (*The Mysteries of Mithra,* Chicago Open Court Publication Co., (Chicago 1911) p. 167, 191) Christians in Rome, anxious to separate themselves from their Jewish heritage (Jews were despised), found that the pagans interpreted their religious services on Sunday as something akin to their holiday festivities. Justin Martyr writes:

> But Sunday is the day on which we all hold our common assembly because it is the first day on which God, having wrought a change in

the darkness and matter, made the world; and Jesus Christ our Savior on the same day rose from the dead. (Justin Martyr, *First Apology of Justin Martyr, Ante-Nicean Christian Library*, (Boston 1887) p. 187 Chap 67)

The justification he used for holding a common assembly on Sunday is interesting. First, he cites the separation of darkness and light on the first day of Creation as grounds for holding a common assembly, and then the resurrection of Jesus. Martyr offers no scriptural authority for holding an assembly on Sunday, but his remarks do suggest how anxious Christians in Rome were to divorce themselves from the womb of Judaism.

In those days, Christianity had no "central office" and each geographical location adjusted doctrine as they chose. During the last part of the second century A.D., Irenaeus, Bishop of Lyons, became alarmed at a number of heresies that had infiltrated the Christian movement. He was aware of how the Christians in Rome had begun to meet on Sunday and abandon the seventh day Sabbath and he spoke out against it. He wrote:

For He [Christ] did not make void, but fulfilled the law [Ten Commandments]. (Irenaeus, *Against Heresies, Vol 1 Ante-Nicean Christian Library*, (Boston, 1997) p. 471, insertions mine.)

Tertullian, another church father, wrote extensively concerning Christian doctrine. He, like Irenaeus, was alarmed at the practices of certain Christians, especially those who lived in Rome. In regard to the seventh day Sabbath he wrote:

Thus Christ did not at all rescind the Sabbath. He kept the law [Ten Commandments] thereof . . . He restored to the Sabbath the works for were proper for it. (Tertullian, *Book IV, Chap 12, Vol 3 Ante-Nicene Christian Library*, (Boston, 1997) p. 362, insertion mine.)

Considerable discussion on Sunday observance took place in those early days. Archelaus, a bishop wrote in his disputation with Manes:

Again as to the assertion that the [seventh day] Sabbath has been abolished we deny that He [Christ] has abolished it plainly. For He Himself was also Lord of the Sabbath. (Archelaus, *The Disputation with Manes, Vol 4 Ante-Nicean Christian* Library, (Boston 1887), p. 217, insertions mine.)

By A.D. 320, confusion and compromise took a heavy toll on early Christian doctrine. Christians had been scattered by persecution to every province throughout the Roman empire. Christians in Alexandria, Egypt (the South) were beginning to defend views that were different from those in Rome (the North). Church authority was discussed, debated and argued.

Most church leaders agreed that church doctrine needed to be more clearly defined and controlled, but who was going to be in control? Many questions and issues were raised for which there was little agreement. In short, distance, culture, language and social factors were beginning to define Christendom according to geography. Thoughtful men anticipated the result – a highly fractured church. Christianity needed a strong leader and Constantine felt that he was divinely appointed to lead a universal Christian Church. When Constantine came to the throne as sole ruler of the empire around A.D. 312, he had transformed himself into a Christian for political advantage. Constantine was cunning and he saw Christianity as a means of unifying the Roman empire. When he endorsed the "Roman version" of Christianity, Constantine set a powerful sequence of events into motion. In future years, the church in Rome would come to dominate all factions of Christianity.

Hopefully, this information satisfies your curiosity about how Sunday observance began. The Romans were the first to merge Sunday observance into Christianity. Strange as it may seem, they never claimed to have divine authority for this action. In fact, Roman Christians did not consider labor on Sunday as sinful or contrary to the will of God. Of course, this attitude stands in stark contrast to the fourth commandment which forbids work on Sabbath. The attitude toward Sunday observance in Rome was a carryover from the pagan worship of Mithra. Sunday in Rome was regarded as a holiday by many Romans long before Christianity arrived in Rome. Sunday was not a day of fasting or reflection.

When Constantine became "a defender of the faith," he had his army baptized into Christianity by marching them through a river. To promote the universal acceptance of a day of rest, Constantine implemented a Sunday law in March, A.D. 321. This law was a clever compromise. Constantine patronized Christians and pagans alike by declaring a national day of rest. The political benefit of this law was well received by the Romans. Constantine endorsed the desire of the Christian church in Rome by setting Sunday aside as a day of rest and this law also favored a large population in Rome who worshiped the pagan god of Mithra on Sunday. So, the Sunday law meshed with customary Roman practice. It also aligned the desires of the church at Rome and everyone in Rome was quite happy with a national day of rest. Notice that the decree issued by Constantine does not mandate worship on Sunday:

> Let all judges and all city people and all tradesmen, rest upon the venerable day of the Sun. But let those dwelling in the country freely and with full liberty attend to the culture of their fields; since it fre-

quently happens, that no other day is so fit for the sowing of grain, or the planting of vines; hence the favorable time should not be allowed to pass, lest the provision of heaven be lost. (Cod. Justin, III Tit 12, L.3., March 7, A.D. 321)

There is a World Out There

Although the Roman church was already meeting on Sunday when Constantine sent out his decree, other Christians in other locations were not! Most Christians were still observing the seventh day Sabbath. Socrates writes near the turn of the fourth century:

> Such is the difference in the churches on the subject of fasts. Nor is there less variation in regard to religious assemblies. For although almost all churches through the world celebrate the sacred mysteries on the Sabbath of every week, yet the Christians of Rome and Alexandria have ceased to do this. (Socrates, *Ecclesiastical History,* Book V, Chap. 22, *Ante-Nicean Christian Library*, Vol II, (Boston, 1887) p. 132)

Even Constantine's decree did not shut out the importance of the seventh day Sabbath. Something else would have to occur before that could be accomplished. The leaders from the church in Rome needed an elaborate doctrine that dealt directly with the issue of the "Lord's Day" to present a strong case before the Christian body. So, the doctrine of Sunday observance was masterminded by Eusebius, a Christian confidant and advisor of Constantine. Carefully notice his anti-Semitic argument for the observance of Sunday:

> Wherefore as they [the Jews] rejected it [the Sabbath law], the Word [Christ] by the new covenant, translated and transferred the feast of the Sabbath to the morning light, and gave us the symbol of true rest, viz., the saving Lord's Day, the first [day] of light, in which the Savior of the world, after all his labors among men, obtained the victory over death, and passed the portals of heaven, having achieved a work superior to the six-days creation. On this day, which is the first [day] of light and of the true Sun, we assemble, after an interval of six days, and celebrate holy and spiritual Sabbaths, even all nations redeemed by him throughout the world, and do those things according to the spiritual law, which were decreed for the priests to do on the Sabbath. And all things whatsoever that it was the duty to do on the Sabbath, these we have transferred to the Lord's Day, as more appropriately belong to it, because it has a precedence and is first in rank, and more honorable than the Jewish Sabbath. All things whatsoever that it was duty to do on the Sabbath, these we have transferred to the

Lord's Day. (Eusebius's Commentary on the Psalms 92, quoted in Coxe's Sabbath literature, Vol I, p. 361, insertions mine.)

Eusebius was a spiritual advisor to Constantine. He is the first man to claim in writing that Christ changed the day of worship. THEN, Eusebius testifies that he (and others, namely Constantine) had "transferred all things, whatsoever that it was duty to do on the Sabbath" to Sunday. Also notice that Eusebius offers no scriptural authority for the change. Further, no church father or authority from that time period supports Eusebius' claims and notice that he does not quote from another source. As it turns out, Eusebius took the thorny problem of worship in hand and became the father of a false doctrine, which favored the practices of the church at Rome. We need to ask ourselves, "Can mere mortals change the law of Almighty God by making a simple declaration? Who has the higher authority – God or man?" Christians have repeated the failure of the Jews and have dismissed or altered the plainest statements of God's Word. Jesus said of the Jews, **"They worship me in vain; their teachings are but rules taught by men."** (Matthew 15:9)

Even with the Sunday law imposed by Constantine, the seventh day Sabbath did not suddenly disappear in Christian churches. By the year A.D. 460, Sozomen writes:

Assemblies are not held in all churches on the same time or manner. The people of Constantinople and almost everywhere assemble on the [seventh-day] Sabbath as well as the first day of the week, which custom is never observed at Rome or Alexandria. (Sozomen, *Ecclesiastical History, Book VII, chap 19, Ante-Nicean Christian Library*, Vol II, (Boston 1887) p. 390, insertion mine.)

Every student of church history knows that the church in Rome eventually gained complete dominion over Christianity. Eventually the Roman Empire was transformed into the Holy Roman Empire and the bishop at Rome became the "Bishop of the Universal Church." For nearly 13 centuries, the kings and queens of Europe were subservient to the Bishop of Rome. This great period of church dominion is appropriately called the "Dark Ages" because religious dominion is a cruel master. I thank God that I live in the United States which has a pluralistic democracy and a Constitution that continues to separate church from state!

Summary

Sunday observance came about for three reasons. First, the majority of early Christians in Rome were not former Jews. Consequently, the imposing culture and religious practices of Judaism, which included the seventh day Sabbath, were not considered as important in Rome as they were in Jerusalem. Actually, converts from Mithraism brought Sunday observance into the Christian church in Rome. Second, the seventh day Sabbath had been a distinguishing mark of the Jews for about 1,500 years. Anti-Semitism was an enormous motive in those days for distinction and separation between Christians and Jews. Last and most important, the union of church and state produced an enormous surprise. When Constantine converted to Christianity to strengthen his political control of the empire, he initiated a process that ultimately subjected the nations of Europe to the dominion and doctrines of the Roman Catholic Church for 1,260 years!

Satan often works in subtle ways and he was masterful when he led the minds of carnal men to profane God's law. Now, the vast majority of Christians worship on Sunday. Through the ages, experts have hammered on the Bible to make it say that the fourth commandment was nailed to the cross, but their creative claims are hollow. These claims are as silly as the priests of Baal who danced around the altar on Mt. Carmel. Protestant denominations who continue to exalt the sacredness of Sunday show, perhaps naively, submission to the doctrines and authority of the Church in Rome. There is no biblical basis for Sunday sacredness. There is no biblical basis for saying the Lord's Day is Sunday. All that supports the observance and sacredness of Sunday as the Lord's Day is a heap of tradition and the arrogance of man. God's law does not change and the Ten Commandments stand without impeachment. The fourth commandment still points to the seventh day of the week as God's holy day. What will God say to you and me on Judgment Day about our regard and treatment of His holy day?

I would like to close this chapter with three texts. The first text is from King Solomon. He wrote, **"Now all has been heard; here is the conclusion of the matter: Fear God and keep his commandments, for this is the whole duty of man for God will bring every deed into judgment, including every hidden thing, whether it is good or evil."** (Ecclesiastes 12:13,14) Jesus said, **"If you obey my commands, you will remain in my love, just as I have obeyed my Father's commands and remain in his love."** (John 15:10) Since these Scriptures are true, why not surrender your life to Jesus and resolve to keep holy His Sabbath of rest *at any cost.* Think of it this way, God offers you and me a one-day vacation from the cares of this world each week. He promises to sustain everything that we are doing until we return after our rest, so that nothing will be lost. Put your faith in God to the test and make up your mind to obey Him. When you carefully and prayerfully consider His offer, what is keeping you from accepting such a fine offer? Jesus says, **"Come to me, all you who are weary and burdened, and I will give you rest** [Sabbath]**."** (Matthew 11:28, insertion mine.)

Chapter 11
Parallel Temples

The point of what we are saying is this: We do have such a high priest, who sat down at the right hand of the throne of the Majesty in heaven, and who serves in the sanctuary, the true tabernacle set up by the Lord, not by man.

– Hebrews 8:1,2

Introduction

The above text indicates that Jesus serves in the *true* tabernacle which is located in Heaven. The author of Hebrews used the word "true tabernacle" to contrast the sanctuary in Heaven with the "pseudo tabernacle" that Moses erected on Earth. (Hebrews 8:5) Did you know that certain processes or ceremonies in the heavenly tabernacle have direct parallels with the earthly tabernacle? I like to describe these parallels as the "Heaven-Earth-Linkage-Law." Activity in the temples of Heaven and Earth are linked together by law! For example, did you know that more than fourteen end-time events are synchronized with special ceremonies in Heaven's temple? The books of Daniel and Revelation are based on ceremonies in Heaven's temple; therefore, it helps to understand the ceremonies in Heaven's temple to correctly understand Bible prophecy. The only way to properly understand the ceremonies that take place in Heaven's temple is to examine the services that were conducted as a parallel on Earth. **"This is why Moses was warned when he was about to build the tabernacle: 'See to it that you make everything according to the pattern shown you on the mountain.' "** (Hebrews 8:5)

Dual Purpose Palace

The ways of God are revealed in ceremonies that take place in His temples. Because we cannot attend the services in Heaven, God commanded Moses to create a parallel temple system on Earth. God's temple in Heaven is a dual purpose palace. It is like a courthouse and a church. On Earth, church is a place where God's will is studied and examined, and people are encouraged to obey God's will. The courthouse is a place where social needs are codified and implemented through the force of law. To a great extent, the balance of power between the church and the courthouse defines the unique culture of every nation on Earth. The same is true in Heaven. Heaven's temple functions as a courthouse and a church. In Jesus, there is a perfect balance of church and state, He is King of kings and Lord of lords. He is the Revealer of God's will and He is the Executor of the justice of God. These are the privileges and the responsibilities of man's Creator, Jesus Christ – the Alpha and the Omega.

God has unilaterally imposed the rule of His law throughout the universe. If there was no law, chaos would rule. The decisions and declarations of Jesus in Heaven's temple are subject to law. God is not arbitrary. God's rule of law does not have a political bias, nor is it temperamental in nature. Nothing less than "the whole truth" is accepted in Heaven's court, so justice and fairness are always present. Because the truth is more important than winning an argument, God is open to the closest scrutiny. God has nothing to hide. In fact, each issue and investigation only magnifies the righteous-ness of God! Malice and mischief are not found in Heaven's temple. During the temporal presence of sin in the universe, justice and fairness are faithfully maintained in Heaven's temple. Highly intelligent angels observe God and they are delighted to serve Him. They never stop singing His praise because He is flawless and magnificent in everything He does.

A Working Model

Of all the concepts taught in the Bible, the services in God's temple are among the most profound, intricate and beautiful. A proper understanding of these services ties all Bible themes together and they provide a back-drop against which all conclusions about God's will and ways can be tested and verified. This is a crucial point. The truth about the ways of God may appear to be abstract (that is, not tangible or verifiable), but this is not the case. God remedied this problem a long time ago by commanding Moses to set up a careful parallel or shadow of Heaven's *process* so that human beings could study, test and validate their understanding of His marvelous ways. Moses was warned to follow the pattern that God gave him. This makes sense for if the model was flawed, our study of Heaven's temple would also be flawed.

Rituals Were Shadows

Few people know anything about the temple services God gave to Moses. I suspect there are two reasons for this: (a) "because they are Jewish," or (b) "they were nailed to the cross." In my opinion, both reasons have contributed to the hopelessly confused state of Christianity today! Just because the Mosaic covenant with its shadows and parallels was nailed to the cross, this does not mean the significance of the shadows and parallels became useless after the cross. The first five books of the Bible are very valuable in helping us understand Jesus because He does not change. He is the same forever. Therefore, the temple services taking place right now in Heaven's true tabernacle are still parallels of temple services that took place 3,000 years ago on Earth. The Old Testament sanctuary rituals had no divine efficacy or potent powers within themselves. (Isaiah 1:11-17; Hebrews 10:1-4) Contrary to what many religions teach today, religious rituals do not have value in themselves. Instead, God wants man to understand the object lessons that He illustrates through temple ceremonies or rituals. The temple rituals which God commanded the children of Israel to observe were shadows or parallels of actual processes that take place in Heaven.

Consider this illustration. A $5.00 bill (U.S. Federal Reserve Note) has no value within itself. It is merely a small piece of paper with writing on both sides. However, it is a symbol of value and most people think of it, use it and treat it as though it had value, even though it does not. As long as the United States government will exchange something of value for a $5.00 bill, it will have value. My point is that the $5.00 bill is a *symbol* of value, even though it is only a piece of paper. But if the U.S. government ever decides to terminate the use of the $5.00 bill, then all of the U.S. $5.00 bills in the world will be worthless. Some currencies are worthless pieces of paper because the government who initially printed the currency is unable to back it with anything of value. For those worthless currencies, the old saying is true, "it is not worth the paper it is printed on." In like manner, temple rituals have no value within themselves. They are symbolic of real things that God has done, is doing and will do for the salvation of the human race. In terms of a working model on Earth, God required the Old Testament rituals to function until the reality appeared. So, when Jesus came to Earth and died on the cross, the rituals came to an end, even though the processes they represent are still ongoing. Even though the rituals are now null and void as far as God is concerned, they contain the keys that explain the ways of God in Heaven's temple. Therefore, a basic understanding of the earthly temple rituals remains vitally important today.

The Tabernacle

The earthly temple built by Moses primarily consisted of seven items: the Ark of the Covenant, the Table of the Presence (also called the Table of Shewbread), the Altar of Incense, the Altar of Burnt Offering, the

Lampstand, the Laver and the Tent of Meeting (the tent building was about 18 wide by 55 feet long). God designed each piece of furniture and gave the pattern to Moses. The purpose and function of each item offers insight into the ways of God. For example, the Bible teaches that even though God forgives sinners, He does not blot out the sin. Instead, He transfers the guilt of the sinner to the Altar of Burnt Offering. This may sound confusing at first, but here is how it works: The wages of sin or penalty for sin is death *by execution* and there are no exceptions. God's law is not subject to change (an omniscient God is quite capable of declaring an everlasting law). If the sins of Adam and Eve could have been forgiven (blotted out, ignored or overlooked), Jesus would not have had to die. Think about it. If there had been any other means to save Adam and Eve from the penalty of sin, the Father would not have allowed Jesus to die. But within the Plan of Salvation, God allows the *penalty* for sin (which is death by execution) to be *transferred* away from the sinner through the death of a perfect substitute. This transfer occurs under specific conditions (faith). So, sinners who put their faith in Jesus can be set free of the condemnation of death (Romans 8:1-5) even though their specific <u>sins</u> are *never* forgiven! (Please do not throw any stones at me just yet. Hear me out!)

To understand this point a little better, consider the sin offering ceremony that took place in the earthly temple. Sinners were required to bring a perfect lamb to the Altar of Burnt Offering at appointed times. The innocent lamb on the altar served as a perfect substitute for the penalty of sin which requires death by execution. (Keep in mind that the wrongdoer should only seek God's forgiveness at the temple *after* he has voluntarily made restitution to the victim of his wrong actions. Exodus 22; Leviticus 6; Matthew 5:24) When the sinner presented his lamb at the Altar of Burnt Offering, it was firmly secured so that it could not escape (certain death). Then, the sinner placed his hands on the head of the lamb and stated his sin. Then, the sinner executed the lamb by cutting its jugular vein with a knife. As blood spilled from the throat of the dying lamb, an attending priest captured some blood in a small bowl. The priest dipped a small branch of hyssop into the bowl and applied the warm blood to the four horns of the altar – one horn on each corner on the altar. The priest also sprinkled some blood on the altar. This ritual confirms a truth that most Christians do not understand; sin is not forgiven. Instead, the sinner's guilt was *transferred* by the death and blood of the lamb to the horns of the altar. This transfer made the Altar of Burnt Offering unclean and it remained defiled all year long until the Day of Atonement took place. On the Day of Atonement, the altar was restored to a pure state by the shedding of blood (the Lord's goat) and the guilt that had accumulated upon the horns of the altar all year long was transferred once again, this time to the head of the scapegoat. The scape-goat was then taken out into the desert to die a very slow and painful death.

The death of Jesus proves that sin cannot be forgiven (overlooked, erased or forgotten). If Jesus could have excused Adam and Eve from the penalty of sin, He would not have had to die. The stain of animal blood on the horns of the Altar of Burnt Offering confirms that sin is not forgiven, but instead is transferred. This is very good news. God allows the penalty for my sins to be transferred *from* me to the horns of the Altar of Burnt Offering through the death of Jesus, the flawless Lamb of God. The blood of animals symbolizes the actual price of God's grace (the blood of His own Son). Keep in mind, the blood of animals did not provide salvation. The execution and blood of animals did not actually transfer the guilt of sin. The sin offering is a parallel of how God deals with sin. The reality to which the sin offering pointed occurred at Calvary. Jesus, the Lamb of God, died for our sins and if we put faith in Him, our guilt is transferred to the Altar of Burnt Offering in Heaven's temple. (Hebrews 8:1-5; 10:1-4; Romans 8:1-8)

Two Altars

There were two altars in the earthly temple because there are two altars in Heaven's temple. The Altar of Burnt Offering was located near the entrance of the courtyard that surrounded the Tent of Meeting and the Altar of Incense was located in the front room of the tent, or the Holy Place. There are two altars for atonement because God is concerned with two levels of sin: individual sin and corporate sin. The Altar of Burnt Offering was covered with bronze and the Altar of Incense was covered with gold. This difference in medals indicates there is a difference in processing these two types of sin. The bronze Altar of Burnt Offering served the needs of individuals, and the golden Altar of Incense served a higher purpose, the needs of the whole community. Both altars had four horns jutting from their four corners. Throughout the Bible, horns symbolize an entity of power. (Psalm 75:10; 112:9; Jeremiah 48:25; Luke 1:69; Revelation 17:12) Within the context of these altars, the four horns represent the omnipresent work of the Holy Spirit throughout the four corners of Earth: North, East, South, and West. (Zechariah 1:18-21; 4:6; John 16:7-11) He is everywhere at once!

Do Not Sin Against the Holy Spirit

Since the beginning of sin, the Holy Spirit has had an indispensable role in God's administration of grace. The human heart must be softened by the

Spirit before repentance can occur. The Holy Spirit does much more than impress the conscience. The Holy Spirit is God and He has all of the prerogatives of God. In fact, the only sin that cannot be forgiven is rejection of the Holy Spirit! (Matthew 12:31) Carefully consider this point: A sinner could present his offering at the Altar of Burnt Offering because the law of Moses *required* it, or a sinner could present his offering at the altar because he was very *sorry* for his sin and wanted to be free of the condemnation that was upon his head. The motive makes a big difference. In the latter case, if the sinner was sincerely repentant, he proved his sorrow for sin by *voluntarily* making restitution for his sin *before* he came to present his sacrifice to God. Again, the essential point so many people overlook on this topic is that killing animals never atoned for sin. (Hebrews 10:1-4) In other words, presenting a sacrificial lamb at the altar did not guarantee that God would accept the sacrifice and allow the transfer of sin even though the external requirements of the sin offering were met. **"The sacrifices of God are a broken spirit; a broken and contrite heart, O God, you will not despise."** (Psalm 51:17) God is not impressed or moved with religious rituals. Not until the Holy Spirit produces a heartfelt sorrow for sin is the guilt of sin actually transferred. (1 John 1:9; 1 John 2:1-6) When people conclude that atonement with God is possible through some religious ritual, you can be sure that apostasy has taken place!

Sinners are Forgiven

Many Bible writers speak about our sins being forgiven (Leviticus 5:13; Romans 4:7), but it is the *sinner* who is forgiven, not the sin. This distinction is so important because we need to understand that God has a process to deal with the disposal of sin. The disposal of sin involves a legal concept called *vengeance*. God's vengeance is a twofold process that will finally culminate at the end of the 1,000 years of Revelation 20. God's vengeance involves the extraction of restitution from those people unwilling to provide appropriate restitution (judicial equilibrium), and His vengeance also involves destroying everyone who refused the indwelling authority of the Holy Spirit. Judicial equilibrium is the balance between our behavior toward others and our accountability for the welfare of others. Judicial equilibrium is found in the golden rule: **"As you do unto others, the same shall be done unto you"** and **"For in the same way you judge others, you will be judged . . . ."** (See Matthew 7:2,12) God's kingdom is not a republic nor a democracy. It is a monarchy.

Sin Is Not Forgiven

Sinners can be freed from the penalty of their sins even though their sins are not forgotten. At first, this statement may appear contradictory. Many Christians believe that Jesus died for us and that somehow all of our sins have been forgiven! But there is much more to the disposal of the toxic waste of sin than is commonly known. All sinners are under the curse of eternal death unless our guilt is removed. The wages of sin is death. (Romans 6:23) Sin is the transgression of God's law. (Leviticus 26; Deuteronomy 28; 1 John 3:4) However, if a person is ignorant of a specific sin, God does not hold the sinner *accountable* for that sin until the sinner becomes properly informed. (Leviticus 4; 1 Timothy 1:13; James 4:17) When a person commits any sin, he or she violates the whole law. (James 2:10) Sinful acts cannot be recalled or erased because they are a matter of record. The unrelenting claim of God's law is this: "Once a sinner, always a sinner." This is why God evicted Adam and Eve from the Garden of Eden. (Genesis 3:22-24) The consequences for violating God's moral law occur whether we are knowledgeable or ignorant of the offense. This is why the Bible says, **". . . Be sure your sin will find you out."** (Numbers 32:23) Do not let this discourage you because the Plan of Salvation offers a way out of condemnation. The Father has provided a perfect substitute to receive the guilt of our sins and through the blood of Jesus, our guilt can be *transferred* to the horns of Heaven's Altar of Burnt Offering! The result is that repentant believers who put their faith in Jesus are no longer under condemnation. (See Romans 5 and 8:1-12.)

The Sin Offering

When God gave Moses the earthly temple pattern, God defined categories of offerings for different categories of sin. Different offenses required different methods for atonement or resolution. Each offering helps us understand how God deals with various issues involving sin. Because there are different types and variations of sacrificial offerings, the following examples demonstrate a typical process. Although every temple service is not explained in the Old Testament, we can be sure that God has preserved the essential details so we can understand the larger process in Heaven's temple. Likewise, while the New Testament does not contain everything that Jesus said while He was on Earth, we can be sure that God preserved what was essential. (John 21:25.) Do not become overwhelmed by the sheer number of rules and offerings used in the earthly temple services. Concentrate instead on God's orderly and consistent ways in dealing with sin. I have found that diligent study on this topic brings great rewards. As you study the system surrounding the earthly temple services, you will begin to see the beauty of the Plan of Salvation unfold. God's ways are truly marvelous to behold!

Unintentional Sin

The sin offering covers two types of personal sin: willful and unintentional sin. Notice what the law says about unintentional sin: **"If a member of the community sins unintentionally and does what is forbidden in any of the Lord's commands, he is guilty. When he is made aware of the sin he committed, he must bring as his offering for the sin he committed a female goat without defect. He is to lay his hand on the head of the sin offering and slaughter it at the place of the burnt offering. Then the priest is to take some of the blood with his finger and put it on the horns of the altar of burnt offering and pour out the rest of the blood** [into a small basin] **at the base of the altar."** (Leviticus 4:27-30, insertion mine.)

If a person is aware that he had committed an unintentional sin, he had to appear at the Altar of Burnt Offering with the required sacrifice. If he could not afford to offer the required animal, items of lesser value, such as birds or even flour, were acceptable to the Lord. (Leviticus 5:7) A priest, ever present and willing to serve, received the sinner's substitute. The priest examined the sacrificial animal very closely. He was concerned about the condition of the animal as well as the sinner's restitution and heartfelt confession. The sacrificial offering had to be perfect, without defect or blemish for it represented God's Son. After the sinner killed the animal, the priest placed the animal's blood on the horns of the altar as a record of sin. (Leviticus 4:7) Although the sinner could not escape the guilt of sin, he was at least free of condemnation until he sinned again. (Leviticus 4:26)

Willful Sin

The process of atonement for willful sin is more serious than that of unintentional sin. Before an individual could seek atonement at the tabernacle, he or she had to make a generous restitution to the victim. Notice what God said: **"Say to the Israelites: 'When a man or woman wrongs another in any way and so is unfaithful to the Lord, that person is guilty and must confess the sin he has committed. He must make full restitution for his wrong, add one fifth to it and give it all to the person he has wronged. But if that person has no close relative to whom restitution can be made for the wrong, the restitution belongs to the**

Lord and must be given to the priest, along with the ram with which atonement is made for him.' " (Numbers 5:6-8)

Defiance Not Tolerated

Obviously, a person cannot continue very long in a pattern of willful sin and be able to meet the financial demands for restitution required by law. This is why Paul wrote: **"If we deliberately keep on sinning after we have received the knowledge of the truth, no sacrifice for sins is left."** (Hebrews 10:26) It is interesting that God does not see willful sin in the same light as defiant sin, although the penalty is the same in both cases. Notice that defiant sin demands immediate action. **"But anyone who sins defiantly, whether native-born or alien, blasphemes the Lord, and that person must be cut off from his people."** (Numbers 15:30) The term "cut off" meant exile, total banishment from the camp. In the wilderness, banishment meant starvation. So, it is important to understand the meaning of defiant sin. According to Webster, defiance means open and bold rebellion. God declares that there is no other God besides Himself. (Isaiah 45:5) God is King, the owner/master of man and naturally, He would interpret defiance as a willful act of insubordination. Therefore, He told Moses, **"Whoever sacrifices to any god other than the Lord must be destroyed."** (Exodus 22:20) God is a jealous God! (Exodus 20:5) In His great wisdom, He knows that defiance is rebellion and defiant rebellion is unforgivable. (1 Samuel 3:14; Matthew 12:31) God did not offer a plan of salvation for Lucifer and his angels because of their open defiance.

One Sin Contains Two Violations

Temple services reveal that one sin can contain two violations. When a person sins against his neighbor, he or she sins against God as well! Therefore, the sanctuary service demonstrates that God requires a two-step process when we sin against a neighbor. First, the Lord required that a sinner make restitution to the victim, and then, the sinner could make atonement for the sin committed against God at the tabernacle. The amount of restitution varied. In minor cases, restitution was 20%. (See Numbers 5:6-8.) In more severe cases, the amount of restitution could be as high as 500%. (See Exodus 22.) When Zacchaeus became a "born again" believer in Christ, he gave 50% of his wealth to the poor, and then he restored 400% to anyone that he had wronged! (Luke 19:8) The purpose of restitution is very important in God's government. In fact, the earthly tabernacle teaches that at a future appointed time, God will ensure that every wicked person suffers appropriately for every wrongful deed, plus an added penalty. The golden rule is an iron clad rule of God's kingdom and universe. At the end, God will ensure that everyone is treated just like they treated others. (Matthew 7:12) This is the larger meaning of vengeance or judicial equilibrium.

For personal injuries, notice the following decree: **"But if there is serious injury, you are to take life for life, eye for eye, tooth for tooth, hand for hand, foot for foot, burn for burn, wound for wound, bruise for bruise."** (Exodus 21:23-25; Leviticus 24:19-21; Deuteronomy 19:18-21) The basic idea of punitive law in the Old Testament is judicial equilibrium. In other words, if someone plans to maliciously harm another person, the law demands complete restitution before he or she can make atonement before God. For personal injury, the offender must experience the same pain he or she willfully inflicted! Restitution retards the growth of sin, so God placed man under the operation of the golden rule. The rule states: "It will be done to you as you intentionally did to your victim, plus interest and penalty." When Jesus was on Earth, the Jews had twisted the golden rule for self-serving purposes. They used it as legal justification for personal revenge, especially against their hated enemy, the Romans. Jesus rebuked them for not understanding the *intent* of the law when He said, **"You have heard that it was said, 'Eye for eye, and tooth for tooth.' But I tell you, Do not resist an evil person. If someone strikes you on the right cheek, turn to him the other also."** (Matthew 5:38-39) Jesus was affirming an important truth, revenge belongs to God and He will extract every ounce of the restitution that His law demands, plus interest. Paul wrote, **"Do not take revenge, my friends, but leave room for God's wrath, for it is written: 'It is mine to avenge; I will repay,' says the Lord."** (Romans 12:19) This verse should be especially meaningful for people who have been victims of a painful injustice. God ensures that judicial equilibrium will be extracted from the wicked before He creates a new Heaven and a new Earth.

Reviewing the Sin Offering

The service at the Altar of Burnt Offering lays a conceptual foundation for other temple services, so keep the following seven points in mind as we progress through this study:

1. The bronze Altar of Burnt Offering served the needs of individuals.

2. The sinner was required to make restitution before presenting a sacrificial offering.

3. The guilt of the sinner was transferred to the lamb by confession and the death of the lamb transferred the guilt to the horns of the altar.

4. The blood on the horns of the altar was as a record of sin. Until the altar was cleansed on the Day of Atonement, the temple was in a state of desecration.

5. Excess blood from the sacrifice was poured into a small basin at the base of the altar. (Leviticus 4:25)

6. Sin, whether unintentional or intentional, requires atonement.

7. Defiant sin cannot be forgiven (atoned for).

The Altar of Incense

The golden Altar of Incense was physically located in the first room of the earthly temple called the Holy Place. Like the Altar of Burnt Offering, this altar also had four horns, one on each corner of the altar. However, there are several significant differences between these two altars. For example, it was the *priests'* responsibility to keep the fire on the Altar of Burnt Offering burning around the clock (Leviticus 6:12,13), but it is believed the Altar of Incense burned perpetually. Miraculously, *God Himself* ignited and sustained the fire on the golden Altar of Incense and it never went out.
(Note: This conclusion is reached by harmonizing the following two points: Aaron's sons, Nadab and Abihu, carried "foreign" or man-made fire into the Holy Place and God struck them dead for it. (Leviticus 10:1-3) Further, the Bible does not indicate that the priests maintained the fire on this altar as it does for the other altar. These two points suggest the fire on the Altar of Incense was sustained by divine power.)

Evening and morning, the priests burned a special formula of incense on the Altar of Incense. God forbade anyone from duplicating this incense. (Exodus 30:34-38) In the wilderness, the Israelites could smell the distinctive aroma of this incense, depending upon the wind, at the limits of the camp. (Exodus 30:7,8) Like the Altar of Burnt Offering, the Altar of Incense was named according to its primary purpose which was the continual burning of incense.

Corporate Atonement

The services at the golden Altar of Incense represent a higher level of atonement than those at the bronze altar in the courtyard. These services are a little more difficult to understand at first because they are shadows of a larger process that takes place in Heaven. The Altar of Incense was reserved for *corporate* atonement, that is, intercession on behalf of the whole community. Priests conducted services at the Altar of Incense, evening and morning, every day of the year. God required *continual* atonement, night and day. This was done so that Israel could dwell in His continual presence. In other words, atonement for sin was ongoing, 24 hours a day, seven days a week. If an individual or a group of individuals sinned, the continual sacrifice on the Altar of Incense provided atonement for everyone until they could present their necessary sacrifices at the Altar of Burnt Offering. The *daily* atonement made on the Altar of Incense allowed the Israelites to dwell in God's continual presence without being destroyed. (Exodus 25:8) The object lesson found within this service is stunning. We know that sinners cannot approach God or live in His presence without mediation or atonement. (Numbers 8:19) But through the sacrifice of Jesus, God extends much grace to us, hoping that we will eventually show up at the Altar of Burnt Offering for the purpose of reconciliation with Him and be saved. The beauty of grace can be observed here since we are not consumed while wandering about in foolish rebellion! **"For if, when we were God's enemies, we were reconciled to him through the death of his Son, how much more, having been reconciled, shall we be saved through his life!"** (Romans 5:10)

Called the Daily or the Continual

The evening and morning services presented on the Altar of Incense were called "the daily" or "the continual" because they were administered evening and morning – every day of the year – continually. The services included the sacrifice of a perfect one-year-old lamb each evening at twilight and each morning just after sunrise. After the priest killed the "daily" lamb on the Altar of Burnt Offering (in the courtyard), he carried some of its blood to the Altar of Incense and applied it to the horns and sides of the altar. Then the priest placed a scoop of the special incense (using God's specifications) on the glowing coals of the altar. Then the fragrant incense flowed freely throughout the tabernacle. In addition to the blood and incense, priests also placed small servings of wheat or barley flour, oil and wine before the Lord as offerings. (Exodus 29:40,41; 30:9) The reality in Heaven which is represented by the *daily services* at the golden altar on Earth is very meaningful. Whereas the sin offering on the Altar of Burnt Offering pointed *forward* to the death of Jesus as the Lamb of God at Calvary, the service on the Altar of Incense pointed *backwards* to the day sin began. On that day, the Father and Son established a mutual covenant to save the whole world! (Psalms 2)

Psalm 2

When Adam and Eve sinned, Jesus entered into a covenant with the Father agreeing to die as man's substitute. (Psalm 2; Genesis 3:15; Romans 5:19; Matthew 26:28; John 17:4) When Jesus submitted to the terms and conditions required in the Plan of Salvation, He agreed to overcome the power of sin by living a perfect life and dying the death of a condemned sinner. (Romans 5:10; 2 Corinthians 5:21) In fact, from the very day that Adam and Eve sinned, Jesus was called the "Son" of God. **"I will proclaim the decree of the Lord** [the Father]**: He said to me, 'You are my Son; today I have become your Father. Ask of me, and I will make the nations your inheritance, the ends of the earth your possession. You will rule them with an iron scepter; you will dash them to pieces like pottery.' "** (Psalms 2:7-9, insertion mine.) The word *son* means "one subject to" or "one in submission to someone like himself." Consequently, Adam is called the "son of God" and so are all believers because we are created in God's image. (Luke 3:38; Matthew 5:9; 1 John 3:1 [KJV]) The covenant between the Father and Jesus to save man stopped the destroying angel who was about to execute Adam and Eve. On the basis of an agreement between the Father and Jesus, Jesus became man's intercessor the day sin began and He remains in this position even on this very day. (Hebrews 7:25) The law given to Adam in Genesis 2:17 is clear – any violation would result in a swift penalty. However, Jesus stepped *in the way* by offering His life, and every day since that moment, His covenant with the Father has stood between guilty man and the righteous demands of God's law. This is why Jesus is called man's Intercessor. (Hebrews 7:25)

The *daily* intercession of Jesus in Heaven's temple is reflected in the daily ministry of the priests on Earth. **"The point of what we are saying is this: We do have such a high priest, who sat down at the right hand of the throne of the Majesty in heaven, and who serves in the sanctuary, the true tabernacle set up by the Lord, not by man."** (Hebrews 8:1,2) The Father allowed Adam and Eve and their offspring to live because of the daily intercession of Jesus. The corporate benefits of Christ's atonement for the whole world became effective immediately, the day sin began. The covenant to save man is called the Plan of Salvation and it remains intact to this very day. The corporate intercession of Jesus on behalf of the whole world will continue until the *beginning* of the Great Tribulation. The Great Tribulation begins when Jesus declares the end of His corporate intercession. (Revelation 10:6) When this happens, the censer at Heaven's golden Altar of Incense (Revelation 8:2-5) will be cast down indicating the services required at that altar are finished. A few days after the censer in Heaven is cast down, the long-delayed wrath of God for the whole world will begin.

God's wrath will come in two phases, seven first plagues and seven last plagues. Although the corporate intercession of Jesus comes to an end at the *beginning* of the Great Tribulation, the door of salvation remains open for individuals because Jesus continues to intercede on behalf of individuals for 1,260 days – until the time of the seventh trumpet.

Corporate Process

The idea of corporate atonement is new to many Christians, so a short study may be helpful. Notice this text: **"If the whole Israelite community sins unintentionally and does what is forbidden in any of the Lord's commands, even though the community is unaware of the matter, they are guilty. When they become aware of the sin they committed, the assembly must bring a young bull as a sin offering and present it before the Tent of Meeting. The elders of the community are to lay their hands on the bull's head before the Lord, and the bull shall be slaughtered before the Lord. Then the anointed priest is to take some of the bull's blood into the Tent of Meeting. He shall dip his finger into the blood and sprinkle it before the Lord seven times in front of the curtain. He is to put some of the blood on the horns of the altar that is before the Lord in the Tent of Meeting. The rest of the blood he shall pour out at the base of the altar of burnt offering at the entrance to the Tent of Meeting."** (Leviticus 4:13-18)

Two points regarding corporate sacrifice stand out: First, it was possible for the *whole community* to sin against God unintentionally! Again, ignorance does not mean innocence. God's universal laws have no boundaries. When the community becomes aware of its sin, God requires the whole community to make atonement and this atonement is presented at the corporate Altar of Incense, not the Altar of Burnt Offering. Second, a sacrificial bull is required for corporate atonement for the sin of an entire community. A bull was the most valuable animal in the herd. This points to the fact that the Father gave His most valuable gift, the blood of His only Son, to redeem the whole world! Many Christians believe John 3:16 is the most beautiful text in the Bible, but notice what the text really says: **"For God so loved the *world* that he gave his one and only Son, that whoever believes in him shall not perish but have eternal life."** (John 3:16, italics mine.) Did you notice that this text is actually a "corporate" text? **"For God so loved the *world* . . . ."** To appreciate the entire scope of the Plan of Salvation, we must understand that it is much larger than an individual matter. The plan involves all of the descendants of Adam and

Eve, and in order to include all the nations of the world, the plan has to include the entire human race over a period of 6,000 years.

When the community sinned, the bull's blood was sprinkled seven times on the front of the veil (or curtain) that separated the Most Holy Place from the Holy Place in the temple. This action signified that as a community, Israel had violated the law which was written on tablets that were behind the veil in the Ark of the Covenant. (The high priest could not enter the Most Holy Place except on the Day of Atonement. Leviticus 16:2) In order to provide atonement for the community, the priest sprinkled the blood as close to the law as possible. Then, he placed blood on the four horns of the Altar of Incense and the crimson record of sin defiled the Altar of Incense until the cleansing that occurred on the Day of Atonement. (Leviticus 4:7,18)

If the High Priest Sins

If the high priest sinned, his atonement had to be presented on the Altar of Incense rather than the Altar of Burnt Offering because his sin was considered a corporate offense. As a living parallel of Jesus, God held the office of high priest to a higher standard of accountability than that of ordinary people. If the high priest sinned, his actions were considered more denigrating in God's sight than anything a political leader of a country may have done! Therefore any sin committed by a high priest was a sin against God and Israel (a corporate offense) and atonement was required on the Altar of Incense. (Leviticus 4:3-7)

Incense Pleasing to God

The Altar of Incense derives its name from its most obvious function; namely, the continual burning of incense. The object lesson for burning incense before God is this: Approach God with reverence. The sweet smell of incense predisposed God for grace and favor. If we want God to hear us and receive us, then we must approach Him with the sweet fragrance of humility and reverence. Although it has been more than 25 years now, each evening after her bath, our daughter would come running from the bathroom and jump into my lap, ready for a bedtime story. I still remember the scent of freshly shampooed hair that was neatly tied in a pony tail. How could I refuse such a sweet-smelling bundle of love and curiosity? Of course, there were moments throughout the day when she did not smell so good, but all that was forgotten at bedtime . . . .

An offering of sweet-smelling incense is pleasing to the God who made the roses and the fresh smell of spring. The fragrance of incense invites Him to hear our prayers and petitions. Of course, the need for incense says much about man's true condition as a sinner. In our cleanest state, we stink! I am not talking about body odor, but rather the stench of sin. Even the pagans burned incense to predispose their gods for favor. (1 Kings 11:8) In other words, God uses the burning of incense as an object lesson to demonstrate our degenerate and offensive condition to Him. We are sinners and we live in the pig sty of sin. Therefore, it is not possible for us to comprehend our sinful, degenerate state as God sees it. A bath or shower does not remove the guilt of sin. The ever-burning Altar of Incense confirms man's hopeless condition before God, but it also confirms God's faithful promise. Daily, He masks our offensiveness with the fragrance of our prayers so that we can draw near Him with our requests. The burning of incense on this altar is directly associated with the prayers (petitions) of the saints. (Revelation 8:4) He hears our prayers. Few things move the arm of Almighty God like the sweet prayers of humble and contrite believers. (Luke 18:10-14; Hebrews 11:6) It has been said that if you wish to receive God's favor, call Him by the name that He likes most, "Father."

Altar of Incense Summary

Here are six summary points about the Altar of Incense:

1. The Altar of Incense was dedicated to corporate services for the whole community.

2. The daily services on this altar provided continual or daily around-the-clock atonement.

3. The services conducted on the Altar of Incense point backwards to the covenant that was established between the Father and the Son the day man sinned.

4. The daily intercession of Jesus in Heaven will terminate at a point in the near future and the Great Tribulation will begin.

5. Twice a day, evening and morning, atonement was placed on this altar.

6. The Altar of Incense was cleansed of defilement or reconsecrated on the Day of Atonement.

No Veil in Heaven's Temple

The earthly tabernacle had a veil that divided the tiny building into two rooms. The first room was called the Holy Place and the room in the back was called the Most Holy Place. It appears that the heavenly Temple does not have or need a veil. Even if there had been a veil in Heaven's temple, just like the earthly veil, its function would have terminated at the time of Jesus' death. The veil in the earthly temple is important for three reasons:

1. First, as a practical matter, the veil was a wall of protection for the priests who ministered before the presence of the Lord in the tabernacle. The veil protected them from the consuming Shekinah Glory of God. (Exodus 40:3; Leviticus 16:2) Of course our High Priest, Jesus, would not need such a veil in Heaven. He sits at the right hand of the Father and is not threatened by the glory of the Father. In fact, Jesus shares in that glory! (John 17:5)

2. The presence of two rooms in the earthly temple confirms that in Heaven's temple there are two distinct phases in the Plan of Salvation. Just as there were two altars that had unique roles in the earthly process of atonement, there are two rooms representing two unique phases of service. The first room shadows the *daily* services of Jesus as our High Priest in the heavenly temple. The backroom, the Most Holy Place, shadows the services of Jesus as He concludes the Plan of Salvation. In other words, the earthly temple's Holy Place and its *daily* routine parallels the "daily intercessory routines" of Jesus as He intercedes on behalf of the whole world in Heaven's temple. The backroom or Most Holy Place and its annual service on the Day of Atonement parallels the final phase of Christ's work at the end of the world in Heaven's Temple. (Hebrews 9:25,26) So, the veil creates two rooms in the earthly tabernacle because there are two distinct phases in Jesus' ministry in Heaven's temple.

3. Paul uses the veil as an illustration explaining how prior to Jesus' ministry and death, man could only go so far in comprehending the salvation of God. The sanctuary service and its shadows are wonderful, but they are only shadows of the reality found in Jesus. However, when Jesus died, the temple veil was ripped open because temple services were no longer necessary. Paul emphasizes that everyone can see behind the curtain now and watch the ministry of Jesus our High Priest sitting at the right hand of the Father. Paul's point is that we now have a much better revelation of God's plan to save man. (Romans 16:25; Colossians 1:26; Hebrews 6:19,20)

The tiny, earthly sanctuary does not physically compare to the glorious temple in Heaven (Isaiah 66:1), but there are distinctive parallels between them. The Heaven-Earth-Linkage-Law connects the two temples so that the earthly temple reveals the *services and processes of the heavenly.* God's response to sin can be compared to turning a lemon into lemonade. God took the bitterness of sin and used it as an opportunity to reveal certain characteristics about Himself and His government that were previously unknown. Because of sin, the whole universe has seen a drama and a dimension of God's love that could not have been seen in any other way. Angels have a clear understanding of the properties of law, sin, penalty and grace. They understand the reasons why Lucifer was expelled much more clearly now. They also understand why God allowed Lucifer to live. The sin drama has revealed to the angels that there is no justification for rebellion against any of the laws of God, for God's laws have their origin in Infinite Wisdom.

The Ark of the Covenant

Physically, the Ark of the Covenant was a small box of acacia wood, overlaid with gold, about 3 feet wide by 5 feet long and 3 feet tall. (Exodus 25:10) It had two rings on each side through which poles could be inserted. (Exodus 25:12) The poles enabled priests to carry the ark from place to place without touching it. The lid or top of the ark was called the atonement cover or "mercy seat." (Compare KJV Exodus 25:17; 26:34; 30:6 with later translations.) Two golden angel figures (cherubim) stood on top of the box. (Exodus 25:20) The Israelites considered the ark to be the most holy piece of furniture in the earthly temple because the Shekinah glory hovered between the two cherubim on the ark. (Exodus 25:22) We know that a few items were kept *inside* the ark. These items included the Ten Commandments which were written by God's own finger on two tablets of stone, a bowl of manna and Aaron's rod that budded. (Exodus 31:18, 40:20; Exodus 16:33; Numbers 17:10) The ceremonial laws which God dictated to Moses were kept in a "pocket" attached to the outside of the ark. (Deuteronomy 31:26)

A Hidden Ark

The ark was located in the backroom of the earthly tabernacle, inside the Most Holy Place. The High Priest was the only person allowed to see the ark and he could see it for just a few minutes each year on the Day of

Atonement when he entered the Most Holy Place. When preparing the ark for travel, the veil separating the Holy Place from the Most Holy Place was used as the first layer of protection around the ark. Then, the ark was completely hidden from view by a blue covering. (Numbers 4:5,6) When traveling, the Israelites kept a radius of about a thousand yards (seven-tenths of a mile) between them and the Ark. (Joshua 3:4) As the priests prepared the ark for travel, Jewish tradition says they always approached it by walking backwards because to look upon *The Presence* was certain death.

God designed the ark and He hid it from the view of everyone but the high priest. The hidden ark reveals a profound truth about God and sin. Before sin defiled the human race, God's law was written in the hearts of Adam and Eve. They instinctively knew the Ten Commandments and Jesus often communed with Adam and Eve face-to-face in the Garden of Eden. (Genesis 3:8) But when sin separated man from God, the presence of God's law evaporated from their heart. The nature of man changed. Instead of having a proclivity for righteousness, man had a propensity toward rebellion. Furthermore, sinners could not survive the glorious presence of God. (Exodus 19:21) So, God hid Himself from man because He desires to be close to man. At Mt. Sinai it was necessary for God to cover Himself with dense darkness so He could be close to His children without His glorious Presence consuming them. (Exodus 19:18; 20:21) The darkness at Calvary covered the Father's presence. (Matthew 27:45) No doubt the Father wept as He bowed near the cross. God is always near, but we cannot physically see Him because His glory would consume us in a split second. When Moses wanted to see Jesus, Jesus would not allow it. (Exodus 33:20) Consider this paradox: The natural eye cannot see God and live, but the eye of *faith* can behold His presence and rejoice! (2 Kings 6:17)

The Ark of the Covenant was hidden from view in the earthly tabernacle because God's ways are hidden and mysterious to sinners. The carnal eye cannot see the beauty and wisdom of God's laws. (1 Kings 3:7-9,14; Psalm 95:10; Isaiah 55:8; 1 Corinthians 2:14) God understands the tendency of fallen man to make an icon out of religious things. God did not want His people worshiping the Ten Commandments or the ark. Instead, He wanted His people to understand and absorb the intent of His law through love, and worship Him with thanksgiving and obedience. The imprint of the law of God within the human heart is something entirely different from the adoration of a stone relic.

Ark to be Exposed

Some scholars believe that the earthly Ark of the Covenant was hidden away by priests in Jeremiah's day just before Nebuchadnezzar captured Jerusalem. Some people believe it will be found before Jesus comes, while others claim the ark has been found – although no one has yet produced any evidence to verify the claim. Nevertheless, the Bible predicts the true Ark of the Covenant in Heaven will one day be visible to all people on Earth. The book of Revelation describes this dazzling wonder at the conclusion of the seventh trumpet (1,260 days into the Great Tribulation). **"Then God's Temple in Heaven was opened, and within His Temple was seen the Ark of his covenant. And there came flashes of lightning, rumblings, peals of thunder, an earthquake and a great hailstorm."** (Revelation 11:19) *At that time,* God will demonstrate the supreme authority of His holy law which the wicked have trampled upon. God will reveal the ark and its contents, the Ten Commandments, with a dazzling display of power and glory because the Ten Commandments are the legal basis to condemn of the wicked. God's vengeance is always fair, just and legal. Before He inflicts the seven last plagues upon the wicked of the world, God will reveal the basis of His justice. (Revelation 15:1; Revelation 16)

The Mercy Seat

The golden lid on the ark was also called the atonement cover or mercy seat (KJV). When the high priest entered the Most Holy Place on the Day of Atonement, he sprinkled blood on this part of the ark to illustrate atonement for a broken law. (Leviticus 16:14) **"The wages of sin is death."** (Romans 6:23) Notice that Paul also writes: **"In fact, the law requires that nearly everything be cleansed with blood, and without the shedding of blood there is no forgiveness."** (Hebrews 9:22) So, blood was sprinkled on the broken law because the law had been defiled by sin. (Romans 3:23)

Divine Love

The Ark of the Covenant represents the character of God in an interesting way. The Ten Commandments represent justice and the atonement cover or "mercy seat" *above* the law represents grace. The *balance* between God's justice and God's mercy is defined as divine love. This is why John says, **"God is love."** (1 John 4:8) God placed the Ark of the Testimony in the Most Holy Place because His character and government are the most important things He owns. (Leviticus 11:44,45) He will not allow anyone to bring reproach upon His holy name without a response. (Exodus 20:7)

" '. . . For I am a great king,' says the Lord Almighty, 'and my name is to be feared among the nations. ' " (Malachi 1:14)

The Laver

"Make a bronze basin, with its bronze stand, for washing. Place it between the Tent of Meeting and the altar, and put water in it. Aaron and his sons are to wash their hands and feet with water from it. Whenever they enter the Tent of Meeting, they shall wash with water so that they will not die. Also, when they approach the altar to minister by presenting an offering made to the Lord by fire, they shall wash their hands and feet so that they will not die. This is to be a lasting ordinance for Aaron and his descendants for the generations to come." (Exodus 30:18-21)

The bronze basin (NIV) or laver (KJV) has practical and spiritual lessons associated with it. In practice, the previous text reveals that God required a state of physical purity, orderliness and cleanliness among those that served in the temple. The ever-present "desert dust" soiled the hands and feet of the priests who served in the temple and God required them to wash before entering the tabernacle (tent of meeting) so they were clean. Spiritually speaking, the application of water on the hands and feet reveal man's perpetual need to be "made clean" of sin from time to time. Sin (like desert dust) defiles our hands and feet and we, like the priests in the desert, need to be made clean!

Notice the words of Jesus to Nicodemus, **"Jesus answered, 'I tell you the truth, no one can enter the kingdom of God unless he is born of water and the Spirit.' "** (John 3:5) Some people misinterpret this verse to make it say that a person must be baptized in order to be saved. This is not the case. The thief on the cross was not baptized, nor does salvation come through rites, rituals, sacraments or works. (Ephesians 2:8,9) Instead, a willing baptism confirms submission to the purifying experience of God's sanctification. Christians need to be "cleansed" from time to time as they travel along the road of life. Baptism marks the beginning of a purifying experience. At the Jordan River, John baptized people into the kingdom of Heaven after they repented from their sins. (Acts 19:4) Washing one another's feet as our Lord commanded serves as a "miniature baptism," representing the fact that we need our sins to be washed away from time to time. The ordinance of foot-washing reminds us who we are, servants – not masters. (See John 13:6-8.) It is so easy to forget that our righteousness is as "filthy rags" in God's sight. (Isaiah 64:6)

God requires physical and spiritual cleanliness. The laver teaches God does accept sinners for what we are, but He requires, as a minimum, that we clean up before we approach Him. If this is true in the physical realm, what can be said of the spiritual? The Psalmist wrote, **"Who may ascend the hill of the Lord? Who may stand in his holy place? He who has clean hands and a pure heart, who does not lift up his soul to an idol or swear by what is false."** (Psalms 24:3,4) No doubt this text is the basis for the adage: "Cleanliness is next to Godliness." Before we leave the matter of priests cleansing their hands and feet at the laver, consider the implication of this verse concerning those who will occupy mansions in the New Jerusalem: **"Nothing impure will ever enter it, nor will anyone who does what is shameful or deceitful, but only those whose names are written in the Lamb's book of life."** (Revelation 21:27)

The Golden Lampstand

"Make a lampstand of pure gold and hammer it out, base and shaft; its flower-like cups, buds and blossoms shall be of one piece with it. . . . See that you make them according to the pattern shown you on the mountain." (Exodus 25:31,40) The golden lampstand was made of one talent of pure gold (about 66 pounds) and it had seven lamps on top of it. It was placed next to the south wall of the Holy Place, directly across the room from the Table of the Presence. (Exodus 25:37,39; 26:35) The golden lampstand represents God's agent of light or truth on Earth. Jesus reminded the Jews, **"You are the light of the world."** (Matthew 5:14; Acts 13:47) God wanted a special relationship with the trustees of His covenant (Exodus 19:1-6) and the golden lampstand represented the union of the human with the divine.

The lampstand was made of pure gold. Gold is often used to represent faith after it has been purified by trial and tribulation. (Revelation 3:18) The purpose of a lampstand is light and this was the spiritual purpose for Israel. Israel was chosen to be a "light to the world," to represent God's love for man. God required the priests to refuel the seven lamps daily with pure olive oil so the seven lights on the lampstand would burn continually through the night. (Leviticus 24:3) The oil represents the power of the Holy Spirit which enables the light of God's truth to burn continually until the darkness of sin has been finally removed. The responsibility for keeping the lights burning rested on the priests of Israel. If they became negligent or careless, darkness would overtake God's people. Just as God held the priests accountable for keeping the "lights on" in the temple, they were also responsible for carrying the "light of truth" to His people. The priests were "the keepers of the flame." Unfortunately, Israel's priests failed and Israel apostatized many times. History also confirms that, "As priests go, so go the people." In fact, much of today's social rot continues to escalate because of the poor leadership of pastors, priests and rabbis.

The Table of the Presence

"Make a table of acacia wood – two cubits long [44 inches], **a cubit wide** [22 inches] **and a cubit and a half high [33 inches]. Overlay it with pure gold and make a gold molding around it . . . And make its plates and dishes of pure gold, as well as its pitchers and bowls for the pouring out of offerings. Put the bread of the Presence on this table to be before me at all times."** (See Exodus 25:23-30, insertions mine.) This table represents the throne of God. All blessings flow from His throne. The idea that the Table of the Presence represents God's throne may surprise you, since in the earthly tabernacle, the focus is always directed toward the "hidden" Ark of the Covenant located in the Most Holy Place. The Shekinah glory lived within the Most Holy Place, so the second room in the Earthly tabernacle was holier than the first room. The veil obscured the Most Holy Place from the view of everyone but the high priest, indicating its extreme sacredness. These physical facts have led many people to conclude that the Ark of the Covenant must represent the throne of God. Here are three reasons why I believe the Table of the Presence represents the throne of God:

Reason # 1 – Name

"Put the bread of the Presence [shewbread, KJV] **on this table to be before me at all times."** (Exodus 25:30) The table received its name from the twelve loaves of bread that were placed on it each Sabbath morning. (Leviticus 24:8) The priests baked the loaves early on Sabbath morning and placed them on the table while they were still hot. (1 Samuel 21:3-6) At first, this practice seems contradictory to the instructions God gave Israel in regards to appropriate Sabbath behavior when He forbade them to cook and bake on the Sabbath. (Exodus 16:23) However, this bread was "special." The twelve loaves represent "a serving of the bread of life" for each tribe. Jesus is the bread of life. (John 6:48) The fresh bread represented a spiritual meal *for* the twelve tribes from God rather than an offering *from* the twelve tribes to God. Putting "hot fresh bread" on the table each Sabbath morning was a shadow of the responsibility given to the priests. They were to offer "freshly prepared" spiritual food from God's Word every

Sabbath morning. (Matthew 12:5; Luke 4:16) The Hebrew words *lechem* (Strong's: #3899) and *paneh* (Strong's: #6440), mean visible food, having presence, within sight or showing. KJV translators indicate the bread was clearly visible – as in "the bread is showing." Thus they gave it the name, "The Table of Showbread" (Exodus 25:30). The presentation of spiritual food on Sabbath morning through "freshly prepared" words of life is the primary meaning of the twelve loaves of fresh "showbread." It is interesting to me that Jesus fed great multitudes twice with loaves and fishes. When the first multitude of over 5,000 people were fed, Jesus used five loaves. (Matthew 14:19) When the second multitude of over 4,000 people were fed, Jesus used seven loaves. (Matthew 15:36) In all, Jesus fed Israel with twelve loaves of bread.

Twelve loaves of bread (along with other items), one loaf for each of the twelve tribes, were placed on the Table of the Presence for the priests to consume at regular intervals. The Table also had cups, bowls and pitchers. (Exodus 37:16) When a person looks at the Table of Showbread in terms of the utensils and the food placed on it, it becomes obvious that this Table represents "a King's table." The priests were invited to eat from the King's table because they were highly honored to serve in His earthly temple. Eating from the King's table was not only a great honor, but it also showed intimacy with the King. It was common for kings in ancient times to honor special friends by inviting them to eat at their table for as long as they lived! (2 Samuel 9:7) Even the wicked Jezebel knew the value of good cooking! She controlled Baal's prophets by feeding them well at her table. (1 Kings 18:19) It would not surprise me to learn that Jezebel coined the phrase, "A way to a man's heart is through his stomach."

Jesus told His disciples, **"And I confer on you a kingdom, just as my Father conferred one on me, so that you may eat and drink at my table in my kingdom and sit on thrones, judging the twelve tribes of Israel."** (Luke 22:29,30) So, the Table of the Presence in the earthly temple is associated with special privileges granted to priests. It is associated with Jesus as the Bread of Life (John 6:35) who has come down from Heaven. The Table of the Presence reflects the *source* of these blessings because the Bread of Life was served to the people each Sabbath from this table.

Reason # 2 – Location

The Table of the Presence was located on the north side of the tabernacle. In ancient times, the direction of "north" was regarded as the direction of divine residence, divine judgment or divine authority. Divine destruction and/or judgments always came from the north. Notice these five examples (Italics mine.):

Isaiah 41:25   **I have stirred up one from *the north,* and he comes – one from the rising sun who calls on my name. He treads on rulers as if they were mortar, as if he were a potter treading the clay.**

Jeremiah 1:14   **The Lord said to me, "From *the north* disaster will be poured out on all who live in the land."**

Jeremiah 4:6   **Raise the signal to go to Zion! Flee for safety without delay! For I am bringing disaster from *the north,* even terrible destruction.**

Jeremiah 46:20   **Egypt is a beautiful heifer, but a gadfly is coming against her from *the north.***

Jeremiah 50:9   **For I will stir up and bring against Babylon an alliance of great nations from the land of *the north.* They will take up their positions against her, and from *the north* she will be captured. Their arrows will be like skilled warriors who do not return empty-handed.**

Now, notice the location of the Table of the Presence: **"Place the table outside the curtain on the *north* side of the tabernacle and put the lampstand opposite it on the south side."** (Exodus 26:35) No matter where Israel moved the earthly tabernacle, the Table of the Presence always sat on the north side. Look closely at the following text to see what the north side of the temple suggests: **"How art thou fallen from heaven, O Lucifer, son of the morning! How art thou cut down to the ground, which didst weaken the nations! For thou hast said in thine heart, I will ascend into heaven, I will exalt my throne above the stars of God: I will sit also upon the mount of the congregation, in the sides of *the north:* I will ascend above the heights of the clouds; I will be like the most High."** (Isaiah 14:12-14, KJV) Lucifer conspired to place his throne "in the sides of the north" because this is the location of God's throne. He wants the adoration that God alone deserves. The following text under-scores the importance of the "north side" of Jerusalem: **"Beautiful for situation, the joy of the whole Earth, is mount Zion, on the sides of *the north,* the city of the great King**." (Psalms 48:2, KJV) The Psalmist describes the location of God's throne as being "on the sides of the north." These verses suggest the north side of the temple is where the throne of

God is located. Since the Table of *the Presence* was located on the north side of the temple, it is reasonable to say the Table of *the Presence* represents the throne of God. But, there is one final reason that brings the question to a close.

Reason # 3 – The Seat of Christ

Remember that the Ark of the Covenant represents the character of God. The ark symbolizes the divine balance between justice and mercy. Because God is consistent and reasonable, it is possible that He can be understood to some extent by finite minds. God is thoughtful and purposeful in everything He does. God designed the earthly tabernacle to teach men and women about Himself without resorting to an overpowering spectacle. The vastness of God's beauty is always below the surface. The Tent of Meeting was covered with common black seal skins. (Exodus 36:19) In other words, God could have "wowed" the Israelites with a Sinai cathedral dwarfing the tombs and pyramids of Egypt. He could have ensconced Himself in some lofty and glorious grandeur that would have utterly embarrassed Pharaoh and the Philistines. He could have intimidated the Israelites into submission each week by showing great displays of power, miracles, signs and wonders from the mountain. On several occasions, God did perform marvelous miracles on behalf of Israel, but He does not want to be worshiped because He happens to be the greatest King in all the universe who has great authority and owns everything. (Psalm 95:3; Malachi 1:14) No, God desires His children to worship for different reasons. He desires our worship because He gave us life and showed us love. He desires our worship because a loving relationship between the Creator and the created is the only way to the fullness of life which He designed for us. Last, God desires our worship because the more we exalt Him the more we become like Him. The more we understand His character, the more we can appreciate His ways and government.

God seeks our worship, but it is for our good, not His. God will not force Himself on one creature because He is love. Jesus' life is an excellent example of this point. He could have chosen any high-ranking, wealthy parents on Earth, but He chose to live and look like a common person. To God, our understanding of His character, ways and government are of greater value than beholding His glory. The Bible says of Jesus, **"He grew up before him** [the Father] **like a tender shoot, and like a root out of dry ground. He had no beauty or majesty to attract us to him, nothing in his appearance that we should desire him. He was despised and**

rejected by men, a man of sorrows, and familiar with suffering. Like one from whom men hide their faces he was despised, and we esteemed him not." (Isaiah 53:2,3, insertion mine.)

When Jesus returned to Heaven, He was seated at the right hand of the Father. (Hebrews 8:1-5) If the Table of the Presence represents God's throne, then the physical location of Jesus (at the right hand of the Father) puts Him *between* the Ark of the Covenant and the Father – the perfect place for an intercessor! Consider the work of Jesus: He sits on His throne upholding the righteousness of God's government (to His right); He sits on His throne exonerating the righteousness of the Father (to His left) and while in this middle position He is man's representative before Heaven's watching host! What a High Priest!

During the days of the earthly tabernacle, the Ark of the Covenant in the Most Holy Place was the *focus* of worship. The Shekinah glory hid behind the veil in the Most Holy Place because God wanted mankind to *focus* on the principles of His government of love and His righteous ways more than His veiled glory. Still, the evidence indicates that the banquet Table of *the Presence* was the source of the Bread of Life. In addition, the Table of *the Presence* was always physically located on the north side of the temple. The Table of *the Presence* symbolizes the throne where His presence is located. If these conclusions are true, then the physical location of Jesus, at the right hand of the Father, makes a great deal of sense. Jesus sits where you would expect a mediator to sit, *between* God the Father and the Ark of the Covenant.

Summary – Temple Furniture

We have briefly examined the purpose of each item in the earthly temple and how it parallels a corresponding item in Heaven's temple. Much more could be written on this topic, so much so, that it could fill many books. We know that God is thoughtful and deliberate in all that He does and the parallels between the earthly and heavenly temple are no exception. The essential purpose for understanding the earthly tabernacle today is twofold. First, the services of the earthly temple provide a backdrop against which we can test our ideas and understanding of the Plan of Salvation. Second, parallel operations between the earthly temple and the heavenly temple explain a number of processes and events which take place in the book of Revelation. The ways of God in redeeming man are revealed in His temple. We have covered a lot of information, so perhaps a brief summary about temple furniture will be helpful.

1. Services at the Altar of Burnt Offering pointed forward to the death of Jesus as man's perfect substitute.

2. Daily services at the Altar of Incense pointed backward to the day intercession by Jesus began for sinful man. The covenant Jesus made with the Father to save man currently stands between the wrath of God and a condemned world.

3. The Ark of the Covenant represents the government of God. The wonderful balance between justice and mercy is called divine love.

4. The Laver illustrates the spiritual cleansing that man regularly needs.

5. The Lampstand represents the agents or trustees of God's salvation who are to let their light shine before others for the glory of God.

6. The Table of the Presence, on the north side of the temple, represents the throne of God.

7. The Heaven-Earth-Linkage-Law indicates that earthly tabernacle services and processes are parallels of heavenly tabernacle services and processes.

Chapter 12
Parallel Temple Services

If he [Jesus] **were on earth, he would not be a priest, for there are already men who offer the gifts prescribed by the law. They serve at a sanctuary that is a copy and shadow of what is in heaven. This is why Moses was warned when he was about to build the tabernacle: "See to it that you make everything according to the pattern shown you on the mountain.**

— Hebrews 8:4,5
(insertion mine)

Shortly after the Exodus, God commanded Israel to observe six religious services each year that are parallels of six processes within the Plan of Salvation. After the time of King David, males were required to attend three of these religious services in Jerusalem. These three feasts were associated with three crop harvests. (Exodus 23:14-17) God designed these earthly events so that participants would consider the real events that would take place in Heaven. The six services were:

1. The Feast of Passover*

2. The Feast of Unleavened Bread

3. The Feast of Weeks or "Pentecost"*

4. The Feast of Trumpets

5. The Day of Atonement

6. The Feast of Ingathering or "Tabernacles"*

   *Attendance was required in Jerusalem.

The first three services took place in the spring and the last three took place in the fall. The timing of these services was very specific.

End Time Parallels

As we examine these six services, we will focus on how they shadow key events that transpire within the Plan of Salvation. When God implemented these six services, He already knew how He was going to bring the drama of sin to an end. So, the story of Israel's miraculous deliverance from slavery in Egypt contains several important parallels about the saints being delivered from the bondage of sin. Think about this. God knows the end from the beginning. He did marvelous things long ago that prove to be awesome parallels of coming events! With this thought in mind, let us consider the story of the night the Lord passed over Egypt.

The Lord said to Moses, **"Tell the whole community of Israel that on the tenth day of this month each man is to take a lamb for his family, one for each household. If any household is too small for a whole lamb, they must share one with their nearest neighbor, having taken into account the number of people there are. You are to determine the amount of lamb needed in accordance with what each person will eat. The animals you choose must be year-old males without defect, and you may take them from the sheep or the goats. Take care of them until the fourteenth day of the month, when all the people of the community of Israel must slaughter them at twilight. Then they are to take some of the blood and put it on the sides and tops of the doorframes of the houses where they eat the lambs. That same night they are to eat the meat roasted over the fire, along with bitter herbs, and bread made without yeast. Do not eat the meat raw or cooked in water, but roast it over the fire – head, legs and inner parts. Do not leave any of it till morning; if some is left till morning, you must burn it. This is how you are to eat it: with your cloak tucked into your belt, your sandals on your feet and your staff in your hand. Eat it in haste; it is the Lord's Passover. On that same night I will pass through Egypt and strike down every firstborn – both men and animals – and I will bring judgment on all the gods of Egypt. I am the Lord. The blood will be a sign for you on the houses where you are; and when I see the blood, I will pass over you. No destructive plague will touch you when I strike Egypt."** (Exodus 12:3-13)

The Rest of the Story

"The Israelites did just what the Lord commanded Moses and Aaron. At midnight the Lord struck down all the firstborn in Egypt, from the firstborn of Pharaoh, who sat on the throne, to the firstborn of the prisoner, who was in the dungeon, and the firstborn of all the live-stock as well. Pharaoh and all his officials and all the Egyptians got up during the night, and there was loud wailing in Egypt, for there was not a house without someone dead. During the night Pharaoh summoned Moses and Aaron and said, 'Up! Leave my people, you

and the Israelites! Go, worship the Lord as you have requested. Take your flocks and herds, as you have said, and go. And also bless me.' The Egyptians urged the people to hurry and leave the country. 'For otherwise,' they said, 'we will all die!' " (Exodus 12:28-33)

The Passover described in Exodus 12 occurred in 1437 B.C. For centuries the Jews have observed the Feast of Passover to commemorate their deliverance from Egypt. However, the Feast of Passover is more inclusive than that. It is a parallel of what God plans to do at the end of time. Consider these seven parallels:

1. First Passover – God's people were miraculously delivered from slavery.
   End-time Parallel (ETP) – God's people will be sealed and then physically delivered from the bondage of mortality.

2. First Passover – Everyone in Egypt was notified that the firstborn (man and beast) had been placed under the curse of death. This announcement produced two groups of people: believers and unbelievers. Believers put blood on their doorposts.
   ETP – The inhabitants of the world will be notified they are under the curse of death. There will be two groups of people: believers and unbelievers. The believers accept Christ's atonement and will obey the message which the 144,000 will proclaim.

3. First Passover – God kept His covenant with Abraham and took Abraham's descendants to the "Promised Land."
   ETP – Jesus will keep His promise and return to Earth at the appointed time. He will take the saints to the "Promised Land," that is, the Earth made new.

4. First Passover – There was a Sabbath rest test in Egypt and persecution before the Exodus.
   ETP – There will be a Sabbath rest test and persecution for the inhabitants of Earth before the great Exodus of the saints at the Second Coming.

5. First Passover – God "passed over" every house in Egypt and He checked the door posts of every house to see who believed His word.
   ETP – God will "pass over" every human being and save each person who believes His word.

6. First Passover – God sent ten plagues upon a defiant Egypt.
   ETP – God will send 14 plagues upon a defiant Earth during the Great

Tribulation (seven first plagues called seven trumpets and seven last plagues called seven bowls).

7. First Passover – God destroyed Pharaoh and his army with water. ETP – God will destroy the Antichrist and his armies with fire.

The Passover is a end-time parallel of God's judgment of man. The judgment of mankind is a topic of utmost importance and yet, few people know anything about it. The Bible says, **"For we must all appear before the judgment seat of Christ, that each one may receive what is due him for the things done while in the body, whether good or bad."** (2 Corinthians 5:10) For now, simply remember that the observance of a Passover feast was far more significant than merely celebrating an escape from Pharaoh and Egypt. God not only sees the past, but also knows where He is going and wants His children to know His plans!

The Feast of Unleavened Bread

"Celebrate the Feast of Unleavened Bread, because it was on this very day that I brought your divisions out of Egypt. Celebrate this day as a lasting ordinance for the generations to come. In the first month you are to eat bread made without yeast, from the evening of the fourteenth day until the evening of the twenty-first day. For seven days no yeast is to be found in your houses. And whoever eats anything with yeast in it must be cut off from the community of Israel, whether he is an alien or native-born. Eat nothing made with yeast. Wherever you live, you must eat unleavened bread." (Exodus 12:17-20)

The observance of Passover and the Feast of Unleavened Bread are inseparably joined. The Passover was celebrated on the 15th day of the first month and the Feast of Unleavened Bread began on the same day. The term "feast" may be misleading since God required Israel to search their homes for yeast and then dispose of it. They were to eat yeast-free bread for seven days. The Hebrews understood that yeast produces fermentation. Consequently, a little bit of yeast will "infect" the batter. (1 Corinthians 5:6-8) On the other hand, unleavened bread has no yeast. God aligned the Feast of Passover with the Feast of Unleavened Bread because He wanted Israel to see the connection between deliverance and purity of heart. God's goodness and grace do not lessen His demands for a pure heart. (Revelation 21:27; 22:15) This is why sinners need the sealing so badly! The Hebrews were to thoroughly search their homes for yeast and remove any trace of it before Passover began. The Feast of Unleavened Bread was to remind them that they needed to be constantly on guard against the yeast of sin in their homes and lives. We still need to guard against the yeast of sin, especially as we wait for the final "pass over" and appearing of our Lord. We must search our heart often and remove any known sin. The devil is a master at gradualism. Sin creeps in slowly, but steadily. Sin will overtake an individual, as well as a whole nation, if it is not firmly resisted. The history of Israel (indeed, all nations) confirms this point.

In the Scriptures, the figurative use of yeast represents the fermenting process of sin and is demonstrated to be vain, foolish, even intoxicating ideas of man. (Mark 8:15; Luke 12:1; Revelation 18:3) Men and women may try to excuse sin, justify sin, defend sin, rename sin, promote sin, exalt sin or extol the benefits of sin, but make no mistake – sin is deadly! God hates sin and He forbade the Jews from presenting any offerings to Him that contained yeast! (Exodus 23:18) Jesus warned His disciples, "'. . . **But be on your guard against the yeast of the Pharisees and Sadducees.' Then they understood that he was not telling them to guard against the yeast used in bread, but against the teaching of the Pharisees and Sadducees.**" (Matthew 16:11-12) These words are certainly applicable today. There are seven religious systems in the world today. Each one is full of yeast. The doctrines of the world's religious systems have fermented and are unacceptable to God. In the last days, the servants of God, the 144,000, will present the unleavened bread of Life to the world and every person on Earth will have an opportunity to choose life or reject the truth. Revelation's story indicates that many, if not the majority of people, will reject the bread of Heaven because they prefer soft bread; doctrines fermented with the yeast of sin.

Three Presentations of Firstfruits

Passover always occurs in the spring, between April 3 and May 2. On the Sunday following Passover, the high priest presented the "firstfruits" of the winter harvest before the Lord. (Leviticus 23:11) This presentation of firstfruits (wheat, barley, oil and wine) was a shadow of a resurrected Jesus presenting Himself before the Father. Jesus is the Firstborn of the dead, the preeminent One risen from the tomb. (Revelation 1:5) Because the firstfruits at Passover were always presented on Sunday, so Jesus presented Himself to the Father on Sunday morning as the Firstfruits of the dead. (John 20:17)

Consider the elements of the Passover feast: The Passover Lamb represents Jesus, the Lamb of God. The yeast-free bread eaten at Passover represents a sinless Jesus, the unleavened Bread of Life that came down from Heaven. (John 6:35) The life and teachings of Jesus have no impurity or fermentation in them. The unfermented wine used at Passover represents the pure blood of Jesus that was shed for our sins. (Luke 22:20) Jesus could not be a perfect substitute for us if there had been any sin in His life.

The first harvest of the year occurred at the time of Passover. As a winter harvest, it was also the smallest harvest. This harvest foreshadows the ascension of Jesus with a small, but triumphant group of people who were resurrected from the cold winter of death. This group of people includes the 24 elders mentioned in Revelation. (Matthew 27:52,53; Ephesians 4:8; Revelation 4:4; 1 Corinthians 15:20) The 24 elders, two witnesses from each of the twelve tribes, are representatives of the human race. These 24 elders were taken to Heaven in A.D. 30. to serve as human observers in Heaven's court. They will testify to all the saints in days to come about the courtroom process when Jesus "passed-over" the records of every person to determine their eternal destiny.

The Feast of Weeks (Pentecost)

"Count off fifty days up to the day after the seventh Sabbath, and then present an offering of new grain to the Lord. From wherever you live, bring two loaves made of two-tenths of an ephah of fine flour, baked with yeast, as a wave offering of firstfruits to the Lord." (Leviticus 23:16,17) The Feast of Weeks was celebrated at the time of the spring harvest. The spring harvest was larger than the winter harvest at Passover. This one-day feast occurred in late spring or early summer (June/July). In Christ's day, this feast was called "Pentecost" because the Greek word for Pentecost means "fiftieth day." The count of fifty days began with the waving of firstfruits on Sunday after Passover. The count of fifty days included seven seventh day Sabbaths (or seven full weeks). Then, on the 50th day (always on a Sunday), the Feast of [seven] Weeks was celebrated with a presentation of firstfruits from the spring harvest.

Farmers understand that when there is zero rainfall there is zero harvest. This feast illustrates the essential work of the Holy Spirit. The work of the Holy Spirit is to soften and influence the human heart toward spiritual matters. (1 Corinthians 2:14) Unless a person is born of the Spirit, he or she cannot enter the kingdom of God. (John 3:5) This feast demonstrates that God is able to bring life, even a bountiful harvest, from the cold soil of a carnal heart if individuals will open up and receive the outpouring of the

Holy Spirit. God wanted the Jews to understand that men may work the soil of the heart and plant seeds of truth, but it is only through the power of the Spirit of God that spiritual life occurs. The beauty of the shadow of this feast is that even though the human heart may be cold or even dead to spiritual things, God can produce a wonderful transformation through the power of the Spirit!

Acts 2 records a wonderful event that illustrates the shadow of this feast. Ten days after Jesus ascended, the Holy Spirit descended on the disciples at Pentecost and 3,000 people became baptized believers in Christ that day! (Acts 2:41) This harvest of souls came from the toil of Christ Himself. He had traveled from village to village, healing the sick, lame and blind. He had preached freedom to people ensnared by twisted religion and superstition and He removed the yeast of foolish dogma with pure words of life. The disciples and these 3,000 baptized believers were the firstfruits from the gospel of Christ. (Matthew 7:28,29) Their conversion was the result of the work of the Holy Spirit!

God's timing is always perfect and the event described in Acts 2 was no exception! Attendence at Pentecost was required so Jewish males came to Jerusalem from many nations. (Acts 2:9-11) The outpouring of the Holy Spirit was verified by signs and wonders and Peter boldly took advantage of the occasion. What a tremendous opportunity to tell of a risen Jesus to those Jews who had gathered from every corner of the world! As a result of *that* Pentecostal event, Israel was widely and powerfully informed about the appearing of Messiah, their corporate guilt for rejecting and killing Him, and the ascension of the risen Savior! Through the convicting power of the Holy Spirit, 3,000 Jews became convinced that Jesus was the Messianic fulfillment of Scripture! (Acts 2:22; Acts 13:48) I also suspect that the testimony of those resurrected with Jesus 50 days earlier gave immutable proof that Jesus was indeed risen from the dead. (Matthew 27:52,53)

Passover, Pentecost and Ingathering

Consider the three presentations of firstfruits. The presentation of firstfruits at Passover represents a risen Jesus. He is the firstborn (the preeminent of men) among those who have died. (Revelation 1:5) The small winter harvest at Passover represents a small group of people that Jesus took to Heaven at the time of His ascension including the 24 elders. The second presentation of firstfruits occurred at Pentecost and these firstfruits from the spring harvest foreshadowed the disciples and the 3,000 people that were baptized at Pentecost in Acts 2. These were the first Christians. The

Pentecost, recorded in Acts 2, is the only Pentecost that stands out in the history of Israel since the initial Exodus. It is widely known because the Holy Spirit *rained* on those gathered in Jerusalem in A.D. 30 to celebrate this Pentecost. The outpouring of Holy Spirit power changed hearts and produced "born again" people. (Romans 8:5; 1 Peter 4:3-6) Since that day, the gospel of Christ has not stopped. The gospel continues to spread throughout the world (Colossians 1:6) and the reverberations of that Pentecost continue! The gospel of the kingdom is still alive and the early rain of the Holy Spirit is still producing a harvest. The time has almost come for Earth's final harvest represented by the Feast of Ingathering. There is going to be a powerful out pouring of Holy Spirit power upon the whole world. (Joel 2:27,28) The fall harvest is the largest harvest and the book of Revelation says the 144,000 servants of God will be the firstfruits of the final harvest. (Revelation 14:4) John also says that the final harvest will be so great that no one can count the number of those who come out of the Great Tribulation! (Revelation 7:9-14) God designed these feasts thousands of years ago because He wants us to understand His plan to save us!

Feast	Firstfruits	Three Harvests
Passover	Jesus	A small group including the 24 elders were taken to Heaven
Pentecost	Disciples + 3,000	All who have received the gospel of Jesus Christ between A.D. 30 and the Tribulation
Ingathering	144,000	All who will receive the gospel during the Great Tribulation

The Feast of Trumpets

The Feast of Trumpets was the first of three convocations held in the seventh month of the year. According to Jewish history, the seventh new moon of the year (or Tishri 1) was marked by a very noisy feast. Priests were arranged in groups and these groups took turns throughout the day sounding their trumpets! Even after the feast was over, trumpet blasts could be heard evening and morning for eight more days. The Bible simply says, **"On the first day of the seventh month hold a sacred assembly**

and do no regular work. It is a day for you to sound the trumpets."
(Numbers 29:1)

The Old Testament does not provide much detail about the Feast of Trumpets. However, we can easily determine the purpose for the Feast of Trumpets with a little investigation. The sounding of trumpets in ancient times was the equivalent of sounding a siren. (Joel 2:1) The trumpet was used in ancient war much like the bugle was used in the Civil War that happened in the United States in the 1860's. The sounding of the trumpets was designed as a warning to every man, woman and child that the ultra-serious Day of Atonement was about to arrive. *God's love for humanity moves Him to notify people when the time of judgment arrives.* The ancient Day of Atonement was regarded as an extremely solemn event because that day marked the end of mercy. God required all known sins be transferred to the sanctuary *before* sundown on the tenth day of the seventh month. (Leviticus 16; 23:27-32) Remember, in ancient Israel a new day began at evening, so the evening of the tenth day is followed by the morning of the tenth day.

To show the children of Israel just how serious He was about the end of mercy, God told Moses that if any household was found guilty of unconfessed sin on the Day of Atonement, that household was to be cut off from the camp. In other words, the heritage of each Jewish family was at stake on the Day of Atonement. So, the Feast of Trumpets served as an impressive announcement that something very serious was about to take place. According to Jewish literature, the priests warned Israel of the approaching Day of Atonement for nine days as they sounded their trumpets throughout the nation. Although no work was allowed on the Day of Atonement, it was unlike the other annual feasts because it was truly a day of fasting and supplication.

The Feast of Trumpets notified the nation of Israel that only a few days remained to make sure everyone was fully reconciled with each other as well as with God. The first nine days of Tishri were dedicated to soul searching and reflection. Each person within the household was to be sure their sins had been *transferred* to the Altar of Burnt Offering. According to Jewish rabbis, the phrase, "Prepare to meet thy God, O Israel" was often spoken during the first nine days of the seventh month. Meeting with God was not a casual matter. The Hebrews understood that God's displeasure could be aroused and fire from God could consume thousands in a matter of seconds. (Numbers 16, Psalm 78:21) They also knew, however, that God was a God of love who does not want one person to be destroyed. (Deuteronomy 7:9; Isaiah 55:6-7; Matthew 18:14)

End-Time Trumpet Parallel

The parallel between the Feast of Trumpets and the Seven Trumpets described in Revelation is obvious and important. The sounding of trumpets at the Feast of Trumpets is a shadow of the sounding of seven trumpets in Heaven during the Great Tribulation. Consider this parallel for a moment: In ancient Israel, God terminated the offer of salvation at sundown on the 10th day of the seventh month (the Day of Atonement). In our time, God will terminate the offer of salvation when the seventh trumpet sounds. (Revelation 10:7; 11:15-19) God's love for humanity moves Him to notify people when the time of judgment arrives. Consequently, when the seven trumpets begin to sound in Heaven, there will be corresponding events on Earth. (Remember the Heaven-Earth-Linkage-Law?) As the trumpet judgments fall on Earth, 144,000 servants of God will proclaim to the world, **"Fear God and give him glory, because the hour of his judgment has come. Worship him who made the heavens, the earth, the sea and the springs of water."** (Revelation 14:7) When the seventh trumpet sounds, God's generous offer of salvation to mankind will be finished. Everyone will have made a decision for or against the gospel by the time the seventh trumpet sounds. Everyone who refuses to accept the generous offer of salvation and the perfect atonement which is offered through faith in Christ will be "cut off" from eternal life.

The seven trumpets of Revelation are linked with seven terrible judgments that will fall on Earth. These judgments cause the Great Tribulation. The Bible predicts four global earthquakes, meteoric showers of burning hail which burn up large portions of Earth, two asteroid impacts, great darkness covering one-third of the Earth – caused perhaps by a large number of volcano eruptions and more. Jesus said, **"For then there will be great distress, unequaled from the beginning of the world until now – and never to be equaled again. If those days had not been cut short, no one would survive, but for the sake of the elect those days will be shortened."** (Matthew 24:21,22) Terrible events and overwhelming suffering will cause everyone to consider or reconsider reconciling with their neighbors and with God. People who love God and His truth will repent of wrong doing. They will accept the terms and conditions for salvation which the 144,000 will proclaim. The seventh day Sabbath will become, as in the days just before the Exodus, a great test of faith. People with hearts like Pharaoh will take their stand on the side of rebellion against God.

Even though God's mercy is great and His salvation is free, there is a limit to His patience with rebellion and sinners. God's willingness to forgive sinners is beyond comprehension, however, His patience with sinners does not last forever. (See Genesis 6:5-7; Romans 2:5-8; Revelation 14:9-10; and Revelation 18:4-5.) Those who love the Lord will come to see that His holy law declares the seventh day of the week to be holy and will obediently submit to the requirements of the Almighty. Just as standing for God's Sabbath was seen as an act of rebellion against the authority of Pharaoh, so in like manner the saints will be tested. All who pass the test of faith will be sealed and delivered from sin's destruction. God has promised to do this! The duration of the seven trumpets and the time allocated for sealing the saints will be 1,260 days. The 144,000 are sealed first (Revelation 7:1-4) and others will be sealed as time passes. (Revelation 10:7)

The Day of Atonement / Reconciliation

The Day of Atonement occurred on the 10th day of the 7th month. This service was the most solemn of the six annual services. The Day of Atonement service involves three vital issues: The reconciliation of man with man, the reconciliation of man with God and the removal of sin *from the temple*. The Day of Atonement indicates there is a terminus, a point in time when God's offer of mercy is terminated. The Hebrew word for atonement, *kaphar* (Strong's H3722) means to placate, cancel, reconcile, pacify, etc. Atonement is sometimes described as a state of *at-one-ment*. The basic idea behind the word *atonement* is reconciliation, being restored to a state of oneness. Notice the requirements for reconciliation: **"The Lord said to Moses: 'If anyone sins and is unfaithful to the Lord by deceiving his neighbor about something entrusted to him or left in his care or stolen, or if he cheats him, or if he finds lost property and lies about it, or if he swears falsely, or if he commits any such sin that people may do – when he thus sins and becomes guilty, he must return what he has stolen or taken by extortion, or what was entrusted to him, or the lost property he found, or whatever it was he swore falsely about. He must make restitution in full, add a fifth of the value to it and give it all to the owner on the day he presents his guilt offering. And as a penalty he must bring to the priest, that is, to the Lord, his guilt offering, a ram from the flock, one without defect and of the proper value. In this way the priest will make atonement for him before the Lord, and he will be forgiven for any of these things he did that made him guilty.' "** (Leviticus 6:1-7) If a person sinned against his neighbor, God required atonement between the two parties *before* He would allow the guilt of that sin to be transferred to the temple. Jesus underscored the necessity for atonement with a brother when He said, **"Therefore, if you are offering your gift at the altar and there remember that your brother has something against you, leave your gift there in front of**

the altar. First go and be reconciled to your brother; then come and offer your gift." (Matthew 5:23,24)

Even though the topic of judicial equilibrium has been introduced, a few comments about this topic are necessary at this point. Atonement for sin is required in God's universe because the presence of sin is not justifiable. If sin could be justified, then God should be held responsible for sin! Since God has done nothing that would make Him responsible for sin, the presence of sin cannot be justified. Therefore, God requires atonement or appeasement for the presence of sin.

God maintains a state of judicial equilibrium throughout His vast kingdom. God is the Guardian, the Executor and the Supreme Court of the universe and He insures that judicial equilibrium is ever present. There is no separation of powers in God's government. Instead, there is a separation of entities, the Father, the Son and the Holy Spirit. These three are united in purpose, plan and action. Together, They uphold and honor a rule of law based upon judicial equilibrium. Judicial equilibrium is defined as the perfect balance between the demands of God's law and His offer of grace. (Remember the Ark of the Covenant represents the balance between justice and mercy.) Judicial equilibrium does not lessen the demands of God's law nor does judicial equilibrium elevate the provisions of grace above the demands of law. The justice side of judicial equilibrium is illustrated by an eye for an eye, a tooth for a tooth, a bruise for bruise and most of all, a life for a life. (Exodus 21) The golden rule spoken from the justice perspective is this: "It will be done to you as you did to others." (Ecclesiastes 12:14; Matthew 7:12) The other side of judicial equilibrium is called mercy. Mercy is extended through a process called reconciliation or atonement. The first step toward atonement for wrong doing is restitution. God requires human beings to make restitution for any sin committed against another (Matthew 5:23,24), and He also requires that we accept atonement for any sin committed against us. This requirement is summed up in the Lord's prayer, **"Forgive us our debts, as we also have forgiven our debtors."** (Matthew 6:12) We noticed earlier in Leviticus 6 that God requires two atonements for sin committed against our neighbor. First, God expects us to voluntarily make atonement with our offended neighbor by offering suitable restitution, then God required atonement at the Altar of Burnt offering by offering an acceptable sacrifice. As far as the sinner was concerned, this was the end of the matter. Still, a wrong had been committed and even though atonement had been made, the guilt of sin remained upon the horns of the altar. This guilt was removed from the temple on the Day of Atonement and placed on the head of a scapegoat.

God Has Set a Day to Judge the World

If sins were not transferred to the tabernacle *before* the Day of Atonement began, those sins could not be forgiven. It was forever too late for any subsequent atonement. The Day of Atonement service illustrates the fact that God has set a day when there will be no further atonement for sin. (During the Great Tribulation, the offer of mercy ends with the seventh trumpet.) If a person neglected to transfer his sins to the altar, the sinner received the penalty of his sins upon his own head. But, all who transferred their sins to the temple prior to the Day of Atonement were set free of sin's penalty. With these thoughts in mind, consider the Day of Atonement service.

The Day of Atonement Process

Early in the morning on the tenth day of the seventh month, the Day of Atonement service began with a close investigation of the life of the high priest. Before the high priest could officiate on behalf of the nation of Israel, God examined him to determine if he was worthy to conduct the service. Imagine how sobering it must have been for the high priest to realize that he must stand in God's presence and be examined before he was allowed to officiate for the children of Israel as their intercessor. The examination of the life of the high priest foreshadowed the investigation which Jesus underwent before He could serve as man's judge. (See Daniel 7:9,10,13,14; Revelation 4 and 5.)

To illustrate how serious the worthiness issue was, the high priest had to slaughter a ram as a sin offering for his family and a bull for himself (remember, the high priest is considered a corporate officer, a representative of Jesus). Then, with a censer and some of the atonement blood from the bull in his hands, the trembling high priest went behind the veil to stand in the brilliant glory of Almighty God. There, surrounded by smoke and the sweet fragrance of incense, the high priest sprinkled some of the blood on the lid of the Ark of the Covenant. Then, he communed with God. If God considered the high priest's life and his offering acceptable, the high priest would be allowed to continue with the higher service, the cleansing of the temple. As the high priest left the Most Holy Place, he set the bull's blood aside for a short period of time. (See Leviticus 16, 21 and 22.)

The Cleansing of the Temple

The second phase, the cleansing of the temple from the guilt of sin, involved several steps. First, two perfect goats were presented to the high priest in the courtyard. Lots were cast to determine which goat would die for the *penalty* of sin. Then, the high priest killed the **Lord's goat** on the Altar of Burnt Offering. With a censer and some of the goat's blood in a cup, the high priest entered behind the veil a second time to stand in God's presence. He then sprinkled the goat's blood on the atonement cover of the Ark and again communed with God. If God was pleased with the sincerity and faithfulness of the people, the high priest was permitted to continue with the final phase of cleansing the temple. After leaving the Most Holy Place, the high priest retrieved the bull's blood from his personal sacrifice and mixed it with the blood from the Lord's goat and put some of the mixed blood on the Altar of Incense. This action removed the defilement of the Altar of Incense. Then, he went out of the temple into the courtyard to the Altar of Burnt Offering and cleansed that altar by sprinkling mixed blood on it. After this was done, the high priest approached the remaining goat (the scapegoat) and placed his hands on the head of the scapegoat.

This final action of placing his hands on the head of the scapegoat transferred all of Israel's guilt which had accumulated in the temple to the scapegoat. Then, a very capable man ("a fit man," [KJV]) led the scapegoat far out into the desert so that the goat would die of starvation. The scapegoat's lengthy starvation shadows the necessity in God's government for full and complete restitution for sin itself. Even though the penalty for sin is death by execution (Lord's goat), sin is never forgiven or justified. Someone must make atonement for the *presence* of sin. Since the creator of sin is Lucifer, Lucifer must bear the responsibility for sin upon his own head. As the father and perpetrator of sin upon angels and the human race, Lucifer has to make restitution for his actions. God's vengeance demands it. The scapegoat received all of the guilt that had been stored in the temple because the scapegoat foreshadows the one who is responsible for the presence of sin in the universe. Death for Lucifer, as represented by the scapegoat, will be slow and painful.

Notice how judicial equilibrium functions. **Justice** demands the following: The father of sin must bear the penalty for creating sin. Further, the creator of sin must also bear the guilt of sin which was transferred away from sinners to the temple. **Grace** offers the following: Sinners under the penalty for sin can have their sins transferred to the temple by presenting a perfect substitute. Here we see the perfect balance between justice and mercy. The Lord's goat represents the mercy that God has extended to sinners: Jesus, the Lamb of God. The scapegoat represents the justice that God demands of sinners: restitution and death.

Confirmations of Truth

The Day of Atonement ceremony confirms several important truths that harmoniously coexist within the Plan of Salvation. The Old Testament tabernacle service confirms that the demands of God's law do not eclipse the offer of God's grace nor does the operation of God's grace make the law void. Clearly, law and grace work together harmoniously within the tabernacle parallels. The law condemns a sinner to death, but grace provides a way for the guilt of the sinner to be transferred so that the sinner may go free. Jesus had to die to save man because God's law could not be changed. God did not have the option of just "forgetting" that Adam and Eve had sinned. Once Adam and Eve committed sin, a series of immutable events began. For example, man became carnal by nature. Also, death came upon all men through Adam. Therefore, Jesus was required to live a perfect life before He could die as our perfect substitute. The guilt of our sins could only be transferred to the altar through One who was above condemnation.

This may begin to sound like a broken record, but it is a critical point. The tabernacle service confirms that sin is neither forgiven nor forgotten until the scapegoat is led away to die. The tabernacle service also confirms that Jesus does not bear the responsibility for sin. Sin cannot be justified. Rather, Jesus is our reconciliation with God and through His perfect blood, our guilt can be transferred to the Altar of Burnt Offering. We have also learned that the temple is cleansed of guilt at an appointed time and the *consequence* of sin is transferred to the one responsible for sin. The suffering of the scapegoat provides restitution. Bottom line: The life of every sinner will be examined. Solomon wrote, **"For God will bring every deed into judgment, including every hidden thing, whether it is good or evil."** (Ecclesiastes 12:14) If our sins are transferred to the altar through Christ's blood, we are not under condemnation! (Romans 8:1-10) If our sins are not transferred to the altar, then God's vengeance requires the wicked to provide restitution for their sins and suffer the penalty for sin.

Two Goats

Some Christians think that both goats used on the Day of Atonement represent Jesus since both goats are used for the purpose of atonement. Notice this text about the scapegoat: **"But the goat chosen by lot as the scapegoat shall be presented alive before the Lord to be used for making atonement by sending it into the desert as a scapegoat."** (Leviticus 16:10) The scapegoat is presented before the Lord while it is *alive*, whereas the Lord's goat was *slain* on that day. Although both goats were used to provide atonement, the atonement they provide is not identical. If the atonement they offer was identical, one goat would have sufficed. The Lord's goat provides atonement with its blood because the *penalty* for sin is death by execution, the other goat provides atonement through starvation and dehydration because *restitution* for sin must be made. Even though the Bible does not explicitly say the scapegoat dies after it is taken into the desert, the implication is that the scapegoat disappears forever and it is never seen or heard from again. This suggests that once sin is removed from God's temple in Heaven, it will never occur again because the creator of sin will be no more!

The Saints Review the Wicked

The scapegoat does not die on the Day of Atonement, so the atonement it offers does not occur that day. The end-time parallel reveals that Lucifer is not destroyed until the end of the 1,000 years. (Revelation 20) In fact, the scapegoat does not provide atonement through its death, it provides atonement (as in restitution) through its suffering. The restitution for sin will be suffering. *Suffering will be inflicted upon the wicked before the penalty for sin is executed.* During the 1,000 years, the saints will reign with Jesus and judge the wicked. **"I saw thrones on which were seated those who had been given authority to judge. And I saw the souls of those who had been beheaded because of their testimony for Jesus and because of the word of God. They had not worshiped the beast or his image and had not received his mark on their foreheads or their hands. They came to life and reigned with Christ a thousand years."** (Revelation 20:4) During the 1,000 years the saints will review the records of the wicked and determine the appropriate amount of suffering that will be necessary for restitution. Judicial equilibrium requires full restitution. For example, Hitler not only deserves to die for his sins and outrageous conduct, but he also owes restitution to millions of people for the suffering he inflicted on them. After a lengthy period of indescribable suffering by fire, Hitler will eventually be burned up in the fire sent from God because the penalty for sin is death by execution. The saints, complying with the requirements of God's law, will determine the amount of suffering that Hitler must endure – proportional to the suffering he caused. If more people understood God's requirement for restitution, the world would be a much different place in which to live! Paul wrote, **"It is a dreadful thing to fall into the hands of the living God."** (Hebrews 10:31)

Notice the golden rule at work: "As you do unto others, it will be done unto you – eye for an eye, tooth for a tooth, bruise for a bruise, etc." Paul says the saints will judge the wicked saying, **"Do you not know that the saints will judge the world? And if you are to judge the world, are you not competent to judge trivial cases? Do you not know that we will judge** [the evil] **angels? How much more the things of this life!"** (1 Corinthians 6:2,3, insertion mine.)

Keep in mind that the saints do not determine whether a person receives eternal life or eternal death. Jesus alone is Creator and Judge of mankind, and by the time of the Second Coming, He will have made an eternal decision about every person. However, the judgment which the saints conduct concerns the issue of restitution. The saints (in many cases the victims of the wicked) will review the actions of the wicked and they will sentence the wicked to a law-full amount of suffering – full restitution will be extracted from the wicked for the suffering they caused. God ensures this process and He calls it His vengeance. **"The Lord is a jealous and avenging God; the Lord takes vengeance and is filled with wrath. The Lord takes vengeance on his foes and maintains his wrath against his enemies. The Lord is slow to anger and great in power; the Lord will not leave the guilty unpunished. His way is in the whirlwind and the storm, and clouds are the dust of his feet."** (Nahum 1:2,3) Paul wrote, **"Do not take revenge, my friends, but leave room for God's wrath, for it is written: 'It is mine to avenge; I will repay,' says the Lord."** (Romans 12:19)

The Scapegoat is a "Fall Guy"

Most people have heard or used the term "scapegoat" when pinning responsibility on someone for something that went dreadfully wrong. In sanctuary terms, the same is true. The scapegoat represents the one responsible for sin! In other words, the scapegoat represents Lucifer because he is responsible for sin. As the responsible party for sin on Earth, Lucifer's guilt cannot be atoned for. He is the father of sin and he must suffer the torment he has caused the saints. (The wicked will suffer for their own sins, but Lucifer must suffer restitution for the sins of the saved.) A protracted death through starvation and dehydration is a form of restitution just like a life sentence is a form of restitution in our penal code today. Remember, the scapegoat does not bear the consequences of sin for the wicked. The guilt of the wicked will be on their own heads.

Some readers may wonder why the scapegoat provides restitution for the sins of the righteous when the saints are required to make restitution for their sins *before* they go to the altar. When full restitution for sin is made between people, the guilt for sin remains to be dealt with. However, many sins go beyond the possibility of restitution. For example, what restitution can be made for malicious slander, adultery, rape, sexual abuse, breaking up a marriage, or driving under the influence of alcohol and killing twenty children? If a person commits an evil deed and makes a gallant effort to restore whatever he or she can, truly repenting of the sin and seeking God's mercy, God will make Lucifer, the originator of sin, provide the restitution for the wrong that goes beyond what man can offer.

Why Two Goats?

It may be that God used two goats on the Day of Atonement instead of two lambs because goats differ from lambs in many ways. Perhaps the most obvious difference is a goat's independence. Every shepherd knows that sheep are followers and goats are leaders. This point illuminates some interesting thoughts. First, Michael (Christ) and Lucifer were once the closest of friends. Lucifer was the first angel that Jesus created. In form, Lucifer looked very similar to Michael. Both were angels, but Michael was the Archangel. Michael was God in the form of an angel. Lucifer, on the other hand, was the highest of *created* beings. Michael and Lucifer held the highest offices in Heaven and had a great deal of latitude in which to exercise their prerogatives. Over time, Lucifer became filled with envy and jealousy and eventually coveted Michael's position. When the Father rebuffed him, he chose to rebel against God. He became the self-appointed leader of sympathetic angels who also came to believe that God was unfair. When open rebellion broke out in Heaven, these two angels became great foes. Perhaps God used two goats on the Day of Atonement because a wild goat can lead an entire herd of sheep astray. Casting lots to determine which goat was the Lord's goat on the Day of Atonement suggests that Michael was the Chosen One to lead the angelic host.

The Feast of Ingathering (Tabernacles)

The last feast of the religious year was the Feast of Ingathering. The feast began on the 15th day of the seventh month and it lasted for seven days. The Jews presented their last and largest collection of firstfruits to the high priest five days after the Day of Atonement service had passed. This feast took place at the end of the summer harvest and as the name reflects, it was a time for rejoicing over the bountiful harvest that had been "gathered in." This feast was also called the Feast of Tabernacles because every Jewish male was required to go to Jerusalem and participate in the feast. Because there was a shortage of housing in Jerusalem, the Jews erected temporary tents (or tabernacles) for this joyous occasion.

The Feast of Tabernacles parallels a very interesting process that takes place *at the end* of the world. The 144,000 are taken to Heaven before the Second Coming, about the time of the seventh trumpet. (Revelation 11:12) At the Second Coming, Jesus will approach Earth with all His angels and the 144,000 attending, and He will call the righteous dead to life. The righteous living will join with the resurrected dead to meet the Lord in the air. (1 Thessalonians 4:16,17) A triumphant Jesus with all His saints will return to the holy city, New Jerusalem. There will be a great feast as Jesus celebrates and drinks the pure wine of the grape with the redeemed. (Matthew 26:29) The saints will remain in the city for 1,000 years as a temporary residence. At the end of the 1,000 years, the holy city will descend from Heaven. (Revelation 21:2) The wicked will be resurrected and notified of their sentence. Jesus will call fire down out of Heaven and purify the Earth. Then, He will create a new Heaven and a new Earth, which will become the primary home of the saints.

Consider some of the Feast of Ingathering parallels:

1. Feast: The Feast of Ingathering was the last and largest harvest of the year. It began five days after the Day of Atonement had passed.

   ETP: (End-time parallel): The last and largest ingathering of saints will occur at the end of the world. The harvest of souls will be numberless. Just as the Feast of Ingathering took place after the Day of Atonement, so the Second Coming occurs after the close of mercy.

2. Feast: All Jewish males were required to go to Jerusalem for this feast.

   ETP: All of the redeemed will be taken to New Jerusalem for the wedding banquet.

3. Feast: The feast and the time spent in Jerusalem was temporary (seven days).

   ETP: The saints will temporarily live in the New Jerusalem during the Sabbatical Millennium.

4. Feast: The firstfruits of this harvest were presented to the high priest before thank offerings from the harvest were presented to the

ETP:　　Lord.

ETP:　　The 144,000 are the firstfruits of the final harvest. The 144,000 are taken to Heaven and presented to Jesus a few days before the Second Coming. Then, at the Second Coming, the great harvest of souls are gathered in.

The firstfruits of the last great harvest foreshadow the 144,000 prophets of God who are selected for a special mission just before the Great Tribulation begins. (Revelation 14:4; 7:1-4) Of course, without rain there is no harvest or firstfruits. In the land of Canaan, there are two essential rains each year. They are called the early rain and the latter rain. These terms, "early and latter" are used with respect to the crops. For crops that mature in late summer, the latter rain brings them to maturity. For crops that mature in early spring, the term "latter rain" refers to rains that bring these crops to maturity. The latter rain finishes the maturing process that began with the early rain!

In a spiritual sense, there are also two rains. Both rains are shadows representing the work of the Holy Spirit. The first work of the Holy Spirit is to lead us to acknowledge our need for a Savior. This spiritual awakening is caused by "the early rain" work of the Holy Spirit. The Feast of Tabernacles shadows the concluding work of the Holy Spirit on behalf of mankind (a latter rain illustration). A great outpouring of Holy Spirit empowerment will occur just before Jesus comes and this latter rain will bring souls to perfect maturity! (Joel 2:28-32; James 5:7; Revelation 11:3) The concluding work of the Holy Spirit's ministry will be highly visible and God's truth will be presented in the clearest terms to every person in the world. (Revelation 14:6-12; Zechariah 4:6) *Everyone* will hear the terms and conditions of salvation. Everyone will have an informed opportunity to know God's will and make a decision about salvation. People who follow the Spirit now will rejoice to hear greater truth. (John 16:13) Many people who are currently indifferent, negligent or perhaps not willing to listen to the Holy Spirit will have a change of heart when they see the display of God's wrath and thoughtfully consider the curse that rests upon their heads. Unfortunately, many people who are in rebellion against God right now will remain in rebellion. They will be deceived and led to their destruction when the Antichrist appears. (2 Thessalonians 2:9-10) Individuals who love God's ways and truth will have their *faith* severely tested. By remaining faithful to God, they will receive the most wonderful gift that God can give to His people while still on Earth. He will give His children the "gift" of a sinless nature – a nature that will have no propensity or attraction to sin and is in complete harmony with His laws. (Hebrews 8:10-13; Romans 1:17; 1 John 3:2)

The gift of the Holy Spirit demonstrates God's great compassion for the human race and His deep desire to save every person that is willing to be redeemed. Man's need for a Savior does not become a reality until the Holy Spirit impresses us with the condemnation and fate that faces every sinner. When an individual responds to the Spirit's prompting, he or she will recognize a desperate need for Jesus, the perfect Lamb of God. When we are "born again," we are happy to submit to the gospel of Christ. There is an inner joy when we walk with the Lord. (John 14:15; 1 John 2:5) At the present time, when a person surrenders his or her will to do God's will, that person is reckoned as righteous through the imputed righteousness of Christ, even though the sealing has not occurred. (Romans 8:1) During the time period of the Great Tribulation, circumstances will force everyone to respond to the gospel. If a person submits to the laws of Babylon, his or her choice will be considered an act of rebellion against God. If a person submits to the law of God, his or his choice will be considered an act of rebellion against the authority of the world's governments. Either way, the consequences will be deadly. The firmness of each person's decision will be tested. If a person passes his test of faith, the righteousness of Christ will be *imparted* to him or her! This is the sealing. (Colossians 1:27; Revelation 7:1-4; 10:7) When God finishes sealing His people, the need for an intercessor or mediator in Heaven will be over. Only then will God's children have a righteous character "sealed" within them. Jesus marks the end of salvation's offer in Heaven by declaring, **"Let him who does wrong continue to do wrong; let him who is vile continue to be vile; let him who does right continue to do right; and let him who is holy continue to be holy."** (Revelation 22:11)

144,000 Will Belong to Jesus

When Passover and Pentecost (the earlier harvests of the year) arrived, the firstfruits were presented to the high priest and they became his personal property. The parallel is true of the final harvest. The firstfruits of the final harvest will be 144,000 men and women who will be servants of God; special prophets during the Great Tribulation. (Revelation 7:1-4; 14:4) Since the firstfruits of the harvests become the exclusive property of the high priest (Numbers 18), the 144,000 "firstfruits" will belong to our High Priest, Jesus Christ. As a reward for their dedication and suffering for the cause of Christ, the 144,000 will become special administrative assistants who accompany Jesus throughout eternity and serve Him wherever He goes. The 144,000 will be the first to experience God's gift of a new nature. They will receive the imparted "gift" of a sinless nature *first* because they are sealed first. (Revelation 7:1-4) The 144,000 will have the Spirit of prophecy resting upon them. They will prophesy just like the prophets of old. Those who heed their message and chose to *live by faith* will be sealed in the same way the 144,000 are sealed. The Bible indicates the 144,000 will wear the name of the Father and Jesus on their foreheads. (Revelation 14:1; 22:4) This will be a beautiful sign revealing their rank and position in God's government. I am not sure how this will be done, but we can be certain it will be beautiful and glorious. The names of the Father and Jesus upon the foreheads of the 144,000 stand in stark contrast to the tattoo that Satan puts on the foreheads of his servants. (Revelation 13:16)

Conclusion

We have a friend in Jesus. Not only does He understand our needs, but He also understands our limitations, weaknesses and foolishness. He is willing to be our High Priest and to present us before God without a blemish. He is willing to save us and grant us power to overcome the ravages of sin. He is willing to release us from anxiety, doubts and bad habits. He has the power to do all of this and so much more! He is willing – are you? Why not surrender your life to Him right now? Why not say, "Lord, I am willing to go, be and do all that you ask." If you are willing to say this to Him, He will enable you to succeed in all that He wants you to do! The good news is that you and I have a friend in Heaven's temple who loves us so much that He was willing to die the second death for us. We cannot easily comprehend such love. That is why we sometimes find it difficult to call on Him to help us with our problems. But be sure of this: He is qualified to deal with any problem we face. We may not like His answers on every occasion, but what child loves every answer from his parents? Jesus knows what is best for us and He responds accordingly. So, go ahead, ask Him to help you. He is ready. Give Him your life and He will deliver you from your worries and fill you with a peace that passes understanding! He is the Alpha and the Omega!

Jesus is righteous in everything He does. **"He is the Rock, his works are perfect, and all his ways are just. A faithful God who does no wrong, upright and just is he . . . ."** (Deuteronomy 32:4) The earthly and heavenly temples confirm so many wonderful truths about Jesus. His actions are open, upright and just. His works are perfect and His righteousness is illustrated in the services of His temple.

Chapter 13
What Happens at Death?

No one can come to me unless the Father who sent me draws him, and I will raise him up at the last day.

– John 6:44

Introduction

Some people in the Bible are remembered for their good deeds, while others are remembered for their rebellion. King Saul, the first king of Israel, is remembered for his rebellion against God. His life is an object lesson showing how quickly self-centeredness can lead to a ruined life. The Bible says that Saul died a tragic death – he took his own life when he was 61 years old. In an attack on Shunem about 1000 B.C., the Philistines critically injured Saul. Rather than let his enemies gloat in victory, he fell upon his own sword and died. (1 Samuel 31:4) Many Christians believe that King Saul went directly to hell that afternoon. According to the doctrine of an eternally burning hell, King Saul and millions of people like him are writhing and jumping about in the flames of hell fire this very minute. Advocates of an eternal hell claim that once God sends a person to hell, there is no escape and no relief. The torment is said to be painful and torturous beyond words!

According to the scenario above, King Saul has been on fire for about 3,000 years. He must be discouraged beyond words since there is no second chance – no way out of hell. His cries for relief are no doubt drowned out by the roar of hell's furnaces. Think about it. If there is a burning hell where sinners, young and old, writhe in eternal torment, it must be the most awful place in the whole universe! There is no way out, no hope, no end. I can just imagine how the hostages of hell curse God and cry out for immediate release from their misery every time the devil turns up the thermostat. Many Christians believe this scenario to be true, or something similar to it and they use the parable Jesus told about the rich man and Lazarus to prove it. (Luke 16:19-31) Unfortunately, many non-Christians refuse to believe in God because they find this doctrine about God's justice to be repugnant. About 15 years ago, George Gallup surveyed American Christians regarding their views on Heaven and hell. Almost 87% of the individuals surveyed believed they were going to

Heaven and 91% said they knew someone in hell or someone who was going there. In recent years, the cruelty of hell has been lessened by some theologians. Consequently, recent surveys reveal that larger numbers of Christians do not believe that hell is a literal place where the souls of wicked people writhe in eternal flames. So, is there a hell? Where is it? What is it like? When does a person go to hell?

Nobody is Burning in Hell Yet

The idea of an eternally burning hell is based on the idea that man's soul is immortal or not subject to death. Therefore, man's soul continues to live an intellectual life after it leaves the body. For this reason Christians often speak of deceased friends saying, "They have gone on to be with the Lord." This comment raises a good question. Do you think Abel and every-one else who has died "in the Lord" are in Heaven, playing harps and eating the delicious fruit that grows on the Tree of Life? Do you think Cain, the first murderer, King Saul, and everyone who has died in rebellion against God are writhing in eternal hell? For the following reasons I am convinced that King Saul is not in hell and Abel is not in Heaven:

1. First and foremost, Jesus paid the penalty for our sins. (Romans 5:9; 1 Corinthians 15:3) If the penalty for sin is an endless burning in hell, then Jesus did not pay the penalty for sin. Jesus was resurrected on the third day! (Acts 10:40) We also know that Jesus returned to Heaven forty days after His death. (Acts 1:3) So, why would God require human beings to burn *forever* for their sins when He required far less of man's Sin Bearer? (2 Corinthians 5:21) The Bible indicates the Father does not impose more on fallen man than He put upon Jesus.

2. God is fair. (Psalm 89:14) God does not torture people forever just because they lived in rebellion for a few years. Eternal punishment for 70 years of rebellion is not fair. A judicial system is fair if it upholds the principle that punishment is commensurate with the crime. (Matthew 7:1,2) Does God do less? No! Should King Saul be tortured with fire for billions of years when he only lived a mere 61 years? No. In fact, the Bible says that God will not torture the wicked for eternity, but instead reduce the wicked to ashes. (Malachi 4:3)

3. God is love and the new Earth will be a wonderful place to live. (1 John 4:8; 1 Corinthians 2:9; Revelation 21:1-4) However, it would be impos-sible for the saints to remain content and happy with God's government and justice if they had to observe their loved ones in the flames of hell day after day.

4. The Bible teaches there will be two resurrections. (John 5:28,29; Revelation 20:4,5) The first resurrection occurs at the Second Coming. At that time, the righteous will be resurrected and they will meet the Lord in the air. (1 Thessalonians 4:16,17) The second resurrection occurs at the end of the 1,000 years. At that time the wicked will be resurrected and they will face their Maker as He announces their sentence. Why are there two resurrections if people are already in Heaven or hell? Why would God resurrect the wicked at the end of the 1,000 years (who are alleged to be in hell already), for the purpose of putting them back into an earthly body and then throwing them into a blazing fire again? (Revelation 20:7-15)

Things Do Not Add Up

Is it possible that the Bible teaches that good people do not go to Heaven when they die and wicked people do not go to hell the day they die? Consider the following:

1. The Bible teaches there is a resurrection for the righteous and a resurrection for the wicked. If the righteous go immediately to Heaven when they die, why does Jesus say that the righteous are resurrected *at the last day*? **"For my Father's will is that everyone who looks to the Son and believes in him shall have eternal life, and I will raise him up at the last day." "No one can come to me unless the Father who sent me draws him, and I will raise him up at the last day." "There is a judge for the one who rejects me and does not accept my words; that very word which I spoke will condemn him at the last day."** (John 6:40, 44; 12:48) Some scholars claim that God's purpose for resurrecting the righteous at the last day is to reclaim an earthly body. This argument does not make any sense. If the soul is a living entity that can exist outside the body, why is a body necessary? For example, if Abel has been in Heaven for almost 6,000 years, why would he want or need a body now? Besides, the Bible says that flesh and blood cannot inherit eternal life! (1 Corinthians 15:50) Even more, what about those individuals who suffer with physical deformities while they are alive? Would their soul want to return to a deformed and degenerate body again? Certainly not. If a body actually returns to dust after death as the Bible indicates (Psalm 104:29; Ecclesiastes 3:20), then why would Jesus wait until the Second Coming to gather some dirt to create a new body for the deceased? He could certainly create a new body at any time.

2. The Bible teaches there is an appointed time for the people of Earth to be judged. (Ecclesiastes 12:14; 2 Corinthians 5:10; Acts 17:31; John 12:48) If people go to Heaven or hell at the time of death, God would have to judge them at the time of death. This is not what the Bible teaches and contrary to what many people believe. Neither Abel, the first man to die about 6,000 years ago, nor King Saul, who died on the battlefield 3,000 years ago, were sent to their eternal destinations at the time of their death.

3. Even more compelling are the Bible verses that confirm that the dead know nothing (Ecclesiastes 9:5) and that they are in a state of "sleep." (John 11:2-15) God foreknew the devil would use man's curiosity about death to trap people with his sophisticated lies. (2 Chronicles 33:6) Therefore, God expressly forbade man from trying to communicate with people who had died. God said, **"Let no one be found among you who sacrifices his son or daughter in the fire, who practices divination or sorcery, interprets omens, engages in witchcraft, or casts spells, or who is a medium or spiritist or who consults the dead."** (Deuteronomy 18:10,11)

4. Revelation 20:15 reveals that God will put an end to sin at the end of the millennium and everyone not found in the Book of Life will be burned up. Here is the problem as I see it. Eternal life in Heaven or in hell requires immortality; however, God grants immortality only to the saints at the Second Coming. (See 1 Corinthians 15:51-53.) The wicked never receive immortality. Therefore, the souls of the wicked are not immortal. In fact, the Bible clearly says, **"the soul who sins is the one who will die."** (Ezekiel 18:4) Think about it. If wicked people were immortal and suffered in hell forever, the presence of sinners and rebellion within the universe would last throughout eternity!

Conditional Mortality

To understand man's condition in death we must begin with the book of Genesis. When God created Adam and Eve, He granted them *conditional* immortality. They could live indefinitely as long as they had access to the Tree of Life. But, when they sinned, God separated them from the Tree of Life so they would eventually die. **"And the Lord God said, 'The man has now become like one of us, knowing good and evil. He must not be allowed to reach out his hand and take also from the tree of life and eat, and live forever.' So the Lord God banished him from the Garden of Eden to work the ground from which he had been taken. After he**

drove the man out, he placed on the east side of the Garden of Eden cherubim and a flaming sword flashing back and forth to guard the way to the tree of life." (Genesis 3:22-24)

At the very beginning of life Jesus warned Adam saying, **" . . . You are free to eat from any tree in the garden; but you must not eat from the tree of the knowledge of good and evil, for when you eat of it you will surely die."** (Genesis 2:16,17) This text does not mean that the body would die and the soul would live on. No! This text means that man would cease to exist. This issue is at the heart of the lie which the devil wanted Eve to believe. Remember, Satan said to Eve, **"You will not surely die . . . ."** (Genesis 3:4) Satan led Eve to believe that if she ate of the forbidden fruit that she would become immortal like God. If she had immortality, she could not be subject to death! What a clever deception!

God did not insert an everlasting soul in Adam's body. Instead, Adam *became* a living soul when God created him. **"The Lord God formed the man from the dust of the ground and breathed into his nostrils the breath of life, and the man *became* a living being."** (Genesis 2:7, italics mine.) In other words, God united Adam's body of dust with His own breath of life and Adam became a living being. When Adam died at the age of 930 years, his soul ceased to exist because the human soul cannot live as a separate entity outside the body. The soul of man results from a combination of two parts – a human body and the breath of life. Here is an illustration that might help to illustrate this concept. A light bulb comes to "life" when the power of electricity is applied to it. Light occurs when the light bulb is combined with electricity. If the power is removed, there is no light. Likewise, if there is no breath of life in the body, there is no soul. A man's soul is mortal which means it is subject to death. God alone is immortal and not subject to death. When Jesus died for humanity, He had to lay His immortality aside! (John 10:17,19) When the Father resurrected Jesus, the Father restored immortality to Him. (Revelation 1:18) But notice what God said about man at the time of Noah's flood, **"Then the Lord said, My Spirit will not contend with man forever, for he is mortal; his** [remaining] **days will be a hundred and twenty years."** (Genesis 6:3, insertion mine.) Each time the word immortal is used in the Bible, it pertains to God, not man. **"Now to the King eternal, immortal, invisible, the only God, be honor and glory for ever and ever. Amen . . . God, the blessed and only Ruler, the King of kings and Lord of lords, who alone is immortal and who lives in unapproachable light, whom no one has seen or can see. To him be honor and might forever. Amen"** (I Timothy 1:17; 6:15,16) Paul expounds on this point by writing that God will grant the gift of immortality to the saints at the Second Coming! **"When the perishable** has been clothed with the imperishable, and the mortal with immortality, then the saying that is written will come true: 'Death has been swallowed up in victory.' " (1 Corinthians 15:54) If the righteous receive immortality at the Second Coming, it is obvious that they do not have immortality before that time!

Therefore, no one has knowledge or intelligence before he or she is born and there is no knowledge or intelligence in death. Death is a state of nonexistence. Many people, of course, disagree with this view and Christians offer certain texts to demonstrate otherwise. Let us examine these texts and see what the Bible actually says:

Spirit Returns to God

"And the dust returns to the ground it came from, and the spirit [*ruach*] **returns to God who gave it."** (Ecclesiastes 12:7, insertion mine.) Some people use this text to prove that the spirit of man returns to God when he dies. Although this text does not say so, the alleged implication is that something intelligent returns to God at the time of death. Advocates of the external soul reason that when the body and the spirit are separated, the spirit (or "ruach") returns to God who gave it. The Hebrew word "ruach" means wind or breath. Notice how this word is translated a few verses earlier: **"As you do not know the path of the wind** [ruach]**, or how the body is formed in a mother's womb, so you cannot understand the work of God, the Maker of all things."** (Ecclesiastes 11:5) The ruach of the righteous, as well as the ruach of the wicked, returns to God at death! The text is clear on this point: The "breath of life" is a gift from God to all people at birth and the "breath of life" [ruach] returns to God who gave it when we die, regardless of our moral behavior!

Job's use of the word "ruach" helps clarify the meaning even further. He says, **"As long as I have life within me, the breath** [ruach] **of God in my nostrils, my lips will not speak deceit."** (Job 27:3,4 [KJV]) An unrefined translation of Job's comment might read, "As long as I have life within me and the breath from God in my nose, my lips will not speak lies." Neither Solomon nor Job used the word "ruach" to mean a conscious spirit roaming the heavens.

King David also knew that death brought an end to consciousness. He said, **"Do not put your trust in princes, in mortal men, who cannot save. When their spirit** [*nephesh*] **departs, they return to the ground; on that very day their plans come to nothing."** (Psalms 146:3,4) The Hebrew word "nephesh" also means breath. This word is used many times in the Bible to describe the breath of living creatures. Notice: **"And the Lord God formed the man from the dust of the ground and breathed into his nostrils the breath** [nephesh] **of life, and man became a living being."** (Genesis 2:7) Concerning the flood, the Bible says, **"Everything on dry land that had the breath** [nephesh] **of life in its nostrils died."** (Genesis 7:22, insertion mine.)

King David believed the dead were in their graves and not in Heaven praising the Lord. He said, **"It is not the dead who praise the Lord, those who go down to silence; it is we** [the living] **who extol the Lord . . . ."** (Psalm 115:17,18, insertion mine.) The Apostle Peter also confirmed this point. On the day of Pentecost he spoke about King David saying, **"Brothers, I can tell you confidently that the patriarch David died and was buried, and his tomb is here to this day . . . For David did not ascend to heaven . . . ."** (Acts 2:29,34)

Solomon leaves no room for doubt regarding this topic. He explains the state of man in death very clearly. He said that the dead are unaware of anything that occurs on Earth. He wrote, **"For the living know that they will die, but the dead know nothing; they have no further reward, and even the memory of them is forgotten. Their love, their hate and their jealousy have long since vanished; never again will they have a part in anything that happens under the sun."** (Ecclesiastes 9:5,6)

Jesus Called Death "Sleep"

Many Christians do not correctly understand man's condition in death. More than 50 times in the New Testament, death is called *sleep.* There are two reasons for this: First, death is actually like a sleep. (See John 11:11-14.) There is no awareness in death (or during a good night's sleep). Second, the first death is temporary (just as sleep is temporary), whereas the second death lasts forever. When Lazarus, the brother of Mary and Martha died, Jesus referred to Lazarus' death as sleep. (John 11.) Why did Jesus refer to Lazarus as being asleep? For an obvious reason – the death that Lazarus experienced was *temporary,* just like sleep is temporary. When we sleep deeply, we are unaware of our surroundings. However, sleep does not last forever. Think of the "resurrection" as a powerful awakening. Every person who lives and dies will live again and God will awaken from their sleep everyone who dies in one of two resurrections. The Bible indicates there are two resurrections – one for the saints and the other for the wicked. The first resurrection occurs at the Second Coming. This means there will be a judgment of human beings *prior* to the Second Coming, because Jesus will decide who is righteous and who is not before He comes. Therefore, those judged to be righteous will be resurrected at the Second Coming. (1 Thessalonians 4:16) The people judged to be wicked will be resurrected at the end of the millennium. (Revelation 20:5)

This is a critical point: Natural death (the first death) is not the *penalty* for sin. Natural death comes as a consequence of being separated from the Tree of Life. The penalty for sin, however, is death by execution and God will implement the penalty for sin at the end of the millennium. (Revelation 20:14,15) Once the distinction between these two deaths is understood, it becomes clear why no one could be burning in hell right now. The second death by execution has not been implemented! The *penalty* for sin has not been imposed on anyone except Jesus and that happened when He died on Calvary. When Jesus died on the cross, He suffered the penalty for our sins, namely, death by execution.

Did Jesus Preach to the Spirits in Hell?

The following text is sometimes offered as a proof text showing that Jesus preached to the souls of dead people after He died on the cross. 1 Peter 3:18-20 says, **"For Christ died for sins once for all, the righteous for the unrighteous, to bring you to God. He was put to death in the body but made alive by the Spirit, through whom also he went and preached to the spirits in prison who disobeyed long ago when God waited patiently in the days of Noah while the ark was being built . . . ."** Did Jesus preach to the spirits of the antediluvians after He died on the cross? If Jesus did this, what did He offer them? Did Jesus grant them a pardon for their rebellion or did He shake a divine finger at them and say, "Eternal hell is the reward you deserve – you vile unbelievers?" Is it possible to escape from hell after being sent there? Did Jesus release any hostages from hell? If so, where is the evidence? Since hell is believed to be the worst possible torture chamber ever devised, would repentance come from a contrite heart or would a charbroiled sinner say anything in order to get relief from anguish? Although most Christians believe the soul remains alive after death, they generally reject the second chance theory for salvation *after* death, believing that matters pertaining to our eternal reward are determined during our present life on Earth.

So, what does Peter say in this text? Peter teaches that Jesus was brought to life by the *same* Holy Spirit that attempted to bring the antediluvians to their senses before the flood. Notice what the Lord told Noah in Genesis 6:3, **"My Spirit will not contend with man forever."** I think most people would agree that it is possible for a person to be physically alive but spiritually dead. (Romans 8:10) Peter says that Jesus was physically put to death in the body, but made alive by the *same* Spirit that tried to save the antediluvians. Because of decadence and rebellion against God, the antediluvians were dead to the Spirit. Since they were not willing to allow the Spirit to lead them onto the ark, they drowned when the flood came.

The context of 1 Peter 3 and 4 shows that Peter is not saying that Jesus preached to imprisoned antediluvians during the time He was dead. In fact, in the verses that follow Peter flips the topic 180 degrees by saying that people who are "alive in the Spirit" are dead to debauchery, lust, drunkenness, orgies, carousing and idolatry – the very conditions that caused the antediluvian's destruction. Peter concludes by saying, **"They** [those dead to the Holy Spirit] **think it strange that you do not plunge with them into the same flood of dissipation, and they heap abuse on you. But they will have to give account to him who is ready to judge the living and the dead. For this is the reason the gospel was preached even to those who are now dead** [to spiritual matters], **so that they might be judged according to men in regard to the body, but** [change their ways and] **live according to God in regard to the spirit."** (1 Peter 4:4-6, insertions mine.)

Rich Man - Poor Man

In Luke 16:19-31, Jesus told the story of a rich man and a beggar named Lazarus. Many people today use this story to confirm the doctrine of an eternally burning hell. Here is the story:

"There was a rich man who was dressed in purple and fine linen and lived in luxury every day. At his gate was laid a beggar named Lazarus, covered with sores and longing to eat what fell from the rich man's table. Even the dogs came and licked his sores. The time came when the beggar died and the angels carried him to Abraham's side. The rich man also died and was buried. In hell, where he was in torment, he looked up and saw Abraham far away, with Lazarus by his side. So he called to him, 'Father Abraham, have pity on me and send Lazarus to dip the tip of his finger in water and cool my tongue, because I am in agony in this fire.' But Abraham replied, 'Son, remember that in your lifetime you received your good things, while Lazarus received bad things, but now he is comforted here and you are in agony. And besides all this, between us and you a great chasm has been fixed, so that those who want to go from here to you cannot, nor

can anyone cross over from there to us.' He answered, 'Then I beg you, father, send Lazarus to my father's house, for I have five brothers. Let him warn them, so that they will not also come to this place of torment.' Abraham replied, 'They have Moses and the Prophets; let them listen to them.' 'No, father Abraham,' he said, 'but if someone from the dead goes to them, they will repent.' He said to him, 'If they do not listen to Moses and the Prophets, they will not be convinced even if someone rises from the dead.' "

When telling this parable, Jesus addressed two theological issues which the Sadducees and Pharisees often debated. The Sadducees did not believe in a resurrection (they were "sad you see"), but the Pharisees believed in a resurrection and any mention of this topic would start a hotly contested debate. Paul used this contentious subject to cleverly distract his accusers so he could escape with his life! (See Acts 23:8,9.) The doctrine of prosperity was a second theological issue hotly debated between these two sects of Jews. The Sadducees believed that wealth and prosperity were physical signs of God's approval and poverty was a terrible curse for wrong doing. (People today still debate this doctrine.) In other words, poor people were gross sinners because the absence of prosperity proved they were under God's condemnation. (See Deuteronomy 28.)

Jesus' use of this parable about a rich man and a poor man allowed Him to cleverly merge these two issues together. Jesus' purpose was to present a larger truth that is found at the end of the story. In the parable, the rich man represents the self-centered, richly-blessed nation of Israel. God had given them every blessing and instead of sharing God's blessings, they appropriated the blessings of God to themselves. The beggar, Lazarus, represents the impoverished Gentiles, who had received only a few spiritual crumbs from the bountiful table of the Jews. Notice how Jesus reversed the rewards in the next life. The beggar (the Gentile) goes to Heaven, but the rich man (the Jew) is sent to hell. From hell the rich man cries out for relief to Abraham, the exalted grandfather of Israel who was residing in Heaven. Abraham explains that justice is being served and the time had come for the poor to be blessed and the rich to suffer. When the rich man realizes his fate, he wants to warn his brothers about hell, but Abraham refuses to release Lazarus (the Gentile) from Heaven to help them. Abraham rebukes the rich man (the Jew) in hell saying, **"Your brothers have Moses and the Prophets** [the Scriptures]**; let them listen to them."** But, the rich man pleads, **"If someone** [like Lazarus is resurrected] **from the dead** [and he] **goes to them** [the Jews]**, they will repent."** (Luke 16:29,30)

By using theological issues that were common points of contention, Jesus had the crowd's full attention with this story. Knowing that the Pharisees and Sadducees were ready to start debating His words, Jesus concluded the story in a way that left no debate! Jesus said, **"If they** [the Jews] **do not listen to Moses and the Prophets** [the Scriptures, Luke 24:27], **they will not be convinced even if someone rises from the dead."** In one sentence Jesus obliquely predicted His rejection. This was (and is) a point that many people fail to grasp. Unless the Holy Spirit dwells within the human heart, it is impossible for religious people to change their minds about truth. Even after Jesus arose from the dead and appeared before more than 500 people (1 Corinthians 15:6), the Jewish nation refused to admit that He was alive. This story is an illustration masterfully told. The specifics of this parable do not harmonize with a host of other Scriptures on this topic, therefore it is fair to conclude that the objective of this parable is an illustration concerning Israel's rejection of Jesus. Jesus often spoke figuratively and this story is no exception. Jesus said, **"Though I have been speaking figuratively, a time is coming when I will no longer use this kind of language but will tell you plainly about my Father."** (John 16:25)

Do Dead Souls Talk Back?

The concept of dead people living in Heaven or hell after they die opens a door for communication with the dead. God expressly forbids any communication with the dead. (Leviticus 19:31; 20:6; Deuteronomy 18:10,11; Isaiah 8:19) The reason is simple. The state of man in death is as a sleep; man knows nothing. (Ecclesiastes 9:5,6) Therefore, God forbids any communication with spirits or with the spirits of the deceased because demons can masquerade as deceased people. When a person communicates first hand with a loved one that is deceased, the power of deception is as good as it gets. Demons know us well. Because they observe and study our behavior, demons can speak about personal matters that are surprisingly accurate and true. Their sole objective is to lead us into rebellion against God.

A few years ago, a lady I know began communicating with her deceased mother through a medium. At first, she was skeptical that communication with her deceased mother was even possible. However, depressed and lonely for her mother's company, she decided to give it a try. During the seance she asked a question that only her mother could correctly answer. When the voice speaking through the medium gave the correct answer, she was overwhelmed with the thought that she was truly in her mother's presence. Do not be like Eve and underestimate the power of demonic deception. I have found that once a person communicates with a deceased loved one, Scripture no longer seems convincing. The delusion is that powerful! People who communicate with spirits or "channel" for spirits have real encounters. The experience is just as real as two people speaking to each other. King Saul visited the witch of Endor and he had a real encounter with a demon that pretended to be Samuel! So, beware of demons. They can and do talk back! (See 1 Samuel 28 and Matthew 8:28-34.)

Sometimes, the following text is used as Bible proof that communicating with the dead is possible. At first glance, this text seems to indicate that the souls of martyrs talk with God and He responds. **"When he opened the fifth seal, I saw under the altar the souls of those who had been slain because of the word of God and the testimony they had maintained. They called out in a loud voice, 'How long, Sovereign Lord, holy and true, until you judge the inhabitants of the earth and avenge our blood?' Then each of them was given a white robe, and they were told to wait a little longer, until the number of their fellow servants and brothers who were to be killed as they had been was completed."** (Revelation 6:9-11)

Bible writers occasionally use a literary device called personification to make a point. Personification is a literary technique for giving something inanimate a lifelike quality, so that the object speaks and acts as though it were alive. For example, when Cain killed Abel, God spoke to Cain saying, **" . . . What have you done? Listen! Your brother's blood cries out to me from the ground."** (Genesis 4:10) Abel's blood did not literally "cry out" to God for justice. Instead, God used this form of personification to emphasize that Abel's death required justice. God demanded an answer from Cain for what he had done. The shedding of innocent blood always "cries out" for justice and eventually, God's vengeance will be served and restitution will be extracted for every wrongful death. (Jeremiah 19)

John also uses personification to convey the largest possible story with the fewest words. In Revelation 6:9-11 the blood of innocent martyrs "cries out" to God for justice, asking Him to end the senseless martyrdom occurring during the Great Tribulation. God responds by telling the martyrs to be patient. Jesus knows what He is doing. He has a larger purpose in mind and His plan must be accomplished first. He assures the martyrs of salvation and tells them to wait for His plan to be fulfilled. The martyrs are given white robes which indicate they are sealed with the righteousness of Christ. (Compare Revelation 2:10, 3:5; John 6:39; Matthew 16:25; Revelation 22:12.)

When the martyrdom of the fifth seal actually begins, the words of Revelation 6 will become very comforting to the saints. Even as the saints cry out to God for help, He has already assured them with the message written in Revelation 6:9-11. This text also reveals that there is a greater purpose that needs to be accomplished before martyrdom comes to an end. As people witness the faithfulness of the martyrs, there will be some who will finally surrender their rebellion against God. Christian history proves that no argument is more powerful or persuasive than the blood of martyrs who willingly lay down their lives for the cause of Christ.

What About Forever and Ever?

Here is another difficult Bible text: "**. . . If anyone worships the beast and his image and receives his mark on the forehead or on the hand, he, too, will drink of the wine of God's fury, which has been poured full strength into the cup of his wrath. He will be tormented with burning sulfur in the presence of the holy angels and of the Lamb. And the smoke of their torment rises for ever and ever. There is no rest day or night for those who worship the beast and his image, or for anyone who receives the mark of his name.**" (Revelation 14:9-11) This text does not mean the wicked are burning forever and ever. Revelation 20:9 states that the wicked are "devoured" at the end of the millennium. The purpose of hell fire is not eternal torment. I believe God has chosen to use fire at the end of the 1,000 years for three reasons: restitution, penalty and purification! The wicked will suffer proportionately to the deeds they refused to make right (restitution). The wicked will be put to death by fire (the penalty for sin is death by execution). Sin and its horrible consequences will be destroyed in the lake of fire and the cancer of sin will cease to exist (purification). **"Whatever they plot against the Lord he will bring to an end; trouble [sin] will not come a second time."** (Nahum 1:9, insertion mine.) After Jesus purifies Earth with fire, He will create a new Heaven and a new Earth. John says, **"Then I saw a new heaven and a new earth, for the first heaven and the first earth had passed away, and there was no longer any sea."** (Revelation 21:1) The smoke rising from the destruction of the wicked and the purification of the world ascends upward forever and ever – *just like ordinary smoke does today.*

What About Night and Day?

Let us go back to Revelation 14:10,11 and notice something else. The wicked: "**. . . will be tormented with burning sulfur in the presence of**

the holy angels and of the Lamb. And the smoke of their torment rises
for ever and ever. There is no rest day or night for those who worship
the beast and his image, or for anyone who receives the mark of his
name." The issue we need to understand in this text concerns the lack of
rest – day or night. Look again at the verse: "There is no rest day or
night for those who worship the beast and his image, or for anyone
who receives the mark of his name." (Revelation 14:11) Some people
use these words to indicate the wicked writhe in the flames of hell day and
night for ever and ever. These words, however, are not describing the
experience of the wicked at the end of the 1,000 years. These words are
describing the experience of the wicked *during* the Great Tribulation! This
verse reveals the intensity of the work the Holy Spirit does during the Great
Tribulation. When the 144,000 powerfully present the gospel to everyone,
people who refuse the gospel will ultimately have no choice but to submit
to the devil (the Antichrist). Those who submit to the demands of the devil
will not only violate their conscience; they will emotionally wrestle with
every effort the Holy Spirit puts forth. The Holy Spirit will vigorously disturb
every soul who persists in rebellion in an attempt to persuade them to
submit to God's authority. (Joel 2:28-32) This is why Revelation 14:11 says,
"There is no rest day or night for those who worship the beast and his
image, or for anyone who receives the mark of his name." Guilt-ridden
and stubborn in their rebellion against God, they will not have peace day or
night because the Holy Spirit will not give up on them until God's offer of
salvation is terminated at the seventh trumpet. (See Revelation 10:7;
11:15-19; John 16:8-11.) Eventually, they will no longer hear the Holy Spirit
prompting their conscience and the wicked will cooperate with the
Antichrist's forces to kill and torture the saints.

What About the Thief on the Cross?

"Then he said, 'Jesus, remember me when you come into your kingdom.' Jesus answered him, 'I tell you the truth, today you will be with
me in paradise.' " (Luke 23:42,43) The Bible indicates that Jesus did not
go to Heaven the day He died. Instead, He ascended to the Father on
Sunday morning. (John 20:17) The original Greek in the New Testament
does not use commas, and the punctuation inserted by translators to make
reading easier can be misleading. One simple misplaced comma can make
the words of Jesus appear to mean something He did not say. Notice how
a comma can change the meaning in the following sentence: "I tell you the
truth today, you will be with me in paradise." This punctuation appears
to be correct since it is supported by the weight of biblical evidence.

Tormented Day and Night Forever

We will examine one last text in Revelation: **"And the devil, who deceived them, was thrown into the lake of burning sulfur, where the beast and the false prophet had been thrown. They will be tormented day and night for ever and ever."** (Revelation 20:10)

If we separate this verse from all other Scripture, it would be easy to conclude that God will throw people into the lake of fire at the end of the millennium and torment them day and night forever and ever. If we ignore the presence of numerous texts and exclusively use this text, the concept of an eternally burning hell could be defended. However, sincere Bible students know that fundamental doctrines require broad support from many Bible writers. More importantly, there has to be harmony from the sum of *all the parts*. Let the entire Bible speak and then weigh the evidence!

If we reconcile all that the Bible has to say on the subject of death and the resurrections, we will find a harmonious solution to John's statement in Revelation 20:10. John says that the wicked will be tormented day and night, forever and ever, which means they will be tormented as long as they exist. Apparently, the burning process (the restitution process) takes longer for some people than others. In other words, people who have been extremely wicked will suffer longer according to their deeds. This means that Satan will burn the longest! (Exodus 22:9; 2 Corinthians 5:10; Revelation 14:10) Remember, the saints will determine the amount of restitution! Jesus told his disciples: " . . . **I tell you the truth, at the renewal of all things, when the Son of Man sits on His glorious throne, you who have followed me will also sit on twelve thrones, judging the twelve tribes of Israel."** (Matthew 19:28) **"Do you not know that the saints will judge the world? . . . Do you not know that we will judge angels?"** (1 Corinthians 6:2,3)

You may be surprised to learn that the biblical use of the word "forever" does not necessarily mean throughout endless ages of eternity. Consider how the word "forever" is used in this text, **"[King] Achish trusted David and said to himself, 'He has become so odious to his people, the Israelites, that he will be my servant forever.' "** (1 Samuel 27:12) This verse does not mean that David was to be a servant to King Achish for eternity. Instead, Achish wanted David to be his servant for as long as he lived. In a similar way, the marriage vow ends at death – "until death do us part" – because forever can only be possible as long as both people in the marriage exist. The torment of justice described in Revelation 20:10 lasts until God's vengeance is satisfied. When sin and sinners are finally destroyed, death and sorrow will be history. **"When the perishable has been** clothed with the imperishable, and the mortal with immortality, then the saying that is written will come true: 'Death has been swallowed up in victory. Where, O death, is your victory? Where, O death, is your sting?' " (1 Corinthians 15:54,55)

Without the Resurrections – We Are Dust

For me, the book of Revelation clarifies the subject of death as it describes the judgment process. Since the subject of death involves a number of prophetic issues that are not covered in this book, perhaps a "big picture" scenario might be helpful. The following is a brief overview of how death, the judgment of the dead and living, the two resurrections and the destruction of the wicked with fire harmonizes with Bible prophecy:

The judgment of mankind has two phases: The judgment of the dead and the judgment of the living. The judgment of the dead involves a close review of each person's history as recorded by angels. (Malachi 3:16) Jesus makes a determination on each person for eternal life or eternal death on the basis of this record. (Daniel 7:9,10; John 5:22, 2 Corinthians 5:10) The first person to be judged was Abel because he was the first to die. During the Great Tribulation, the living will make choices which will indicate their faith or lack of faith in Jesus. The "mark of the beast test" will ultimately separate the wicked living from the righteous living. (Revelation 3:10) Our eternal destiny will have been determined by the time Jesus returns to Earth at the Second Coming. (Revelation 22:12) This may seem obvious, but it is a crucial point. When Jesus returns, people like Abel, who are a part of the righteous dead, will be called to life (resurrected) and they will rise up out of their graves to meet Jesus in the air. (John 6:39,40) This is the first resurrection. Then, Paul says the righteous living will join with the righteous dead to meet the Lord in the air. (1 Thessalonians 4:16,17)

The wicked who have died through the ages, like Cain, are not resurrected at the Second Coming. In fact, the Bible states that Jesus slays the wicked who are alive on Earth at the time of His appearing. (Revelation 19:15-21) The net effect is that the wicked, from Cain to those living at the time of the Second Coming, sleep on until the 1,000 years in Revelation 20 have ended. During the millennium, Earth will be left desolate because Jesus takes the saints to the Holy City which is in Heaven for "The Feast of Ingathering!" The devil remains on Earth with no one to deceive during the millennium. Meanwhile, the saints are in Heaven and they will review the records of the wicked. They will satisfy themselves that the eternal decision which Jesus made on every person was fair and appropriate. The saints will also judge the wicked by determining the appropriate restitution that each wicked person must suffer after they are resurrected. (1 Corinthians 6:2,3)

At the end of the 1,000 years, the Holy City will descend to Earth with the saints inside. After the Holy City rests on Earth, Jesus will resurrect the wicked. This is the second resurrection. Every wicked person who ever lived on Earth will see the reality of God. Think about it; every person will meet his or her Maker! Everyone who has ever lived will see the Holy City, the saints, the devil and his angels. With one last blast of lies and fury, Satan incites a great multitude of wicked people to attack the City of God (Revelation 20:7-8), but Jesus suspends the attack with the same authority He calmed the angry Sea of Galilee. Jesus turns the tumult of battle into silence so that He can present the facts to the wicked. Jesus will reveal to each wicked person why He could not save him or her. He will also declare the verdict of the saints indicating how much restitution will be extracted before death in the lake of fire. After the truth has been presented and the wicked see how fair and just Jesus has been, every wicked person will bow before Jesus Christ admitting that God is fair and His judgment is righteous. (Isaiah 45:23,24; Romans 14:11,12; Philippians 12:10) As the realization sets in about the outcome of their life decisions, the wicked become overwrought by their sense of loss, fear and loathing disgust. In an effort to avoid the suffering God has imposed upon them, they try to kill themselves. God initiates the executive phase of judgment by calling fire down from Heaven and ultimately, God burns up the wicked and every trace of sin is gone. (Revelation 20:9,15)

Missing Heaven Will be Hell

This chapter may not fully resolve the question of an eternally burning hell for the reader. However, the weight of evidence throughout the Bible must be considered if we are to properly understand what God is doing. One thing is certain, God is love. Because His love is great and everlasting, we want to spend eternity with Him. His government is fair and His mercy is overwhelming! God's truths are too wonderful to describe and His peace too deep to explain. Missing Heaven after realizing all that God offers – will be hell. In summary, ponder the following statements:

1. The wages of sin is eternal death, not eternal life in the torture of hell.

2. There are two deaths, the first is temporary and it is called "sleep," the second death occurs at the end of the 1,000 years and is eternal.

3. There are two resurrections, the first one is for the righteous and occurs at the Second Coming. The second resurrection is for the wicked and occurs at the end of the 1,000 years.

4. A soul is formed when the body and the breath of life are united. A soul ceases to exist when the breath of life is separated from the body. Regardless of behavior, the spirit or breath of life returns to God when a person dies.

5. The soul of man is not an immortal entity. The soul that sins will die.

6. The parable of the rich man and the beggar is an object lesson. The object lesson of the parable is stated in the parable.

7. God forbids any communication with the dead because such communication is with demons. The dead know nothing.

8. God is fair. His punishment is commensurate with the crime. Jesus did not suffer eternal torture in hell and neither will the wicked. Eternal torture is not fair.

9. God has appointed a time for the judgment of human beings. With the exception of a few people taken to Heaven "on a credit card" (Enoch, Elijah, Moses, the 24 elders, etc.), human beings do not receive their eternal reward at the time of death. We must wait until either the resurrection at the Second Coming or the resurrection at the end of the 1,000 years.

10. No one can be in hell at this time because the second death (the penalty for sin) is not implemented until the end of the 1,000 years.

Chapter 14
Which is Next – the Rapture or the Second Coming?

Two men will be in the field; one will be taken and the other left. Two women will be grinding with a hand mill; one will be taken and the other left. Therefore keep watch, because you do not know on what day your Lord will come.

– Matthew 24:40-42

There are six apocalyptic prophecies in the book of Daniel and they "stack" on top of each other much like the layers of a wedding cake. Each prophecy has a beginning and ending point in time and each prophecy contains an orderly sequence of events. For example, Daniel 2 is the bottom layer or "foundation" prophecy and its time-span reaches from 600 B.C. to the Second Coming. The second apocalyptic prophecy (Daniel 7) stacks on top of Daniel 2 and covers the same time-span as Daniel 2. The third prophecy or layer starts around 538 B.C. and reaches to the Second Coming. The fourth prophecy begins in 457 B.C. and ends with A.D. 33, etc. By layering the prophecies of Daniel on top of each other, God eliminated several problems before they even began! First, when we examine these six layers, a large amount of information unfolds that is otherwise unknown. By linking the six layers together with prophetic events, God says a great deal with the fewest possible words. This is an important consideration because books of the Old Testament were duplicated by hand for almost 3,000 years. Second, by layering the prophecies on top of each other, God implemented a process which scholars call repetition and enlargement. It allows the Bible student to confidently arrange and define all the prophetic elements within each prophecy. As each layer of prophecy is added to the "stack," the underlying layers have to be correctly interpreted and chronologically arranged or the next layer will not make sense. Last, by layering the prophecies, God hid the meaning of these prophecies in the book of Daniel until the time of the end would arrive. (Daniel 12:4,9) I believe God did this so the last generation on Earth could quickly understand the fulfillment of 26 centuries of prophecy. In other words, an ordinary person can now understand the sweeping prophetic progression of 26 centuries with just a few hours of study. Now that the layering of the prophecies has been discovered, people can determine which elements of apocalyptic prophecy are in the past and which are forthcoming! A brief discussion about the six layers in Daniel has been presented because of this statement: "The six prophecies of Daniel do not support the idea of a pre-tribulation or mid-tribulation rapture of the saints."

There are twelve apocalyptic prophecies in the book of Revelation and these also "stack" on top of each other just like the six layers do in the book of Daniel. Even more, the twelve layers of Revelation harmoniously align with the six apocalyptic prophecies in Daniel. When all eighteen prophecies are viewed together, there is one marvelous prophetic story that unfolds in chronological order. All eighteen prophecies are interconnected. Each layer has a starting point in time and an ending point in time, and the events in each prophecy (or layer) occur in the chronological order given. When a person understands how past fulfillments of prophecy conform to this well-defined architecture, it is possible to determine with some certainty the chronological timing within God's prophetic plans. It is important to understand that the chronological layers of Daniel and Revelation do not support a pre-tribulation or mid-tribulation rapture.

When the eighteen layers of apocalyptic prophecy are arranged correctly, the progressive fulfillment of prophecy is confirmed by recorded history. This occurs because apocalyptic prophecy produces a chronological "time-line" showing past, present and future events. A knowledge of this time-line prevents a misapplication of end-time statements that occur throughout the Bible. For example, the opening text for this chapter (Matthew 24:40-42) is often used by proponents of the pre-tribulation rapture to justify a sudden snatching away of people from Earth. There are two problems with this assertion. First, the chronological order of Daniel and Revelation does not support a pre-tribulation rapture and second, the context itself does not mandate a pre-tribulation rapture. If a person has the notion of a pre-tribulation rapture *already in mind*, Matthew 24:40-42 can be presented in a way that makes it appear to support a pre-tribulation rapture. Before a sincere Bible student draws a conclusion, efforts should be made to reconcile many texts that are not in harmony with a pre-tribulation rapture. We need to ask, can we "pick and choose" texts that only favor our notions and ignore those we do not understand or like? Truth is found in the harmony that comes from the sum of all its parts. There is an explanation for Matthew 24:40-42 that harmoniously aligns with the chronological order given in Daniel and Revelation, as well as all the other texts that do not harmonize with the doctrine of a pre-tribulation rapture.

New World Order

The world stands at the door of a great transition. The nations of Earth as we currently know them, are about to undergo a radical change. I am not describing another world order based on political realignment. Political realignment has been an ongoing process ever since nations came into existence. Instead, I am describing the destruction of earthly nations and the creation of a *new world* whose order God will establish. The Bible is the *only* source of truth on this subject and it is the only book that contains a comprehensive roadmap of soon coming events. The Bible is the only authority that speaks for God on this matter. For these reasons, people should carefully consider the prophecies in Daniel and Revelation. The people of Earth need to understand that the Most High God is about to bring this world of sin to an end.

Many people sense that something big is about to happen and indeed, something very big is about to happen. Jesus is going to startle billions of people with an enormous demonstration of divine authority. Confusion, mayhem and extreme suffering will be everywhere and a trustworthy roadmap explaining the forthcoming actions of Jesus will be indispensable. Although the roadmap of Bible prophecy does not reveal a pretty picture for the immediate future, it does provide the light of eternal hope shining through a short, but very dark tunnel. For this reason, the information contained in the Bible should receive our highest attention. After investigating Bible prophecy for many years, I am convinced that whether we agree or disagree with the events described in Bible prophecy, man's opinions do not affect God or His actions. He will do what He has said He will do. What we may believe about God has nothing to do with God's behavior – all that He has predicted will come to pass. Therefore, it is imperative that we approach Bible prophecy from an honest perspective for the purpose of understanding the ways of God. The Father has put Jesus in control of closing events. With this thought in mind, let us consider what the Bible has to say about the Second Coming and the concept of a pre-tribulation rapture.

Views on the Rapture

Protestants basically support one of four views about the gathering of the saints. Many Protestants believe in a pre-tribulation rapture. A smaller, but significant number, believe in a mid-tribulation rapture (e.g., Christians are taken to Heaven midway through the seventieth week of seven years). A third group of Protestants believe in a pre-wrath rapture (e.g., Christians are taken to Heaven just before the outpouring of the seven last plagues). Last, a minority of Protestants believes in a post-tribulation gathering of the saints at the Second Coming. The concept of a rapture (regardless of timing) is a complicated study because so many ideas are involved. In fact, the study of Bible prophecy is a lot like weaving a potholder out of many pieces of colored yarn. Small pieces of yarn are not very strong or important by themselves. However, if a person weaves the yarn together just right, the result can be an attractive and durable potholder. The same is true with the study of prophecy. Eventually, every student of prophecy ends up creating his or her own "prophetic potholder" out of the yarn given to him or her! (Sorry for the pun.) As so often happens, many rush out to assure others about the superiority of their potholder and the weakness of all others. (If this topic was not so serious, I would find this entire process, which also includes my work, to be amusing.) The object of owning a potholder is to keep from getting burned and a parallel can be drawn for a prophetic potholder as well. (Again, sorry for the pun.) Each week I receive multi-paged letters from people who assure me that I am totally wrong because my prophetic potholder could not possibly come from a logical study of God's Word. My standard response (defense?) is that the arrangement of the yarn makes the difference! Be assured, time will confirm all that God has said. *Nothing* but the passage of time can confirm how close or how far we are from rightly interpreting God's Word.

With that said, however, I want you to know right up front that even when I put the chronological order of Daniel and Revelation aside for a moment, there are numerous scriptural reasons why I cannot accept the doctrine of a pre-tribulation rapture. Let me address a few of these issues:

Just One Gathering of the Saints!

Some Christians say the righteous dead do not participate in the pre-tribulation rapture and others say the righteous dead are included. What does the Bible say? When are the righteous dead resurrected? Jesus said, **"And this is the will of him who sent me, that I shall lose none of all that he has given me, but raise them up at the last day. For my Father's will is that everyone who looks to the Son and believes in him shall have eternal life, and I will raise him up at the last day."** (John 6:39,40) When does "the last day" occur? Does it occur at the *beginning* of the 70th week (of seven years)? No! Paul wrote, **"According to the Lord's own word, we tell you that we who are still alive, who are left till the coming of the Lord, will certainly not precede those who have fallen asleep. For the Lord himself will come down from Heaven,** with a loud command, with the voice of the archangel and with the trumpet call of God, and the dead in Christ will rise first. After that, we who are still alive and are left will be caught up together with them in the clouds to meet the Lord in the air. And so we will be with the Lord forever." (1 Thessalonians 4:15-17) These verses contain four important points:

a.   The living do not precede the dead to Heaven.

b.   Jesus Himself will come down from Heaven.

c.   He will call the righteous dead to life with a loud command.

d.   As the dead ascend, the living will join with them to meet Jesus in the air.

Look again at the text. Paul says, **"After that** [e.g., resurrection of the righteous], **we who are still alive and are left will be caught up to meet the Lord in the air."** Some people distort Paul's words to mean, "after that [the rapture], we who are still alive and are left [behind] will be caught up to meet the Lord in the air [later on at the Second Coming]. . . ." But this is not the meaning of Paul's remarks. Consider verse 15 again: **"According to the Lord's own word, we tell you that we who are still alive, who are left till the coming of the Lord, will certainly not precede those who have fallen asleep."** Paul states two things: First, the living *will not precede* the dead to Heaven. The two groups meet the Lord at the same time. Second, Paul refers to individuals who are alive at the coming of the Lord in the sense that "we" [the living] who are *alive when* the Lord appears will unite with the dead to meet Jesus in the air. Paul's idea is quite different from being "left behind after a rapture." Review verses 15-17 and notice Paul's use of the pronoun "we." Why does Paul use the inclusive pronoun "we" in these texts? Paul thought that he, with other living believers ("we"), would live to see Christ appear in the clouds and the dead raised from their graves without experiencing death themselves. (1 Corinthians 7:29,30) Paul did not believe in or teach a pre-Second Coming rapture.

Paul has more to say about the resurrection of the righteous. Notice this text which was written a few years after 1 Thessalonians: **"Listen, I tell you a mystery: *We* will not all sleep, but *we* will all be changed – in a flash, in the twinkling of an eye, at the last trumpet. For the trumpet will sound, the dead will be raised imperishable, and *we* will be changed."** (1 Corinthians 15:51,52, italics mine.) Did you notice that the Apostle Paul uses the inclusive pronoun "we" three times in this text? He used the third person plural pronoun *"we"* because he believed that he would live to see Jesus return. Of course, Paul had no idea time would last 2,000 more years.

On the basis of what we have read, the Bible teaches there is one gathering of the saints, both the dead and the living, at the last day. This fact proves the rapture doctrine to be deficient because it requires two gatherings of the saints, one gathering at the beginning of the 70th week and one gathering at the Second Coming.

When Does the Judgment Occur?

A pre-trib rapture *mandates* a pre-trib judgment *before* the rapture can take place because Jesus has to decide who can be raptured and who cannot. The fact that Jesus judges the people of Earth *before* the Second Coming is well supported in Scripture, but no scriptural support exists for a judgment of *the living before* the Great Tribulation begins. In fact, I find the opposite to be true. One of the primary purposes of the Great Tribulation is to judge the living. (Revelation 3:10) The contest between obeying God and observing His Ten Commandments versus obeying the Antichrist (the devil) and receiving his mark will separate the people of Earth into one of two camps. Notice what Jesus says about the Second Coming: **"When the Son of Man comes in his glory, and all the angels with him, he will sit on his throne in heavenly glory. All the nations will be gathered before him, and he will separate the people one from another as a shepherd separates the sheep from the goats. He will put the sheep on his right and the goats on his left . . . "Then he will say to those on his left, 'Depart from me, you who are cursed, into the eternal fire prepared for the devil and his angels. For I was hungry and you gave me nothing to eat, I was thirsty and you gave me nothing to drink, I was a stranger and you did not invite me in, I needed clothes and you did not clothe me, I was sick and in prison and you did not look after me.' "They also will answer, 'Lord, when did we see you hungry or thirsty or a stranger or needing clothes or sick or in prison, and did not help you?' "He will reply, 'I tell you the truth, whatever you did not do for one of the least of these, you did not do for me.' Then they will go away to eternal punishment, but the righteous to eternal life."** (Matthew 25:31-46)

Jesus clearly establishes *when* the sheep are separated from the goats. This happens, Jesus said, **"When the Son of Man comes in his glory . . . All the nations will be gathered before him, and he will separate the people one from another. They** [the wicked] **will go away to eternal**

punishment, but the righteous to eternal life." In this text, Jesus describes the scene that occurs on the last day, the day when the eternal reward is given. Nothing is said about gathering up His sheep *before* the Second Coming. Nothing is said about granting eternal life to millions of people seven years before the Second Coming.

Notice these verses: **"He [Jesus] answered, 'The one who sowed the good seed is the Son of Man. The field is the world, and the good seed stands for the sons of the kingdom. The weeds are the sons of the evil one, and the enemy who sows them is the devil. The harvest is the end of the age, and the harvesters are angels. As the weeds are pulled up and burned in the fire, so it will be at the end of the age. The Son of Man will send out his angels, and they will weed out of his kingdom everything that causes sin and all who do evil. They will throw them into the fiery furnace, where there will be weeping and gnashing of teeth. Then the righteous will shine like the sun in the kingdom of their Father. He who has ears, let him hear.' "** (Matthew 13:37-43) These verses conflict with the notion of a pre-trib rapture. The harvest is the end of the age and we know from an earlier verse (verse 30) that the weeds (the wicked) and the good seed (the righteous) grow *together* until the time of the harvest. When the Son of Man sends His angels, they will gather up the good seed and throw the weeds into the fiery furnace. Nothing is said about sparing the weeds for seven more years after the good seed is taken up to Heaven.

[Jesus said] **"As for the person who hears my words but does not keep them, I do not judge him. For I did not come** [this time] **to judge the world, but to save it. There is a judge for the one who rejects me and does not accept my words; that very word which I spoke will condemn him at *the last day*."** (John 12:47-48, insertion mine.)

This may seem strange, but "the last day" issue rises again. Jesus makes an interesting point about *the last day* in these verses. From earlier study we know that "the last day" occurs at the Second Coming. Therefore, no one *actually knows* whether he or she is saved or condemned until the Second Coming or the last day. Keep in mind that I am writing of *knowing*, not about believing. A person may believe he or she is saved or even lost, but faith is not the same thing as knowledge. Hebrews 11:1 (KJV) says, **"Now faith is the substance of things *hoped* for, the evidence of things not seen . . . ."** Knowledge, on the other hand, is a matter of fact. This is why the tree in Genesis was called "the *knowledge* of good and evil." Humankind had no knowledge of sin until sin occurred. God gave instructions about sin (Genesis 2:17) and Adam and Eve knew that sin could occur, but they did not know what sin was. However, once sin was experienced, it became a matter of fact. The point in John 12 is timing: According to Jesus, no one will *know* whether he or she is saved or condemned until the last day which occurs when the righteous are resurrected. Righteous people cannot be raptured to Heaven (saved), if the rest of the living have not been condemned to death yet! According to the words of Jesus in John 12:47,48, everyone left behind after a rapture would be condemned to eternal death. Notice what Jesus said about His appearing: **"Behold, I am coming soon! My reward is with me, and I will give to everyone according to what he has done . . . Blessed are those who wash their robes, that they may have the right to the tree of life and may go through the gates into the city. Outside are the dogs, those who practice magic arts, the sexually immoral, the murderers, the idolaters and everyone who loves and practices falsehood."** (Revelation 22:12-15)

John 12 and Revelation 22 are in perfect harmony. When Jesus returns, His reward of salvation or condemnation *is with* Him. When He arrives, all people will have been judged according to their deeds (works, KJV) and Jesus Himself will physically distribute everyone's reward at His appearing. Jesus will execute the condemned (the goats, or the wicked) by a single command (the sharp sword that comes out of His mouth). (2 Thessalonians 2:8; Revelation 19:21) The righteous dead will come to life and rise from the Earth upon command (Revelation 1:18), and the righteous living will join the resurrected saints and "fly away" to meet the Lord *in the air* "at the last day. (1 Thessalonians 4:16)

The Bible teaches that the judgment of man takes place *before* rewards are handed out at the last day: **"Now all has been heard; here is the conclusion of the matter: Fear God and keep his commandments, for this is the whole duty of man. For God will bring every deed into judgment, including every hidden thing, whether it is good or evil."** (Ecclesiastes 12:13-14)

This verse confirms that God will "pass over" or judge each person that lives on the face of the Earth. He will review every deed during the judgment process and make a determination regarding each person, whether for salvation or condemnation. If a person lives by faith, then his or her deeds or works will confirm his or her faith. (James 2:17) This is why we are judged by our works. Notice this confirming verse: **"For we must all appear before the judgment seat of Christ, that each one may receive what is due him for the things done while in the body, whether good or bad."** (2 Corinthians 5:10)

Did you notice that Paul uses the inclusive pronoun again? **"For *we* must all appear. . . ."** Paul knew that he too must stand before the judgment seat of Christ. So *everyone*, good and bad, including Protestants believing in a pre-trib rapture, has to stand before the judgment seat of Christ. The judgment of the *living* occurs during the Great Tribulation. God is going to test the faith and loyalty of the living with tribulation! (Revelation 3:10) In fact, this is why God permits the worldwide mark of the beast test to be established – to see who will obey Him and live by faith, even to the point of death.

The Church at Philadelphia

"Since you have kept my command to endure patiently, I will also keep you from *the hour of trial* that is going to come upon *the whole world to test* those *who live* on the earth." (Revelation 3:10, italics mine.) This text is often used by pre-trib rapture believers to defend their escape from the Great Tribulation. So, let us carefully examine this text and its context. To be fair, if the Bible had one verse in it, and this was its only verse, I could be persuaded that the Bible supported the idea that the saints will escape the hour of trial that is coming upon the whole world. However, when compared with everything the Bible has to say about the end-time, this verse does not actually say what it is purported to say. This verse was directed to the church at Philadelphia. So, we need to ask, will the church at Philadelphia be *the only* church to escape the hour of trial that is going to come upon the whole world? I do not believe this to be true. There are six more churches in Revelation, and we need to discover what happens to them during the Great Tribulation.

Review Revelation 3:10 and observe these two points: First, Jesus says an hour of trial is going to come upon the whole world *to test the living*. For reasons beyond the scope of this study, I agree with pre-trib rapture believers that the Great Tribulation is imminently before us! I believe this verse points to a final tribulation that has no equal in world history. (Matthew 24:21; Daniel 12:1,2) When a person first reads this text it may appear that the church of Philadelphia (Revelation 3:7) will be kept *from* experiencing the hour of trial, that is, they will escape this testing time. Unfortunately, many Christians have come to regard this verse as proof that Christians will escape the suffering that will overcome the world during the Tribulation. Actually, this verse does not teach that Christians will be taken to Heaven before the Tribulation begins, but instead indicates that believers will be sustained *beginning from* (Greek word 'ek) the hour of trial until Jesus appears.

One of the world's best lexicons on early Christian use of the Greek language is *A Greek Lexicon of the New Testament* (Bauer, Arndt and Gingrich, 1952, Fourth Ed.). The word in question is the Greek preposition *'ek* and it is translated "from" both in the NIV and KJV. Therefore, the phrase reads, "**. . . I will keep you *from* the hour of trial . . .**" However, this tiny preposition is also translated in a variety of other ways in both versions of the Bible and has more than a dozen different English equivalents in meaning. For example, *'ek* can mean "from, out of, away from, coming out of, descending from, by, because of, beginning from, begins from, for," etc. On page 235 of this lexicon, the authors indicate that when the preposition is followed by a measurement of time – as in "the hour of trial," *'ek* can convey the meaning "beginning from." In other words, a person is justified in reading this verse as follows: "I [Jesus] will also keep you *beginning from* the hour of trial that is going to come upon the whole world. . . ."

When one word, especially a preposition, determines the meaning of a pivotal verse, we must be very careful in our research. We can and should turn to additional lexicons and other word study helps for insight. Although this effort may be valuable, it is not the highest authority regarding the intended meaning of the verse. Higher and more weighty evidence must come from the Bible itself. So, here are three points for your consideration about why this verse should be understood as *"beginning from* the hour of trial":

a. Jesus told His disciples, "**. . . And surely I am with you always, to the very end of the age [world (KJV)].**" (Matthew 28:20) This verse should be taken at face value. Jesus plainly said He will be with His children to the very last day when He physically and gloriously appears in the clouds. This idea concurs with Revelation 3:10: "I [Jesus] will also keep you *beginning from* the hour of trial that is going to come upon the whole world. . . ."

b. Several verses in Revelation indicate that the saints are on Earth during the Great Tribulation. The word "saints" is mentioned twelve times in Revelation (NIV) and thirteen times in the KJV. Except for the 144,000 servants who are taken to Heaven after the seven trumpets end and the 24 elders who were taken to Heaven at the time of Christ's ascension, Revelation does not place the *living* saints in Heaven before the Second Coming. In fact, Revelation places the saints on Earth! Notice what happens to the saints in these verses: "**Then the dragon was enraged at the woman and went off to make war against the rest [the remnant, (KJV)] of her offspring – those who obey God's commandments and hold to the testimony of Jesus . . . He [the beast] was given power to make war against the *saints* and to**

---

conquer them. And he was given authority over every tribe, people, language and nation . . . If anyone is to go into captivity, into captivity he will go. If anyone is to be killed with the sword, with the sword he will be killed. This calls for patient endurance and faithfulness on the part of the *saints* . . . ." (Revelation 12:17; 13:7; 13:10, italics mine.)

I do not find support in Scripture for the idea that some saints are enjoying the bliss of Heaven while others are living through a hellish tribulation on Earth. Instead, the purpose of the Great Tribulation is to test those people who live on Earth and to expose who the saints really are! Revelation 14:12 confirms the saints will suffer because they obey God. John says, **"This calls for patient endurance on the part of the saints who** [suffer because they] **obey God's commandments and remain faithful to Jesus."** The point is that Revelation clearly puts the saints on Earth during the Great Tribulation. Therefore, Revelation 3:10 should read, "I [Jesus] will also keep you *beginning from* the hour of trial that is going to come upon the whole world. . . ."

c. Let us review the comments of Jesus to all seven churches. The meaning of Revelation 3:10 will become clearer when placed within its larger context. Does Jesus intend to honor the people in the church at Philadelphia with a pre-trib rapture and punish the other six churches by putting them through the Great Tribulation? Besides, who belongs to the church of Philadelphia today? How can we tell? Study the chart on the following page to see what Jesus says to each church.

I regard the seven messages to the seven churches as local and timely messages. This means that when these messages were given in A.D. 95, they were directed at seven specific churches that existed in John's day. Therefore, we have to understand these messages within their local situation, their day and time. (Similarly, we have to treat the epistles of Paul to the Thessalonians in the same manner.)

To appreciate the meaning of these messages, put on John's sandals and stand where he stood. I do not find any justification from Scripture revealing that the seven churches represent seven phases of historical development within the Christian church over the past 2,000 years as some people claim. Neither do I find the message given to the first century church of Philadelphia uniquely applicable to those people who believe in a pre-trib rapture *today*. I do find these seven churches in Asia Minor to be typical of Christians during all ages. Therefore, the messages should not be promoted as apocalyptic prophecy, but as warning and edifying messages for all Christian churches. Jesus sent timely messages to seven Christian

Church	Item	Censure	Reward
Ephesus	You've lost your first love for the gospel	The removal of your lampstand	Overcomers will have the right to eat from the tree of life
Smyrna	You're about to suffer persecution for ten days	None	Overcomers will not be frightened by the second death
Pergamum	You're eating food offered to idols and sexual immorality	I'll destroy you with the sword that comes out of my mouth	Overcomers will receive hidden manna and a white stone
Thyatira	You're eating food offered to idols and sexual immorality	I'll fully repay you according to your evil deeds	Overcomers will be given authority over the nations
Sardis	Your deeds indicate you are alive but you are spiritually dead	Wake up or I will come upon you like a thief	Overcomers will never be blotted out of the Book of Life
Philadelphia	You are weak, but you have been loyal and faithful to me	None	Overcomers will be pillars in the temple of my God
Laodicea	You're compromising and lukewarm	I'm about to spew you out of my mouth	Overcomers will sit with me on my throne

churches that had problems in John's day, so that Christians everywhere could see that Jesus closely observes those people who proclaim His Name. (Incidently, more than seven Christian churches existed in John's day, but Jesus chose these seven because their corporate behavior represented Christian churches everywhere. The number seven is often used as a number of "completeness" and therefore, *seven* messages to *seven* churches suggest Jesus' comprehensive analysis of Christian behavior.)

Specific to Smyrna

Notice how the message to Smyrna is limited to their time-period and locale: **"Do not be afraid of what you are about to suffer. I tell you, the devil will put some of you in prison to test you, and you will suffer persecution for ten days. Be faithful, even to the point of death, and I will give you the crown of life."** (Revelation 2:10) The ten days of persecution and the circumstances remain a mystery today. However, the essential question we should ask is why would Jesus allow those people in this church to suffer, even to the point of death, yet spare members in the church at Philadelphia from the Great Tribulation? Today, if some people belong to the church of Philadelphia, who belongs to the church of Smyrna? If we apply the same interpretative logic in Revelation 2:10 as pre-trib believers do in Revelation 3:10, then who would want to belong to the church of Smyrna?

Specific to Philadelphia

In A.D. 95, Christians were suffering oppression from both the Romans and the Jews. All who accepted Jesus Christ as the Son of God were severely persecuted. The Jews hated the Christians because Christians proclaimed all over the world that Judaism was a false religion. The Romans hated the Christians because Christians would not worship the man-god, Caesar. The church at Philadelphia had suffered great losses. John himself was on the isle of Patmos because his loyalty to Jesus prevented him from submitting to the demands of Rome. It was not a good time to be a Christian. Notice how tenderly Jesus spoke to the suffering people in Philadelphia: **"Since you have kept my command to endure patiently, I will also keep you from the hour of trial that is going to come upon the whole world to test those who live on the earth."** (Revelation 3:10) In effect, Jesus was commending that local church for their patient endurance because they had suffered for the gospel. He further assured them that He would continue to sustain them during the hour of trial that was coming upon the whole world (not just their city). No doubt, the Philadelphians were wondering how they could continue to endure additional suffering on a longer or even larger scale. No doubt they knew about the predicted Great Tribulation mentioned in Daniel, Matthew and Luke, but like us, they did not know exactly when it would begin. No doubt, they were asking themselves how things could be any worse! I am sure they took the words of Jesus to mean: Hang on! I will continue to sustain you during the hour of trial that will come upon the Earth to test the whole world.

Summary on Revelation 3:10

Tradition teaches that nine or ten of Christ's disciples were martyrs for their faith. History confirms that millions died for their faith during the Dark Ages. If this is true, then we need to ask ourselves why born again Christians living today, out of all generations, should be spared from the Great

Tribulation? Further, the use of Revelation 3:10 to support a pre-trib rapture of the entire Christian church is simply not justified when we consider the following issues: the timing surrounding the resurrection of the dead, the judgment of the living, the many uses of the Greek preposition 'ek, Jesus' promise to be with His disciples until the very end of the age, the earthly location of the saints during the Great Tribulation mentioned in Revelation, and the messages given to the seven churches that were timely and local (especially as related to the church of Philadelphia).

The Rapture Doctrine is Not a Testing Doctrine!

I have a problem with those individuals who make the pre-trib rapture a testing doctrine. Many Protestants are threatened with eternal loss if they refuse to believe in a pre-trib rapture. Some people say that if you do not believe in the rapture, you cannot be saved *after* it happens – there is no second chance. This is interesting, since this position stands in opposition to the basic premise of the pre-trib rapture. Pre-trib advocates teach that sinners will have seven more years (the 70th week) to "get right" with the Lord. So, condemnation for rejecting the rapture has no scriptural support. When did the rapture doctrine become a testing truth for salvation and who had the authority to establish this test?

The Bible identifies one unpardonable sin (Matthew 12:31,32) and that sin is not the denial of a pre-trib rapture. This type of threat regarding eternal loss is a form of manipulation. Doctrines that trap and hold uninformed people in a prison of toxic faith should be openly refuted. We are not living in the Dark Ages. In most countries today, anyone who wants to own and read a Bible can easily obtain one. As you may surmise, I give no credence to the concept that a person could be lost simply by refusing to believe the doctrine of the rapture. On the contrary, we receive the assurance of salvation (1 John 5:12) when we surrender our life to Jesus Christ as Lord and Master. He is my Shepherd (Psalm 23). He guides me into all truth through the ministry of the Holy Spirit! (John 16:13) *I do not trust any pastor, priest or rabbi to tell me what I must believe or what I must do in order to be saved. My duty is to listen to the Holy Spirit.* (John 3:8) He brings enlightenment and conviction as I study God's Word for myself. Yes, I enjoy listening to religious speakers for study and investigation, but when I study, I follow and obey Jesus as the Spirit convicts me. Let no one deceive you in this: Salvation is a personal matter between you and your Savior. (John 14:21-24; Philippians 2:12,13)

"One Will be Taken and the Other Left"

One of the favorite texts used by people who believe in a pre-Second Coming rapture is found in Matthew 24:40-42. Jesus said, **"Two men will be in the field; one will be taken and the other left. Two women will be grinding with a hand mill; one will be taken and the other left. 'Therefore keep watch, because you do not know on what day your Lord will come.' "**

This verse understandably makes many people nervous. It seems to suggest that the appearing of Jesus will be a sudden and totally unexpected event. On the surface these verses appear to say that two people will be working side by side and poof – one person is taken and the other is left. Sometimes people who support the pre-trib rapture use these verses to make a sharp distinction between a sudden, "thief in the night" kind of gathering of the saints, and the glorious resurrection/ascension of the remaining saints mentioned in 1 Thessalonians 4:16 and Revelation 1:7. Do these verses really teach a secret gathering of the saints before the Second Coming? This is only possible if the context in which these words were spoken is totally ignored. So, let us take a close look at the context of these comments:

The setting for Matthew 24 begins as Jesus is leaving the temple. His disciples caught up with Him and they draw His attention to the magnificent buildings that make up the temple complex. The temple was the pride of the Jews. It was their most sacred religious shrine. Herod had expanded and adorned it with much gold and cedar in an attempt to win the respect and cooperation of the Jews. The Jews believed that God would not allow His "restored" temple to be desecrated again and the disciples wondered when Jesus would establish His throne and rule from His temple. As Jesus looked upon the gleaming walls of the edifice, a deep sadness overcame Him. Then, He uttered this prophecy: **"I tell you the truth, not one stone here will be left on another; every one will be thrown down."** His words, no doubt, stunned the disciples. These were outrageous words! Jesus was predicting something very BIG was going to happen in Jerusalem!

A short time later, while sitting on the Mount of Olives, the disciples came privately to Jesus. Jesus' previous remarks had raised both concern and curiosity within them. **"Tell us,"** they said, **"when will this** [destruction of the temple] **happen, and what will be the sign of your coming and of the end of the age?"** Jesus' response to His disciples is recorded by Matthew and Luke. In both gospels one compelling point surfaces: Jesus consistently speaks of *one* return or *one* coming. He does not allude to a pre-Second Coming rapture. Notice these seven highlights from Matthew 24 (Italics mine.):

a. " . . . he who stands firm *to the end* will be saved." (24:13)

b. ". . . this gospel of the kingdom will be preached in the whole world as a testimony to all nations, and then *the end* will come." (24:14)

c. ". . . as lightning that comes from the east is visible even in the west, so will be *the coming* of the Son of Man." (24:27)

d. "At that time *the sign of the Son of Man will appear in the sky*, and all the nations of the earth will mourn. They will see the Son of Man *coming on the clouds of the sky*, with power and great glory." (24:30)

e. "As it was in the days of Noah, so it will be *at the coming* of the Son of Man." (24:37)

f. ". . . they knew nothing about what would happen until the flood came and took them all away. That is how it will be *at the coming* of the Son of Man." (24:39)

g. "Therefore keep watch, because you do not know on what day your Lord *will come*." (24:42)

These seven statements along with many others within the context of Matthew 24 and 25 are directed at *one* coming of the Son of Man. To insist that Jesus also talks about a pre-trib rapture in two verses is to frustrate everything else He says in the other 95 verses of these two chapters. Consider the immediate context of verses 36-43 where the statement is made, "one will be taken, the other left": **"No one knows about that day or hour, not even the angels in heaven, nor the Son, but only the Father. As it was in the days of Noah, so it will be at the coming of the Son of Man. For in the days before the flood, people were eating and drinking, marrying and giving in marriage, up to the day Noah entered the ark; and they knew nothing about what would happen until the flood came and took them all away. That is how it will be at the coming of the Son of Man. Two men will be in the field; one will be taken and the other left. Two women will be grinding with a hand mill; one will be taken and the other left. Therefore keep watch, because you do not know on what day your Lord will come. But understand this: If the owner of the house had known at what time of night the thief was coming, he would have kept watch and would not have let his house**

be broken into." (Matthew 24:36-43) Three phrases from these verses deserve emphasis:

a. **"No one knows about that day or hour . . . but only the Father."**

b. **"As it was in the days of Noah, so it will be at the coming of the Son of Man."**

c. **". . . and they knew nothing about what would happen until the flood came and took them all away. That is how it will be at the coming of the Son of Man. Two men will be in the field. . . ."**

Matthew 24:36-43 is concerned about the coming of the Son of Man. This point is stated twice. No one but the Father knows the date of Christ's coming (a singular coming). Jesus says there is a twofold parallel between Noah's day and His appearing – most people will be surprised and many will be lost because of willful ignorance. I believe most Christians will agree that two people can work side-by-side every day and yet, one will be saved and the other will be lost. This is the meaning and emphasis of the two verses in question. In other words, salvation boils down to *personal* preparation. We cannot depend on our friends, church membership or the charismatic oratory of a pastor for salvation. Salvation is a personal matter. When end time events unfold, the faithful will be saved and the others will be lost. This point is underscored in the parable of the ten virgins – which is part of this discussion. No doubt, the wise and foolish virgins were close friends. The difference between the wise and the foolish was preparation. When the foolish saw that they were without oil, they went to search for it. Meanwhile, the bridegroom arrived and the wise virgins followed Him through the door and into the banquet. Later, the foolish virgins showed up, but were rejected. (See Matthew 25:1-13.) The key thought in the parable of the ten virgins is daily preparedness.

Jesus said, **"So you also must be ready, because the Son of Man will come at an hour when you do not expect him."** (Matthew 24:44) **"The master of that servant will come on a day when he does not expect him and at an hour he is not aware of."** (Matthew 24:30) **"Therefore keep watch, because you do not know the day or the hour."** (Matthew 25:13)

The issue of readiness found in these verses is beyond controversy. The initial events leading up to the appearing of the Son of Man will come as a surprise to nominal Christians! Notice this verse: **"But you, brothers, are not in darkness so that this day should surprise you like a thief. You are all sons of the light and sons of the day. We do not belong to the night or to the darkness. So then, let us not be like others, who are**

asleep, but let us be alert and self-controlled." (1 Thessalonians 5:4-6) These verses reveal that there is no need to be surprised about the fulfillment of prophetic events if we are awake, alert and prepared. Centuries ago the prophet Amos wrote, **"Surely the Sovereign Lord does nothing without revealing his plan to his servants the prophets."** (Amos 3:7) It seems clear that if we correctly understand the apocalyptic prophecies contained in Daniel and Revelation, there is no need to be surprised. Although we do not know the day or hour of Christ's return, we can know the timing of events in relation to God's prophetic clock. We should always be living as if God's Word is about to be fulfilled!

An Overwhelming Surprise

The overwhelming surprise that Jesus continues to warn us about is not the Second Coming, but the initiation of the sequence of events leading up to His physical appearing. How does the surprise occur? Jesus offers this parallel: **"As it was in the days of Noah, so it will be at the coming of the Son of Man. For in the days before the flood, people were eating and drinking, marrying and giving in marriage, up to the day Noah entered the ark; and they knew nothing about what would happen until the flood came and took them all away. That is how it will be at the coming of the Son of Man. Two men will be in the field; one will be taken and the other left . . . ."** (Matthew 24:37-39) In other words, before the flood, life went on as usual. People were not fasting or praying for understanding. Instead, they were eating and drinking, planning weddings, and living as if the end of the world was only a figment of someone's imagination. (See 2 Peter 3:5-7.) The antediluvians were warned of impending disaster. For 120 years the work and message of faithful Noah irritated the antediluvians. (Genesis 6:3; Hebrews 11:7; 2 Peter 2:5) However, they were busy with life's activities; going about their daily routines with little concern. The antediluvians were warned that the end was coming, but none believed.

So, what did Jesus mean when He said: **". . . and they knew nothing about what would happen until the flood came and took them all away."** In their wildest imagination, the antediluvians did not conceive the enormity or the process of what lay ahead. In the busy and active lifestyles that existed before the flood, the antediluvians did not intimately concern themselves with Noah's message or his "crazy" activities. I am sure Noah's peers considered him a "kook." Then one day, without further notice or announcement, Noah and his family went inside the ark. When the animals came in an orderly fashion to enter the ark, few, if any, spectators were present. Noah's folly had been there for more than a hundred years – it was "a common sight." The Lord Himself closed the great door while the rest of the world was totally *unaware* of the significance of what had just happened. (Genesis 7:16) Everyone outside the ark was doomed and they did not know it! Everyone inside the ark was "sealed" in and they knew it. The townsfolk did not notice that the work *outside* the great boat had stopped. The noisy hillside had become quiet. Excess building materials and other construction items were laying around the perimeter of the big boat, just as they had been for years. Things looked pretty much the same. No doubt, intoxicated revelers went out to jeer or mock Noah at times, but no one was disturbed or worried that last night on Earth. Jesus said, "They were eating and drinking" and planning for another day. What they did not know was that there were no more tomorrows.

Suddenly, a streak of light streamed down from the sky followed by calamitous heaves in the Earth and ocean. These were followed in quick succession by sonic booms and catastrophic crashes. The grumble of a great earthquake could be heard from deep within the Earth. The ground began to rise in places, buildings began to fall and the air was suddenly filled with hot moist vapor. I believe the sky was literally falling! A steady sequence of horrific explosions was heard as fiery meteors and asteroids impacted planet Earth and the fountains of the deep were broken apart. Although the impacts were some distance away from Noah, the sounds of doom were everywhere. Every eye was wide open. Every pulse was racing. Suddenly, as if on cue, everyone remembered Noah! "*So this is how it happens,*" they thought as they grabbed as many precious items as they could carry and fled their shaking houses.

The ark, undisturbed and motionless, was illumined by sheets of lightning. The boat stood as a monument for truth. The tall, smooth sides of the ark prevented anyone from climbing aboard. The size and weight of the ark's only door was more than men could move. I can imagine the sound of frantic pleading – "Noah! Noah! Noah!!! Let us in! Please, let us in. Please!!!" Within minutes of the meteoric impacts, torrents of water converged on the hillside where a crowd had gathered. I surmise that a great tsunami came rushing in from the ocean and pushed inland, followed by rivers of water pouring from the sky. The foolish antediluvians were swept to their deaths within minutes. They knew nothing about the course of events because they had refused to listen.

Jesus makes it quite clear: **"As it was in the days before the flood, so shall it also be at the coming of the Son of Man."** Noah and his family did not escape the flood, but they did escape destruction because of their faith. (Hebrews 11:7) Likewise, the saints will not escape the Tribulation, but they do have the assurance of salvation. They know that Jesus has promised to be with them until the very end. After comparing Noah's day with His Second Coming, Jesus brings His remarks into sharp focus. Two people will be working side by side; one will be saved; the other left behind. Jesus was not alluding to a pre-trib rapture. He was speaking about the qualifying experience of faith. Faith in God is not something that can be developed within 30 minutes of terror. Faith in God is something that develops through testing and trials. As Jesus reflected about the time of His return, He saw many parallels between Noah's day and ours. The Great Tribulation will strike the world with a violence unseen since the days of Noah. Again, there will be powerful earthquakes, meteoric showers of burning hail and two asteroid impacts. (The first four trumpets consist of great physical harm to this planet.) And yes, there will be enormous terror and death. Of course, the destruction caused by the seven trumpet events will not be total, as in Noah's day, or no one could live. Although 50% of the Earth's population will survive these horrific manifestations of God's wrath, the time period of the seven trumpets will be filled with gloom, darkness and despair.

Little Has Changed

Little has changed. As in Noah's day, most of the world still refuses to listen. Even devout, religious people refuse to hear. They have created sweet prophetic concepts, counting themselves worthy of escaping the Great Tribulation that will soon occur. Many good people are deceived and an overwhelming disappointment is approaching. Who is to blame for all this misinformation? Everyone – everyone who owns a Bible. God has mercifully put a translation of His Word in almost every language of the world, making sure that everyone who wants to know the truth may have the opportunity. If people were sincerely searching for truth, having open discussions and studies about the prophecies of Daniel and Revelation, Christians would be much better prepared for what is coming.

Like a Thief

The Apostle Peter sums up the approaching Tribulation saying, **"The Lord is not slow in keeping his promise, as some understand slowness. He is patient with you, not wanting anyone to perish, but everyone to come to repentance. But the day of the Lord will come like a thief. The heavens will disappear with a roar; the elements will be destroyed by**

fire, and the earth and everything in it will be laid bare . . . That day
will bring about the destruction of the heavens by fire, and the elements will melt in the heat."** (1 Peter 3:9-12) For most of Earth's inhabitants, the Great Tribulation will begin without knowledge or warning – just
like a thief! The Great Tribulation will be 1,335 days in length. (Daniel
12:11,12) Even if the entire human race were told, few would believe. How
sad! **"But you, brothers, are not in darkness so that this day should
surprise you like a thief. You are all sons of the light and sons of the
day. We do not belong to the night or to the darkness. So then, let us
not be like others, who are asleep, but let us be alert and self-controlled."** (1 Thessalonians 5:4-6) This you can count on! When the seven
trumpets begin, people who have made a habit of studying God's Word
and daily listening to His Spirit, will be ready. People who "played church"
will be left . . . left wondering what went wrong.

Summary

If we harmonize all that the Bible has to say about the Second Coming, a
comprehensive picture begins to form. It will be a most awe-filled day. John
wrote, **"Look, he is coming with the clouds, and every eye will see
him, even those who pierced him; and all the peoples of the earth will
mourn because of him. So shall it be! Amen."** (Revelation 1:7) The
prophet Joel saw the great day of the Lord, **"Before them** [the warriors of
the Lord] **the earth shakes, the sky trembles, the sun and moon are
darkened, and the stars no longer shine. The Lord thunders at the
head of his army; his forces are beyond number, and mighty are
those who obey his command. The day of the Lord is great; it is
dreadful. Who can endure it?"** (Joel 2:10,11, insertion mine.) Given the
preponderance of evidence throughout Scripture, we have to conclude
there is one gathering of the saints – at the Second Coming.

Chapter 15
The Seventh Millennium

And I saw an angel coming down out of heaven, having the key to the Abyss and holding in his hand a great chain. He seized the dragon, that ancient serpent, who is the devil, or Satan, and bound him for a thousand years. He threw him into the Abyss, and locked and sealed it over him, to keep him from deceiving the nations anymore until the thousand years were ended. After that, he must be set free for a short time.

– Revelation 20:1-3

Introduction

I believe the 1,000 years of Revelation 20 will be a sabbatical millennium when Earth gets a rest from the works of sin. Bible chronology indicates the 6,000[th] anniversary of sin could occur somewhere between 1998 and 2017. *If* the Second Coming were to occur at the end of the 6,000[th] year of sin, the 1,000 years of Revelation 20 would be a sabbatical millennium. Of course, no one knows when the 6,000[th] year will occur and the Bible does not say that Jesus is going to return at the end of 6,000 years, but the progressive fulfillment of apocalyptic prophecy confirms the Second Coming of Jesus is very near. The Bible says that no man knows the day or hour of Christ's return (Matthew 24:36), but the Bible does say that we can know when the end is near! (Daniel 8:17,19; 12:4,9) We should thoughtfully consider clues about the timing of the Second Coming in the Bible. (1 Thessalonians 5:3-9) Eighteen apocalyptic time-periods are mentioned in the books of Daniel and Revelation and these time-periods are pieces of a big puzzle that reveal God's timing. God is always on time (Exodus 12:40-42, Galatians 4:4) and with Him, timing is the basis for everything.

God's Use of Clocks

The Bible teaches that God created four clocks during Creation's week by which He measures Earth time. Three clocks are based on planetary motion: The "day clock" is based on one rotation of Earth on its axis; the "month clock" is based on one orbit of the moon around Earth; and the "year clock" is synchronized with the positions of the Sun and moon in the spring of the year. The weekly cycle also began at Creation and it remains synchronized with Creation's week to this very day! About 2,500 years after Creation, God introduced five more clocks. It is interesting to note that these clocks are based on the template of the weekly cycle. Notice:

1. Week of seven months (Israel's religious year)
2. Week of seven years (7 years)
3. Week of seven weeks or one Jubilee cycle (49 years)
4. Great Day = ten Jubilee cycles (490 years)
5. Great Week = a week of Great Days (3,430 years)

In addition, if you add up the genealogical records found in the Bible, the prophetic time-periods mentioned in Daniel and Revelation and the 1,000 years of Revelation 20, the Bible record covers a total time span of 7,000 years. Using the weekly cycle template, two more clocks appear to be at work:

6. Grand Day = ten centuries (1,000 years)
7. Grand Week = a week of seven Grand Days (7,000 years)

I have asked myself, why did God create seven clocks based on the weekly template? After much study, I have concluded that each "weekly" clock points man toward God's Sabbath rest and God's Sabbath rest at every level says something significant about the duration of sin. (See my article, *Great Clocks From God* for an in depth explanation. It can be downloaded from the Wake Up America Seminars web-site at www.wake-up.org or a printed copy can be obtained for a minimal cost by contacting the office.)

Four Prophetic Views

Students of Bible prophecy usually accept one of four basic views regarding the 1,000 years mentioned in Revelation 20. Of course, there are also variations within each view. They are:

1. Premillennialism

2. Postmillennialism

3. Amillennialism

4. Panmillennialism

The most popular of the four views is called Premillennialism. Adherents of this view are so called because they believe that Christ's kingdom on Earth will be established *before* the millennium begins. In essence, premillennialism teaches there will be a pre-trib rapture. Seven years later Jesus is supposed to return to Earth and resurrect the righteous. Then, it is believed that Jesus will reign for 1,000 years in peace and righteousness from the throne of David located in the city of Jerusalem. At the end of the 1,000 years, there will be a final resurrection, judgment and a renewal of the heavens and Earth. Many premillennialists believe that the promises and covenants God gave to ancient Israel in the Old Testament will be fulfilled during the 1,000 years. (Premillennialism is largely based on the doctrine of dispensationalism.) There is some dispute among premillennialists concerning the identity and role of the saints during the millennium. Some scholars teach that the saints will rule as priests and kings with Christ over the unconverted. Others believe the Jews will be converted to Christianity as a result of the rapture and they will rule over the Gentiles. The net effect in either case is that the saints will rule over the wicked.

The opposite of Premillennialism is Postmillennialism. Bible students who believe in Postmillennialism teach that Christ's kingdom will be established on Earth *after* the 1,000 years are over. One group of postmillennialists believe that the world will continue as it is, getting more and more Christianized as a result of Christians sharing the gospel on a wider scale (i.e., worldwide TV, shortwave radio, Bibles printed in many languages, etc.). When the world has been reached with the gospel, a long period of peace and prosperity will exist for 1,000 years. At the end of the 1,000 years, Christ will return to Earth, resurrect the dead, perform the final judgment, give the saints eternal life and destroy the wicked. Other postmillennialists believe that Christ will establish His kingdom on Earth at the end of the 1,000 years, but they believe the Earth will be desolate of mankind during the 1,000 years.

The third view of the 1,000 years is called Amillennialism. Advocates of this view maintain that the 1,000 years is not a *literal* period of peace and righteousness. They believe the millennium alludes to the present reign of deceased souls with Christ in Heaven. This will be followed by Christ's Second Coming, a resurrection, final judgment, and Christ's eternal reign over a perfect kingdom on Earth. Just what takes place during the 1,000 years of Revelation 20 is a matter of debate among amillennialists. The millennium, according to amillennialism, is to be understood in an allegorical sense.

There is a "tongue-in-cheek" position on the millennium called "Panmillennialism." People in this category do not attempt to explain or understand Revelation 20. They take a fail-proof position saying the millennium will "pan-out" just as God intends.

So, which view of the millennium is best? Which view is more comprehensive? What is the truth about the 1,000 years of Revelation 20? Do Christians *really* need to know about the millennium right now? Certainly, the subject of the millennium years invites many good questions.

A Completed Picture

It is human nature to dismiss the importance of things we do not understand. An elderly man once said to me, "I've lived 80 years without understanding the millennium. Do you really think I need to know about it *now*?" I smiled and responded, "People lived on Earth for thousands of years without refrigerators. Do we really need them *now*?" We both smiled. I find that God has included "timely" information in the Bible because this information becomes essential to His believers who want to understand the ways of God *when the appointed time arrives*. The better we understand God's actions, the deeper our faith in God can grow! Therefore, I believe the subject of the millennium is important because I believe the time has come to understand a host of prophetic matters that are about to be fulfilled – Revelation 20 brings the big picture of God's plans into focus.

The Sequence of Events

In the previous chapter, I mentioned how the prophecies of Daniel and Revelation are "stacked" onto each other like layers of a wedding cake. As we investigate the 1,000 years of Revelation 20, I would like to present portions of prophecies #16, #17 and #18 so you can see how the layering of prophecies says so much in very few words. The first prophecy we will examine (#16) is taken from Revelation 19:11- 20:10. This prophecy has a beginning point in time and an ending point in time and the events within the prophecy occur in the order in which they are given. It provides an overall big picture of what happens at the beginning, the middle and the end of the 1,000 years. The two short prophecies that follow (#17 and #18) add more detail. Notice how the chronology in each prophecy contributes to the overall story.

Prophecy #16 (Revelation 19:11 - 20:10)

Step 1: Heaven's Army Assembled for the Second Coming

"I saw heaven standing open and there before me was a white horse, whose rider is called Faithful and True. With justice he judges and makes war. His eyes are like blazing fire, and on his head are many crowns. He has a name written on him that no one knows but he himself. He is dressed in a robe dipped in blood, and his name is the Word of God. The armies of heaven were following him, riding on white horses and dressed in fine linen, white and clean. Out of his mouth comes a sharp sword with which to strike down the nations. 'He will rule them with an iron scepter.' He treads the winepress of the fury of the wrath of God Almighty. On his robe and on his thigh he has this name written: KING OF KINGS AND LORD OF LORDS."

Step 2: Jesus Returns to Earth

"And I saw an angel standing in the sun, who cried in a loud voice to all the birds flying in midair, 'Come, gather together for the great supper of God, so that you may eat the flesh of kings, generals, and mighty men, of horses and their riders, and the flesh of all people, free and slave, small and great.' Then I saw the beast and the kings of the earth and their armies gathered together to make war against the rider on the horse and his army. But the beast [Babylon] was captured, and with him the false prophet [the lamb like beast] who had performed the miraculous signs on his behalf. With these signs he had deluded those who had received the mark of the beast and worshiped his image. The two of them were thrown alive into the fiery lake of burning sulfur. The rest of them [the wicked] were killed with the sword that came out of the mouth of the rider on the horse, and all the birds gorged themselves on their flesh."

Step 3: The Antichrist is Returned to the Abyss

"And I saw an angel coming down out of heaven, having the key to the Abyss and holding in his hand a great chain. He seized the dragon, that ancient serpent, who is the devil, or Satan, and bound him for a thousand years. He threw him into the Abyss, and locked and sealed it over him, to keep him from deceiving the nations anymore until the thousand years were ended. After that, he must be set free for a short time."

Step 4: The Saints Judge the Actions of the Wicked

"I saw thrones on which were seated those who had been given authority to judge. And I saw the souls of those who had been beheaded because of their testimony for Jesus and because of the word of God. They had not worshiped the beast or his image and had not received his mark on their foreheads or their hands. They came to life and reigned with Christ a thousand years. (The rest of the dead did not come to life until the thousand years were ended.) This is the first resurrection. Blessed and holy are those who have part in the first resurrection. The second death has no power over them, but they will be priests of God and of Christ and will reign with him for a thousand years."

Step 5: The Wicked are Annihilated

"When the thousand years are over, Satan will be released from his prison and will go out to deceive the nations in the four corners of the earth – Gog and Magog – to gather them for battle. In number they are like the sand on the seashore. They marched across the breadth of the earth and surrounded the camp of God's people, the city he loves. But fire came down from heaven and devoured them. And the devil, who deceived them, was thrown into the lake of burning sulfur, where the beast and the false prophet had been thrown. They will be tormented day and night forever and ever."

Prophecy #17: The Great White Throne Judgment Scene (Revelation 20:11 - 21:1)

A new prophecy begins with Revelation 20:11 because verse 11 breaks the chronological order of the previous prophecy. This prophecy reveals certain details that take place at the end of the 1,000 years, *just after* the wicked are resurrected, but *before* they are destroyed in the lake of fire. After studying the contents of this prophecy, see if you can chronologically harmonize this prophecy with the previous prophecy:

"Then I saw a great white throne and him who was seated on it. Earth and sky fled from his presence, and there was no place for them. And I saw the dead, great and small, standing before the throne, and books were opened. Another book was opened, which is the book of life. The dead were judged according to what they had done as recorded in the books. The sea gave up the dead that were in it, and death and Hades gave up the dead that were in them, and each person was judged according to what he had done. Then death and Hades were thrown into the lake of fire. The lake of fire is the second death. If anyone's name was not found written in the book of life, he was thrown into the lake of fire. Then I saw a new heaven and a new earth, for the first heaven and the first earth had passed away, and there was no longer any sea."

Prophecy #18: The Holy City Descends at the End of the 1,000 Years (Revelation 21:2 - 6)

A new prophecy begins with Revelation 21:2 because verse 2 breaks the chronological order of the previous prophecy. This prophecy reveals certain details that take place *just after* the wicked are resurrected, but *before* the destruction of the wicked.

"I saw the Holy City, the new Jerusalem, coming down out of heaven from God, prepared as a bride beautifully dressed for her husband. And I heard a loud voice from the throne saying, 'Now the dwelling of God is with men, and he will live with them. They will be his people, and God himself will be with them and be their God. He will wipe every tear from their eyes. There will be no more death or mourning or crying or pain, for the old order of things has passed away.' He who was seated on the throne said, 'I am making everything new!' Then he said, 'Write this down, for these words are trustworthy and true. . . .' "

Synthesis

When I align the chronological details in these three prophecies, I reach the following conclusions:

1. When Jesus returns to Earth, the armies of Earth will actually attempt to destroy Him.

2. Jesus will face His enemies and command them to die. (This is represented by the sharp sword that comes out of His mouth.) Incidently, the righteous dead are resurrected by words from the same mouth!

3. The Antichrist (the false prophet) and his global administration (the beast) will be thrown alive in a great lake of fire at the Second Coming. Everyone will be destroyed in that fire, but the fire itself will burn on throughout the 1,000 years. Lucifer and his angels will see the place of their coming execution for 1,000 years.

    Note: Lucifer and his angels are allowed to physically appear on Earth during the fifth trumpet. At that time they will be given *visible* bodies for the benefit of mankind to see. (Revelation 17:8; 9:1-11) These bodies will be taken away from them at the Second Coming and destroyed in the lake of fire. This forces Lucifer and his angels back into the spirit world or the Abyss (from whence they came) and they remain in this state, "chained" to a desolate Earth for 1,000 years.

4. During the 1,000 years, the saints reign with Christ. This means they will share in Jesus' great authority in reviewing the records of the wicked to determine the appropriate amount of restitution as required by law.

5. At the end of the 1,000 years, the holy city, New Jerusalem, descends from Heaven to Earth with the saints inside. The wicked will be resurrected and Lucifer will be "released" to lead the wicked in an all-out attempt to destroy God, the saints and the city. God allows this to occur to demonstrate once again that sin cannot be justified. Sin is nothing but rebellion against the authority of God. When the righteous see the defiant behavior of the wicked in the very presence of Almighty God, this evidence will be more than enough to satisfy any question that may linger about the necessity of destroying the wicked. Every tear will be dried.

6. As the wicked rush the city, the Great White Throne judgment scene takes place. The Maker of Life will stop the great throng as it advances toward His city. Jesus will address His created beings and reveal to each wicked person why He could not save him or her. He will also reveal his or her forthcoming punishment. I presume there will be a few special words addressed to Lucifer, the father of sin. Jesus will lament the rise of sin as He speaks to the being who was once His best and closest friend. It will be an awesome day of reckoning.

7. When the wicked realize their great loss, when they see that their fate was sealed by their own rebellion, when they hear their sentence of restitution and death, panic stricken they go into an agonizing frenzy. Jesus calls fire down out of the heavens and the judgment decided by the saints is applied and ultimately, the penalty of death by execution brings sin to an end.

Some Questions

Perhaps the best way to conclude the study on this topic is to answer nine commonly asked questions.

1. Where are the saints during the 1,000 years and what will they be doing?

They will reign (share authority) with Christ in Heaven. This conclusion is based on four concepts: First, the righteous dead of ages past and the righteous living will be caught up together in the clouds to meet the Lord in the air. *Important point: Christ does not walk upon the Earth at the Second Coming. Instead, He calls the saints up to meet Him in the air.* (1 Thessalonians 4:16,17) Jesus takes the saints back to the holy city, New Jerusalem, where He has been preparing homes for them. (John 14:1-3) Second, when Christ appears at the Second Coming, He commands the wicked to die. (Revelation 19:15-21; 2 Thessalonians 2:8) Third, the saints will have the responsibility of determining the appropriate punishment for wicked people and Satan's angels. (1 Corinthians 6:1-3) Last, at the end of the 1,000 years, the saints descend from Heaven to Earth *in* the Holy City at the end of the 1,000 years. (Revelation 21:2-22:5)

2. Where are the wicked during the 1,000 years and what will they be doing?

With the exception of those who participated in the crucifixion of Jesus, the wicked are not resurrected at the Second Coming. They remain in a state of soul-sleep or death. They wait for the second resurrection and the White Throne Judgment scene. (Revelation 20:5; 20:12,13) At the Second Coming, the devil is forced to return to the spirit world (the Abyss) for 1,000 years. (He was let out of the Abyss during the fifth trumpet. Revelation 9:1-11) Because the Earth is desolate of life, he cannot deceive anyone during the 1,000 years. Furthermore, he is "chained" to his earthly prison and cannot go anywhere to tempt or annoy the other inhabitants of the universe. (Revelation 20:1-3) The devil and his demons will have a lot of time to reflect on their eventful history of rebellion against God and they will churn with depression and anxiety over their coming destruction – especially the restitution phase. Remember from page 238, Lucifer is the scapegoat. All the sins from the temple will be placed on his head.

3. Did God pre-decree a precise period of 1,000 Earth-years or should this time-period be interpreted as a general statement?

Evidence from the Bible suggests the 1,000 years will be a sabbatical millennium. There is nothing in the Bible to prevent the 1,000 years from being a precise time-period that fulfills the weekly template God designed at Creation. (Genesis 2:1-3; Psalm 90:4; 2 Peter 3:8)

4. Does the millennium occur before or after Christ sets up His kingdom on Earth?

Based on the material presented in this chapter and the previous one, Jesus will return for the saints at the beginning of the millennium. At that time, He will take them to "His Father's house," which is located in Heaven, for 1,000 years. During the 1,000 years, the saints will conduct a judgment process upon the wicked, determining the amount of restitution that each wicked person must pay. At the end of the 1,000 years, the Holy City and the saints descend to Earth. At that time, the wicked are resurrected to see the reality of salvation and why He could not save them. Then the punishment begins and ultimately, God cleanses the Earth of every impurity. Hallelujah! After seven millenniums of sin, a new Heaven and a new Earth will be created. Then it can be said, "the Kingdom of God is among men."

5. What event marks the beginning of 1,000 years?

The Second Coming.

6. What event marks the end of the 1,000 years?

It could be called the Third Coming, since the Holy City descends and the wicked from all ages are resurrected to meet their fate.

7. Will the 1,000 years of Revelation 20 be the seventh millennium since sin began, in effect, a sabbatical rest for Earth?

Yes, it appears that way. (See 2 Peter 3:8.) Consider the parallel: The works of sin last for six millennial days (six 1,000-year periods). Earth will then receive its Sabbath rest for 1,000 years before it is put back into proper "working" order at the beginning of eternity!

8. What is God's overall purpose for the 1,000 years?

In addition to the purposes stated in previous questions, God uses the millennium as a time for the saints to prove to themselves that God's judgment of the wicked, His character and His government are righteous beyond question. All issues surrounding the judgement process will be resolved before God *permanently* annihilates anyone. The first 1,000 years of eternal life will also include their judgment regarding restitution from the wicked. God gives this job to the saints at the beginning of their eternal life because He wants the redeemed to carefully consider the seriousness of sin and rebellion from His perspective. Therefore, He requires them to sit in judgment upon human beings as He must do. As a direct result, the saints will be able to testify throughout the endless ages of eternity about the importance of maintaining a nonnegotiable faith in God and His government. Their eternal testimony will thwart the rise of sin forever in God's expanding universe.

9. Although the 1,000 years are only mentioned in Revelation 20, do other Bible writers indirectly speak of this time-period?

No details or comments about the millennium are given by Old Testament prophets. Since God's original plan (I refer to it as "Plan A") to rescue Earth from sin was based on a scheme that directly involved ancient Israel, the original plan did not have a 1,000 year respite from sin. But when ancient Israel failed to meet God's requirements, God introduced what I refer to as "Plan B." The book of Revelation demonstrates how God can take the failure of man and produce an even more glorious outcome. Remember this, the greater the chaos, the greater God's glory for resolving the problem!

Conclusion

We have reached the end of this volume. I have attempted to explain five essential Bible truths (I call them the five S's):

Salvation through faith in Jesus Christ
God's seventh day **S**abbath rest
Parallel **S**anctuaries
The **S**tate of man in death
The circumstances and events surrounding the **S**econd Coming.

Each of these doctrines centers on the generous ministry of Jesus Christ. As we begin to understand the depth of God's plans, it leads the sincere in heart toward a greater appreciation for Jesus. I have written this book for two reasons. First, I want to exalt my Savior, Jesus. Even though I continue to learn more about Him every day, my desire is to share a number of wonderful things I have gleaned from Scripture. No one compares to Jesus. He rightfully deserves to be called, **"The Alpha and The Omega."** He is the most awesome being in the whole universe. Second, this book was written as a primer for prophetic study. The prophecies of Daniel and Revelation are an advanced area of study and a harmonious understanding of the prophecies requires a solid foundation of the five essential truths presented in this book.

For example, Revelation 8:5 mentions the "casting down of the golden censer" at the golden altar. To understand what this means, we need to understand it within the context of services being conducted in Heaven's temple at the Altar of Incense. Since information about services conducted at the heavenly Altar of Incense does not exist in the Bible, we must turn to the parallels and patterns between the heavenly and the earthly sanctuaries. As we examine the ministry conducted at the Altar of Incense on Earth, it helps us to understand the significance of casting down the censer at the heavenly altar.

"Future telling" is not the primary purpose of Bible prophecy. Bible prophecy does involve a study of future events, but not in the way most people assume. Bible prophecy covers a number of topics that believers should want to understand. Ultimately, Bible prophecy reveals how Jesus will resolve all of the problems caused by sin. He will eventually destroy the wicked, both humans and angels. Earth itself is so contaminated with sin that purification by fire is required! The Godhead has been dealing with the sin problem for a long time and they will bring the drama to a close as planned – and this is where apocalyptic prophecy comes into focus.

Unfortunately, the elimination of sin also involves destroying human beings that Jesus deeply loves. The deliberate and final destruction of fallen angels and fallen human beings must be done within a framework of justice and mercy that every survivor can understand. Throughout eternity, the drama of sin will be reviewed and discussed by men and angels. Of course, after the drama is over, God's children will have a host of records to examine which will disclose the whole truth about sin and God's behavior. (1 Corinthians 6:1-4, Revelation 20:4) But, we are presently living before the drama of sin has been brought to a close. So, God has given us who live before the drama comes to a close, an opportunity to understand the sweeping outline of how the sin problem will be resolved. By giving this information to us in advance, our understanding of what He must do to the human race during the Great Tribulation makes sense.

If the balance between God's eternal justice and His unlimited love to save man is not the central theme when studying Bible prophecy, then it is robbed of its sanctifying value, because human beings can do nothing to prevent the things God has determined to do. At the present time, one man says this about Revelation and another says that, so no one can determine the truth. This is about to change. When the Great Tribulation begins, God will make sure all people will see and hear His truth. He will empower 144,000 spokespersons all over the world and they will speak with authority, as did Moses and Elijah.

For now, we must accept by faith that God is unbelievably generous in His grace and His government is based on the equitable rule of law based on love. God's laws are not righteous because He declares them to be righteous. God's laws are righteous and fair because the evidence will show that when sin's drama has ended, His laws will have been proven to be righteous! The eternal well being of His creatures is God's first and highest concern. As I have come to understand His profound love for sinners, I conclude that, "Jesus is the Alpha and the Omega, the First and Last, the Beginning and End. He is the Engineer of everything and the Creator of all creations. He is the Architect of the universe, the Prince of Kindness and the Prince of Peace. But for a few hours in the tomb, He is eternal. He has no beginning and He is alive forever more. He is unmoved, unchanged, undefeated, and never undone. He was bruised but He brought healing. He was pierced but He eased pain. He was persecuted but He brought freedom. He was put to death but He brought life. He is risen and He brings power to those who believe in Him. The world cannot understand Him, the armies of Earth cannot defeat Him, the schools of men cannot explain Him, and the leaders of nations cannot ignore Him. Herod could not kill Him, the Pharisees could not confuse Him, and crowds could not get enough of Him. Pilate could not hold Him in the tomb, Caesars could not silence His followers, traditions cannot replace Him, and modern science cannot explain Him. He is the way, the true light, the bread of life, perfect love and Lord of Lords. He is goodness, kindness and gentleness. He is God, He is the angel of the Lord and He is man. He is holy, righteous, mighty, powerful, and pure. His ways are right, His word is eternal, His will is unchanging, and His expansive thoughts include me. He is my Redeemer and Savior. He is my guide and my peace. He is my joy and my comfort, He is my Lord and He rules over my life. I serve Him because His bond is love, His burden is light, and His objective for me is abundant life. I follow Him because He is the source of truth, the owner of wisdom and all knowledge. He is love. He is sovereign over the kings of Earth, the Ruler of rulers, the Leader of leaders, the Model for overcomers. If His qualifications seem impressive, His demonstration of love is even greater. He desires a wonderful relationship with every human being. If I obediently submit to His call, He will never leave me, forsake me, mislead me, forget me, overlook me, or ignore my prayers. When I fall, He lifts me up. When I fail, He forgives. When I am weak, He is strong. When I am lost, He knows the way. When I am afraid, He gives me courage. When I stumble, He steadies me. When I am hurt, He heals me. When I am broken, He mends me. When I am blind, He leads me. When I am hungry, He feeds me. When I face trials, He assures me. When I face persecution, He sustains me. When I face problems, He comforts me. When I endure loss, He provides for me. When I face the shadow of death, He gives me grace. He is everything for everybody, everywhere, every time, and in every way. He is Almighty God, He is faithful and trustworthy. I am His, and He is mine." (Variations of this statement have been circulated on the internet. I have added a number of statements that spring from my discoveries. Originating author is unknown.)

Bible Cross Reference

About the Author

Larry Wilson, Director of Wake Up America Seminars, became a born again Christian after returning from a tour of duty in Vietnam. The understanding of the gospel, the plan of salvation, and the atonement of Jesus Christ has thrilled his soul for the past 30 years. Since his conversion, he has spent over 25 years intensely studying the prophecies of Daniel and Revelation.

In 1988, he published the book *Warning! Revelation is about to be fulfilled* and since then, has written several books (over 750,000 books in circulation throughout the world in more than 60 countries). He also writes a feature Bible study in the *Day Star* (a monthly publication produced by Wake Up America Seminars). He gives seminar presentations, produces video programs which have been broadcast from various locations throughout the United States, and is a frequent guest on radio talk shows.

About the Organization

Wake Up America Seminars (WUAS) is both a non-profit and a non-denominational organization. With God's blessings and the generosity of many people, WUAS has distributed millions of pamphlets, books and tapes around the world since it began in 1988. WUAS is not a church, nor is it affiliated or sponsored by any religious organization. WUAS does not offer membership of any kind. Its mission is not to convert the world to a point of view. Although WUAS has well defined views on certain biblical matters, its mission is primarily "seed sowing." It promotes the primacy of salvation through faith in Jesus Christ, His imminent return, and is doing its best to encourage people with the good news of the gospel. People of all faiths are invited to study the materials produced by WUAS.

Books

Warning! Revelation is about to be fulfilled

What do the books of Daniel and Revelation have to say about soon coming events? *Warning! Revelation is about to be fulfilled* outlines Revelation's story in an easy to read format. Revelation predicts and describes many incredible events that will soon occur. These events will not happen in random order nor will they be freak manifestations of violent weather. The coming events predicted in Revelation are carefully designed and executed by the Creator of Heaven and Earth.

To learn more about what the prophecies of Daniel and Revelation have to say about coming events, contact the Wake Up America Seminars office at (800) 475-0876 or access the web site at *http://www.wake-up.org*.

Wake Up America Seminars, Inc.
P.O. Box 273
Bellbrook, OH   45305
(800) 475-0876

Books

The Revelation of Jesus

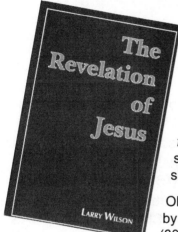

Like a gold mine, the Bible contains very valuable, but hidden treasure. Down through the ages, the Holy Spirit has led men and women to discover precious truths hidden within the Bible. Each new discovery lifts the saving power of Jesus Christ to a new height. *The Revelation of Jesus* expands on the concepts presented in the book *Warning! Revelation is about to be fulfilled* and provides additional scriptural support to amplify the Plan of Salvation and significant end-time prophecies.

Obtain your own copy of this 346 page book by contacting Wake Up America Seminars at (800) 475-0876.

Other Books by Larry Wilson. . .

18 End-Time Bible Prophecies

The Mysteries of Daniel

The Mysteries of Revelation

Wake Up America Seminars, Inc.
P.O. Box 273
Bellbrook, OH   45305
http://www.wake-up.org

Taped Seminar Series

Many seminar series have been recorded on audio and video tape. Call for a free catalog from the Wake Up America Seminars office at (800) 475-0876. Many subjects are available on tape including righteousness by faith, the sanctuary, the Plan of Salvation, the book of Hebrews, God's justice and mercy, and great clocks of God.

The *Day Star* Newsletter

Each month, the *Day Star* features a short Bible study on various end-time topics or a topic that may provide spiritual encouragement. Complimentary subscriptions to United States residents are available by calling the WUAS office at (800) 475-0876. International subscribers can also obtain a subscription for the newsletter at a minimal cost. Check with the WUAS office for current pricing.

Wake Up America Seminars, Inc.
P.O. Box 273
Bellbrook, OH   45305
(800) 475-0876

Coming in 2002 . . .

Jesus
The Rock of Ages

Jesus The Alpha and The Omega provides a basic framework to understand Bible prophecy. This framework, based on five essential Bible doctrines, helps the serious student of Bible prophecy appreciate the prophecies of Daniel and Revelation. *Jesus The Rock of Ages* will not only provide an in-depth study on the apocalyptic prophecies, but also will demonstrate how important it is to develop our faith walk today in light of prophetic events. If you would like to learn more about what God is about to do, order a copy of . . .

Jesus
The Rock of Ages

Wake Up America Seminars, Inc.
P.O. Box 273
Bellbrook, OH   45305
http://www.wake-up.org

We would like to receive comments about this book or questions you may have. Please send your comments to us at the address below. Thank you.

Wake Up America Seminars, Inc.
P.O. Box 273
Bellbrook, OH   45305

http://www.wake-up.org

email: *wakeup@infinet.com*